Common Worship
in Theological Education

Common Worship
in Theological Education

edited by SIOBHÁN GARRIGAN
and TODD E. JOHNSON

PICKWICK *Publications* · Eugene, Oregon

COMMON WORSHIP IN THEOLOGICAL EDUCATION

Pickwick Publications
An Imprint of Wipf and Stock Publishers
199 W. 8th Ave., Suite 3
Eugene, OR 97401

www.wipfandstock.com

ISBN 13: 978-1-60899-045-0

Cataloging-in-Publication data:

Common worship in theological education / edited by Siobhán Garrigan and
Todd E. Johnson.

xii + 200 p. ; 23 cm. — Includes bibliographical references.

ISBN 13: 978-1-60899-045-0

1. Theological seminaries. 2. Worship. 3. Worship (Christian education). I.
Garrigan, Siobhán. II. Johnson, Todd E. III. Title.

BV4022.C62 2010

Contents

Contributors

E. Byron (Ron) Anderson is Styberg Associate Professor of Worship and Director of the Nellie B. Ebersole Program in Music Ministry at Garrett-Evangelical Theological Seminary.

Michelle Baker-Wright is a PhD candidate in Christian Worship at Fuller Theological Seminary and has been Assistant Director of Chapel there since 2007.

Cláudio Carvalhaes is Assistant Professor of Worship and Preaching at Louisville Presbyterian Theological Seminary, where he has also coordinated Chapel worship since 2008.

Patrick Evans is Associate Professor in the Practice of Sacred Music and Director of Music for Marquand Chapel at Yale Divinity School and Institute of Sacred Music. He is also Director of Music at Broadway Presbyterian Church in New York City.

Siobhán Garrigan is Associate Professor of Liturgical Studies, and Associate Dean, for Chapel, at Yale Divinity School and Institute of Sacred Music, where she has directed the daily ecumenical worship program since 2002.

Mary Hess is Associate Professor of Educational Leadership at Luther Seminary. Her most recent book is *Teaching Reflectively in Theological Education.*

Todd E. Johnson is the Brehm Chair of Worship, Theology and the Arts at Fuller Theological Seminary where he directs the PhD program in Christian Worship. Before coming to Fuller, he was Dean of the Chapel at North Park Theological Seminary.

LIST OF CONTRIBUTORS

Lizette Larson-Miller is the Kaehr Professor of Liturgy at the Church Divinity School of the Pacific and the Graduate Theological Union. She is also an Episcopal priest active in parish ministry and the author of numerous works in liturgy and architecture and rites for the sick and dying.

Mark Stamm is Associate Professor of Christian Worship at Perkins School of Theology, Southern Methodist University, where he has served since 2000. As part of his work, he provides oversight for the school's weekday chapel program.

Ron Rienstra is Assistant Professor of Preaching and Worship at Western Theological Seminary in Holland, Michigan. He is the author, along with his wife, of *Worship Words: Disciplining Language for Faithful Ministry*.

Dwight W. Vogel, OSL is Ernest and Bernice Styberg Professor Emeritus of Worship and Preaching at Garrett-Evangelical Theological Seminary in Evanston, Illinois where he was Dean of the Chapel. He is now a resident of Pilgrim Place in Claremont, California.

Preface

MARY HESS

You hold in your hands an immensely important resource: a book of essays on the diverse practices of chapel worship in seminaries and divinity schools, and what it can mean to learn in and through such practices.

At a moment in theological education when there is widespread concern about the embodied nature of theological education—a concern raised, in part, by the growth of diverse digital approaches to learning—the most explicitly embodied and potentially integrative space of theological education (chapel) is also its most under theorized and under explored resource. This book enters our discourse at precisely that place, and offers a rich and variegated set of essays exploring the teaching and learning that take place in seminary and divinity school chapels across the United States.

Craig Dykstra, perhaps one of the most influential voices in the field of practical theology—first as a scholar in his own right, and then through his work at the religion division at the Lilly Endowment—makes two points that are pertinent here. First, "The point and purpose of practical theology are to nourish, nurture, discipline, and resource both pastoral and ecclesial imagination."[1]

He then fleshes out what he means by noting that:

> The first priority in teaching children to swim is to enable them to trust the water. Somehow or another they have to come to a specific kind of knowledge. In a deeply somatic, bodily way—and in a way that is in no small part existential, for it is a knowledge that must be strong enough to address their fears—they must come

1. Craig Dykstra, "Pastoral and Ecclesial Imagination," in *For Life Abundant: Practical Theology, Theological Education, and Christian Ministry*, edited by Dorothy C. Bass and Craig Dykstra (Grand Rapids, MI: Eerdmans, 2008) 43.

to know the buoyancy of the water. Buoyancy is not something you can teach children—or anyone else, for that matter—through a lesson in physics. Objective as it is, for the sake of swimming one has to come to know it personally.

So it is with the life of faith. At the heart of the Christian life there lies a deep, somatic, profoundly personal, but very real knowledge. It is the knowledge of the buoyancy of God. It is the knowledge that in struggle and in joy, in conflict and in peace—indeed, in every possible circumstance and condition in life and death—we are upheld by God's own everlasting arms.[2]

This book of essays is a fascinating entry in the discussions now taking place in practical theology, and seminary chapels are an essential place in which such buoyancy is encountered – or not. To the extent that it is not, there is an implicit curriculum in place that actively counters much of what our seminary curricula explicitly teach.

In her essay in this collection, for example, Siobhán Garrigan notes the striking contradiction between "large numbers of alumni/ae reporting [chapel's] privileged place as a pedagogical site" and the standards of the Association of Theological Schools viewing chapel as one of many "community activities" rather than a key element of the curriculum. Garrigan—and the rest of the fine authors in this volume—powerfully contest that marginalization by paying careful attention to myriad ways in which learning unfolds throughout chapels across the country.

In these pages you will find a keen investigation into a host of specific challenges that are shared across theological education: can learning be both formatively catechetical and critically engaged at the same time? what do our differing understandings of biblical authority contribute to our religious practices? what does it mean to gather in prayer together, when we come from different contexts and denominations? how does God act upon us, and how do we participate in acting with God? in what ways might our practices need to shift as the world around us shifts, and in what ways must we stand firm in claiming practices over time?

On this last challenge consider, for example, a recent essay by Gary Hamel on *The Wall Street Journal* website that emphasized twelve characteristics of what the author labeled the "facebook generation"[3]:

2. Ibid., 55.

3. Gary Hamel, "The Facebook Generation vs. the Fortune 500," Gary Hamel's Management 2.0: A Look at New Ways of Managing, WSJ Blogs, *The Wall Street Journal*,

(1) All ideas compete on an equal footing

(2) Contribution counts for more than credentials

(3) Hierarchies are natural, not prescribed

(4) Leaders serve rather than preside

(5) Tasks are chosen, not assigned

(6) Groups are self-defining and -organizing

(7) Resources get attracted, not allocated

(8) Power comes from sharing information, not hoarding it

(9) Opinions compound and decisions are peer-reviewed

(10) Users can veto most policy decisions

(11) Intrinsic rewards matter most

(12) Hackers are heroes

There are a multitude of ways in which this set of characteristics directly contradicts liturgical practice across a wide variety of denominations and settings. These contradictions create striking challenges in our educational processes, when students who are socialized by the wider culture into such practices enter our theological classrooms. Yet at the same time, as Adán Medrano and others have argued, it is precisely our richly variegated, embodied traditions of ritual practice—writ large in liturgy, or small in daily prayers—that hold some of the most generative resources to draw upon in engaging these challenges.[4]

The authors of this collection explore these resources, and point to specific ways in which chapel practices can help us with formation and integration into the deeply critical and intimately thoughtful patterns of theological scholarship. They bring a wide variety of metaphors to bear in their exploration. Chapel as laboratory, chapel as monastery, chapel as song circle, chapel as classroom, chapel as church—each of these examples offers insight into specific elements of learning that take place, whether we intentionally shape them or not, in the midst of chapel practices. In

---

http://blogs.wsj.com/management/2009/03/24/the-facebook-generation-vs-the-fortune-500/ (accessed June 22, 2009).

4. Adán M. Medrano, "Making Religious Media: Notes from the field," in *Belief in Media: Cultural Perspectives on Media and Christianity,* edited by Peter Horsfield, Mary E. Hess, and Adán M. Medrano (Burlington, VT: Ashgate, 2004) 141–52.

doing so, the essayists in this book also demonstrate a passionate attention to the detail of what is generally termed "the scholarship of teaching and learning." That is, these essays are thoughtfully researched and carefully argued forays into learning in depth from experience.

In addition to metaphors and examples from practice, these authors make specific claims about what constitutes effective ways to lead and shape the formative processes of chapel. One of the most compelling of those claims, for me at least, arose from Dwight Vogel's description of what it means to learn from our mistakes. He offers a thoughtful rationale for openly engaging criticism, and reminds his readers that specific ecclesiological, pneumatological and Christological claims are embedded in these conflicts. Lifting them up and engaging them, rather than ignoring or subsuming them, can lead to transformative practice. Cláudio Carvalhaes also provides compelling testimony to the power dynamics of the spaces we inhabit liturgically, with specific ideas about embodied postures that can free us to worship together in these spaces.

I could go on, but the point is not to read my words—the point is to enter these pages and learn from the richness of what is offered here. Every theological educator needs to think about these questions, and this book offers abundant companions for doing so!

1

Ora et Labora: *Reflections on the (Non-)History of Seminary Chapel*

TODD E. JOHNSON

A History of Failure

This chapter is a failure. It was intended to be a survey of the history of seminary chapel. This chapter was to set the chapters that follow it in broader historical perspective than either the contemporary context or that of recent memory—either personal or institutional. This chapter would establish the original purpose (or purposes) of chapel within the context of formal pastoral education and then identify the changes that occurred in chapels over time within the context of ecclesial and curricular changes of those times. With any luck, this chapter would contain discoveries of historical inaccuracies in previous scholars' studies of seminary chapels, and offer insightful conclusions from history that might help untie the Gordian Knot of the liturgical battles often fought in the places of prayer in schools of ministry. This would have been a chapter to set the tone for what would be a great study of the place of chapel—the place of common worship—within the intellectual, spiritual, and social life of the seminary community. There were high hopes for this chapter.

Unfortunately this chapter does not meet those expectations. The histories of worship in ministry education appear not to exist. There are no competing theories for the time, place, or purpose of the inception of chapel in seminary. Instead of debate or disagreement about the question of seminary chapel's history, there is silence. It would seem there has been little interest in this historical question. This chapter is a failure; or at least, this chapter has discovered a failure—a failure to attend to the importance of worship in the process of educating and forming the ministers of the church. The history of seminary chapel is a failure of historical research. And this chapter does not seek to fill that void. Instead, it now intends to identify what history we do have and then signal possible directions for future investigation.

Seminary Chapel: The Non-History

Given that there is no explicit history of the place of chapel in pastoral education, what can be gleaned from the occasional patches of chapel found in the quilt of the history of theological seminaries? Please note the emphasis upon "occasional." One of the most prolific scholars in this area is Glenn T. Miller, Professor of Ecclesiastical History and Academic Dean at Bangor Seminary. Over the course of his two major works on American seminary education (450 pages covering up to Civil War and another 800 pages from the Civil War to 1970),[1] there is virtually no attention given to the place of chapel worship in the life, ethos, and identity of seminaries. Miller's work is representative of much of the history of seminary education.[2]

To get at the history of common worship in seminary, one must have a general outline of the history of the education of ministers. What we now call seminary education originated out of the need to teach theology to those in ministry (and preparing for ministry). On the one hand, there was the need to teach orthodoxy versus heterodoxy, faithfully preserving the Christian tradition by insuring its transmission; and on the other hand, there was a need to give the student the resources to do the theological reflection necessary for ministry in the church.[3]

---

1. These two works are *Piety and Intellect* and *Piety and Profession.*

2. This is common as well for surveys of the history of ordination, which offer information on clerical education and with them scattered references to common worship. For example, Cooke, *Ministry to Word and Sacraments.*

3. Miller, *Piety and Intellect*, 13–14.

It appears that some of the original theological education for clergy was simply basic Christian catechesis. Ambrose famously was moved through the catechumenate to the episcopacy in Milan in 374 more because of his gifts and abilities as a governor than his education. There were exceptions to this rule, notably the catechetical school in Alexandria led by such noteworthy teachers as Clement and Origen. However, this school was not exclusively for ministry formation and education, as it taught subjects such as science, mathematics, and the arts. It even had a school for the blind. It was designed after the Greek models of academies, in which the best students would later become teachers. We have no extant evidence of common worship within the academy, but one could safely presume that the students participated in the liturgical life of the Christian church in Alexandria.[4] This may be the pattern of common worship for those being educated for ministry in the years to come: common education within the academy, and common worship within the local church.

The Fall of the Roman Empire led to the dissolution of much of the educational system that was in place in the first few centuries of the Common Era, only to be replaced in the late centuries of the medieval era by universities. Although the university has its roots in the academy of Plato (*circa* 380 BCE), the first university was established in Constantinople in the Fifth century CE. Even so, most of the education in the medieval west was not through universities but monasteries, which preserved the learning and crafts of the guilds and philosophers—as well as the theology of the Church's first centuries—and passed them along to women and men religious. Seminaries have their historical roots most directly in the monastery, where the community of people set apart for prayer was also, in part, a community of learning.

As having an education became more sought after in the middle ages, some religious orders used their schools as a means of recruiting possible novices for the order. The Augustinians were not unique in their curriculum, in which the first year would be spent learning the daily offices in order to be eligible to study grammar.[5] As time went on, monasteries began educating boys who were not preparing for religious life, and provided a form of public education.

4. See *The Oxford Dictionary of the Christian Church*, 3rd ed., s.v. "Catechetical School in Alexandria."

5. Orme, *Medieval Schools*, 264.

By the eleventh century there was no standardized education of priests, beyond the requirement of a general education enabling them to at least pronounce Latin well enough to say the Mass. The twelfth century marked an increased emphasis on education within the church. The Third Lateran Council encouraged clergy to offer a free education to their flock, in particular the education of poor clerics and training of scholars at every cathedral church. In response, Cathedral schools were begun and the monasteries became more rigorous in their scholarship. This gave rise to the birth of the medieval university that, in turn, spawned scholasticism in the twelfth and thirteenth centuries. Medieval universities often had no campus *per se*. They met where they found space, usually churches or homes. Worship took place in churches or monasteries.[6]

As the Reformation churches began to take shape, the education of Protestant clerics became an issue. Reformation schools were basically extensions of the University. Miller writes, "The first Protestant leaders . . . (Luther and Melanchthon) . . . , were humanistic university professors who believed that their ecclesiastical vocation was an extension of their teaching office."[7] Further, the Reformed brands of the Reformation (Zwingli and Calvin) were similar in their expansion of the Renaissance model of education that had influenced them. The role of the newly formed Protestant schools was not entirely clear at the time of their inception. For example, when in 1559 the Genevan Academy opened its doors, John Calvin saw the role of this school as primarily the education of Reformed clergy. The Genevan magistrates had a broader view, however, believing that such an academy was less confessional and more a place for the training of the multiple professions needed in society, from ministry to law and medicine. This broad academic training for clergy lead ultimately to the Puritan ideal of pastors as the learned voices in society, well-rounded in their knowledge.[8]

---

6. Miller, *Piety and Intellect*, 13. Nicholas Orme reports that in England in the twelfth century, schools were beginning to develop outside of the monasteries. They could be found in churches in towns and villages. This did not diminish the reach of monasteries in education, but in fact was an indication of the growth of education in general. Monasteries grew in the depth and breadth of their offerings, embracing the growing university model on the continent. Orme, *Medieval Schools*, 255.

7. Miller, *Piety and Intellect*, 13.

8. Karin Maag, *Seminary or University?*, 2–3. George Marsden observed, "Protestantism promoted a well-educated clergy, which quickly became the backbone of the international revolutionary movement . . . In villages throughout Protestant lands

When the waves of the Reformation made their way across the English Channel, resulting in (among other things) the dissolution of the monasteries, it did not mean the dissolution of Britain's educational system. Many of the monasteries were later converted into schools and universities, preserving much the same educational pattern as before the Reformation, including praying the daily offices.[9] As England began to methodically develop its educational system in the sixteenth century, it extended this monastic paradigm to its cathedral schools and later its universities. All assumed the foundation of corporate prayer and theology together with grammar as the essentials of education.[10] Although it cannot be said with certainty, it appears that the first "chapels" in schools were simply the monastic oratories in what were now schools. Regardless, it is clear that the expectation of common worship in education was a norm in Western Europe for all education, whether for clergy or lay.

The Council of Trent, strategizing the Roman Catholic response to the growing Protestant movement in Western Europe, required that each diocese establish a seminary to train diocesan priests. Many of these seminaries were located in or near the cathedral (often at the cathedral school), where the seminarians would participate in the worship life of the church. Almost a century later, the ecclesiastical reform movement known as the French School (led by Jean-Jacques Olier) established seminaries as "apostolic houses," which were places of liturgical and spiritual formation, to supplement the education the seminarians received elsewhere. The liturgies in Olier's group were celebrated in a parish, not in the seminary, but were seen as a supplemental formational resource to the theological education the students were receiving, and were private liturgies for the seminarians. This was another step in the development of worship distinctly for seminarians.[11]

As we jump forward in time and see the development of schools of higher education in the colonies, we see the beginning of institutions primarily for the education of clergy. Harvard, which began in 1636, is

---

for centuries to come, the clergyman would be the best educated citizen and education would be the key to his authority . . . the claims of the Reformers hinged on the interpretation of texts and on a science of textual interpretation sufficient to challenge church authority" (Marsden, *The Soul of the American University*, 41).

9. Orme, *Medieval Schools*, 299.

10. Orme, *Medieval Schools*, 303.

11. Cunningham and Weborg, *Prayer and Life in the Spirit*, 17–18.

emblematic of this pattern. The assumption was that clergy would get training in the humanities, including theology, and would apprentice under another clergyman to learn the pastoral skills required of a minister. Whether clergy or lay, however, all students would be required to attend daily chapel.

Required chapel in colleges and universities was the norm into the late nineteenth century, even at state schools. Required chapels in some state schools lasted into the 1900s. An example of such a chapel service would be the University of Minnesota's chapel, which was lead by the president and faculty, and included a hymn or hymns, scripture reading, and prayer.[12] Further, the University of Illinois, founded in 1868, had from its inception required chapel for all of its students. School began at 6:45am, and chapel was at 8:15am, lasting fifteen minutes. Later it was expanded to thirty minutes, probably to include a sermon. Students were required to attend chapel daily, and then attend church services Sunday morning as well Sunday afternoon chapel. This was standard fare in the late nineteenth century, but became less and less common after the turn of the century.[13] Church-sponsored schools, such as those in the Ivy League, held on to the tradition of a required chapel for all students past 1900. For example, at Yale the college requirement of mandatory chapel attendance and compulsory Sunday worship began to be questioned at the end of the nineteenth century, and its support faded by the 1920s. In the Fall of 1926, Yale had for the first time voluntary chapel attendance.[14]

Between the inception of Harvard and Yale University's loss of mandatory chapel, a watershed in the history of American seminary education occurred: the establishment of Andover Seminary. In the late eighteenth century, the Congregational churches in New England were becoming increasingly Unitarian. This was especially seen in the leadership of Harvard. In the wake of this growing Unitarianism, traditionally orthodox Congregationalists began Andover Seminary at Phillips Academy in Andover, Massachusetts in 1808. This was the first theological seminary in the United States, as it was the first theological school to anticipate that its clergy had a college education. Its three-year curriculum became

---

12. Longfield, "From Evangelicalism to Liberalism," 51.

13. Behle, "Educating *The Lord's Redeemed and Anointed*," 62–63.

14. Attendance at worship for students of the Divinity School remained mandatory. Longfield, "For God, Country, and for Yale," 146–69.

the template for what is now understood as the three-year Master's of Divinity degree.[15]

At its establishment, Andover Seminary met in the local Congregational meeting house and in the homes of its professors. The first building on Andover's campus had a room dedicated as the chapel.[16] The next building erected was Bartlett Chapel, which was dedicated in 1818, ten years after the opening of the school. Chapel was required for both faculty and students, both before and after classes for Morning and Evening prayer. The Trustees set the times for these services. Morning prayer was set for 7am in the Winter, starting fifteen minutes earlier every two weeks until it began at 6am the first of March. The seminary also gathered on Sunday for worship on the Lord's Day. In many ways Andover was established as much as a religious community as it was an educational institution: the students lived and ate together, prayed together, and had limited contact with the greater community, even to the point where the students worshipped almost exclusively on campus, even on Sunday.[17]

Some Andover chapel sermons were published as theological tracts. The earliest I found was from August 17, 1823, which was a Sunday. This gives the impression that sermons were only preached on Sunday in the first decades of the seminary's existence.[18] It also implies that daily chapel was more a way of beginning and ending the day in prayer than offering a service of the Word in the midst of the day of study. The practice of daily prayer was common among the eighteenth-century English puritans, and one can easily imagine this practice was a point of reference for the founders of Andover.[19]

Although Andover created what we would call today "an intentional community," it had little provision for the formation of pastoral practice.

15. Rowe, *History of Andover Theological Seminary*, 13. James Fraser observes that Andover established a paradigm of theological education that has been accepted almost without question. It was a graduate education, it lasted three years, and it formed ministers in the disciplines of Bible study, Theology, History and Preaching. Yet there is little evidence that their rota of chapel prayer had such long lasting affects. See Fraser, *Schooling the Preachers*, 35.

16. Rowe, *History of Andover Theological Seminary*, 24–25, 28.

17. Rowe's description of the Spartan existence the students lived, including the severe illnesses—even death—of the students caused by the meager fare and barely adequate housing (especially heat) echo the ascetic communities of early Christian history.

18. Murdock, *Nature of the Atonement*.

19. See Tripp, *Daily Prayer in the Reformed Tradition*.

Evidence seems to point to faculty leadership of chapel, for example. It appears to have continued the practice of having a ministry student gain their pastoral education in an apprenticeship, in this case after their seminary education, unless they had already come with pastoral experience.

This is evidence of an interesting tension in the nature of Protestant seminary education in the nineteenth and twentieth centuries. What was the relationship between faith (and its practices) and learning? In a study commissioned in 1924 by the Institute of Social and Religious Research, Robert Kelly surveyed American seminary education and found it wanting. He identified a lack of qualified faculty (and students), inadequate library resources, and a significant disconnect from the churches for which they were preparing students, to name a few.[20] This survey is as much an indication of a lack of certainty in direction in seminary education as it is a lack of quality or resources. For example, in the early twentieth century, even the most progressive seminaries saw the purpose of their scholarship to build up—not diminish or destroy—the practices and ministries of the Christian faith. Yet at the same time there was a growing emphasis on establishing theology as a scientific, objective study that could hold its own with any academic discipline. This approach shifted these seminaries further away from praxis-oriented teaching and more toward academic excellence alone.[21]

An illustration of this tension between academics and pastoral practice can be found in the University of Chicago Divinity School of the mid-1900s, which established a "laboratory practice" track to its educational philosophy. In this approach, students would supplement their graduate education in theology with work in churches and social agencies to learn the practical aspects of their vocation. Although a throwback to the apprenticeship model, there was no proposed means for correlation or integration within the course of study, such as there would have been in an apprenticeship. It was strong on content and less intentional about practice.

This would change in the mid-twentieth century with the development of practical or pastoral theology. It would seem that this should have been the time when worship and chapel worship in particular would have had its day. However, in his survey of the development of practical

20. Cherry, *Hurrying Toward Zion*, 13.

21. Cherry, *Hurrying Toward Zion*, 35–36.

or pastoral theology, Conrad Cherry identifies the practical disciplines, particularly emphasizing pastoral counseling. Noticeably absent was any mention of worship, liturgy, or even preaching. Chapel was absent for the entire conversation. This is more typical than not of the place of chapel in theological education.[22] There were exceptions to this rule, however. Nels Ferré, then Professor of Philosophical Theology at Vanderbilt, is a unique voice in the role of the chapel in theological education (though not exclusively seminary education). Ferré saw the integration of faith and learning occurring primarily in the chapel, a vision both unique to its day and ours, as we shall see.[23]

Seminary Chapel: The Non-Conversation

The origins of this essay and this volume began with a conversation at Fuller Theological Seminary in June of 2007. Co-sponsored by Fuller's Brehm Center for Worship, Theology, and the Arts and Calvin College's Institute of Christian Worship, a cross-section of chapel leadership in North America gathered for two days to try to approximate a snapshot of the state of seminary chapel in North America. We who gathered there constituted a representative sample of U.S. and Canadian seminaries in all their theological, denominational, political, and liturgical diversity. Together we discussed what we came to identify as some very common problems. We were struck that without exception we experienced the issue of the chapel being marginalized in conversations about teaching

22. See ch. 4, "Theory and Practice," of Cherry, *Hurrying Toward Zion*, 127–155.

23. Ferré, *Christian Faith and Higher Education*. Two representative quotes show how different Ferré's perspectives were (and are): "In Christian education the chapel always stands central on campus. It should do so geographically; it should do so educationally. By the chapel is meant more than a building; by the chapel is meant the basic attitude of the educational institutional toward the ultimate. The campus worships whether it wants to or not. The more education is right the more the chapel stands at the dead center of higher education as the most vital Reality . . . Worship at its center is a personal relation to Deity that cannot be had apart from decision. To worship aright is to decide about life as a whole, its meaning and conduct" (108–9).

"The academic life, moreover, should itself center in the total life of the Christian community. This means concretely that the worship of God should be primary; the vocation of the college is to find for the world, and to help the world do, the will of God. God becomes real and regnant only through worship. Chapel services should be held daily, and be so integral to the whole purpose and "feel" of the academic community that no compulsion should be necessary" (123–24).

and learning within the faculty. Those who had no faculty appointment in their schools were often shown little respect for their gifts, skills, and training; while those with faculty appointments were often seen as doing less than important academic work, if academic at all.

Reflecting on a comprehensive bibliography of works written on seminary chapel, we began to understand the problem: there had been so little written by or for the academy about chapel, that chapel had gained little respect among our peers in terms of the scholarly, ecclesial, political, and liturgical training and abilities that are required—not to mention the sheer extravagant output of human labor—to create and sustain a chapel program. The idea of this book came out of our desperate attempt to get the seminary chapel a place at the table where the chapel can be seen as an important (if not essential) part of the education and formation one receives in seminary.[24]

What have we learned from our cursory survey of the history of seminary education that might inform our appraisal of the current situation of the place of chapel in Protestant seminaries today? From its inception in North America, common worship was seen as an integral part of higher education in general, and ministry education in particular. Its importance was assumed, though never explained or defended in any public way within the academy. The controversy that ensued in the early years of North American higher education was whether or not chapel should be mandatory in state schools and schools with decreasing connection to the church. These were not seminary issues however. It would appear that there are two factors that have complicated seminary chapels in the past half-century. One is the growth of a variety of liturgical expressions, many of which are more divergent than convergent. It is not uncommon for students from the same ecclesial tradition to have drastically different liturgical experiences in their home churches, such as the influence of the Charismatic movement in one and the influence of the liturgical movement in another.[25] The second influence in this matter is the develop-

24. Information about and from this meeting can be accessed at http://www.calvin.edu/worship/wcom/campus/seminary.php. The bibliography mentioned above can be found at http://www.calvin.edu/worship/wcom/campus/lections.php. Thanks to Ron Rienstra, author of chapter 8, for the extravagant work he performed in collecting, collating, and disseminating materials for and from this meeting.

25. For a survey of the explosion of diverse worship influences in Protestant churches see Redman, *The Great Worship Awakening.*

ment and growth of the area of liturgical studies in Protestant seminaries. Seminaries for the first time have faculty members to teach worship full- or part-time, who have terminal degrees in liturgical studies, not preaching or music or some related sub-discipline. This has upped the ante in terms of the academic expectations on chapel, which may or may not run counter to the trends of liturgical diversity in a seminary community.[26]

There has been a growth in scholarly work in the area of both seminary education and practical theology in the past decade. In particular, there have been two recent and significant volumes, *Educating Clergy* and *For Life Abundant*.[27] The first is a survey of theological schools (Jewish and Christian) in North America assessing their strategies and effectiveness in preparing women and men for ministry. The second is a survey of scholarship on teaching Christian practices and practical theology in general. The two intersect at the point of attempting to create and nurture a "pastoral imagination" for improved pastoral effectiveness.

The volume *Educating Clergy* does contain a section on common worship in seminary education. Although the details of their findings are interesting in that they demonstrate the variety of approaches and levels of investment taken by various theological schools, what is more interesting for our purposes is how the research team categorized chapel. Chapel was a co-curricular program of spiritual formation. Although this research concludes that for schools with either a shared liturgical tradition or diverse liturgical traditions, the chapel is a place of "academic, professional/pastoral and spiritual formation,"[28] the question of how the chapel is related to the curriculum is only raised with one seminary because of its explicit integration of the chapel with their curriculum.[29]

Although the reviewers state how important chapels are for creating a set of shared spiritual practices and helping foster a sense of community among the students, faculty and staff, it is unclear how important they

26. For a series of essays that addresses both of these factors, see White, *Christian Worship in North America*.

27. Foster, Dahill, Golemon, and Tolentino, *Educating Clergy*; and Bass and Dykstra, *For Life Abundant*.

28. Compare Foster Dahill, Golemon, and Tolentino, *Educating Clergy*, 267 and 278.

29. This seminary was the Church Divinity School of the Pacific, the Episcopal seminary in the Graduate Theological Union consortium of schools at Berkley. The Dean of this chapel, Lizette Larson-Miller, authors chapter 5, "Seminary Chapel in a Prayer Book Context."

believe this is to the overall task of educating future clerics for their ministries. Given the scope of this volume, to give the topic of chapel worship only five pages is a bit scant, and may be more revealing of the actual import given to chapel in this study.[30]

This tendency to marginalize the place of chapel surprisingly finds itself also in *For Life Abundant*, particularly because there were two chapters dedicated specifically to worship and religious ritual in the seminary curriculum. "Liturgics" (worship studies) was defined as a practical theology discipline along with homiletics, pastoral care, Christian education, and other disciplines that teach a practice.[31] Disciplines which emphasize practices confirm an epistemological truth that performance generates meaning in ways like no other, creating a "preferential option for practice" over theory alone.[32] The reason for this is that "[p]ractical theologians teach a practice with the expectation that participation in that practice will cultivate the kind of knowledge, *phronesis*, that deepens students' capacities for further participation in the practice."[33] At first blush it would appear that such an approach to learning, especially in terms of learning the field of 'liturgics' would privilege the possibilities for practical knowledge gained through the opportunity for regular participation in common worship.

In the section entitled "Practical Theology in the Classroom," there are two essays on teaching worship, John Witvliet's "Teaching Worship as a Christian Practice" and James Nieman's "Liturgy and Life."[34] Although the parameter of the topic was explicitly the classroom, one would imagine that there might be some mention of the relationship between the classroom and the chapel. For example, Witvliet stresses the importance of not only teaching about the practice, but teaching the practice; we must prepare our worship students, whether undergraduate or seminarian, he argues, to execute what they learn, and evaluate their execution, all to the end of leading the people of God in "full, conscious and active partici-

30. See section entitled , "Cultivating Spirituality Through Common Worship," in Foster, Dahill, Golemon, and Tolentino, *Educating Clergy*, 275–80.

31. Miller–McLemore, "Practical Theology and Pedagogy," 172. Compare to Foley, "Academy Membership," 3–16.

32. Miller–McLemore, "Practical Theology and Pedagogy," 182, 189.

33. Miller–McLemore, "Practical Theology and Pedagogy," 180.

34. Witvliet "Teaching Worship as a Christian Practice," 117–48; and Nieman, "Liturgy and Life," 150–67.

pation" in the prayers of the community. As applicable as chapel would be for a communal place of rehearsing, evaluating, and developing these practices in the community and its members, chapel was not mentioned.

Nieman's essay was slightly more focused, as it addressed four pastoral rites in the Lutheran (ELCA) tradition: baptism, wedding, healing, and funeral. The rites (with the exception of healing rites) are unlikely to find their way into the life of a seminary chapel. However, the goal of training reflective practitioners is an end that squares quite nicely with a goal of a seminary chapel program, and no mention is made of it. This is not a critique of either Witvliet's or Nieman's essays. Instead it is critique of how distant the chapel finds itself from even the most relevant conversations in the academy about teaching, learning, and formation. This is an opportunity lost both for the growth and development of the seminary chapel program and the teaching ministry of the seminary. How can seminary chapel become a full partner at the table? What does the history of ministry education help us see this in lack of engagement with the broader mission of the seminary and possibilities that have yet to be realized?

Plato, Augustine, and Wittgenstein Walk into a Bar . . .

In the previous section we saw how the issues surrounding chapel in the life of the seminary, in particular its relationship to the seminary curriculum, appear to have little voice in the broader conversations in the academy. Even those in the fields of liturgy and practical theology seem to overlook or underestimate the place of chapel in pastoral and theological education. I am suggesting that there is potential benefit by including the chapel in those conversations, both for how it could benefit the chapel and how it could benefit the broader mission of the academy. Chapel appears to be a logical place to root the phronetic of not just worship, but of the lived expression of all the disciplines taught in seminary. I would suggest that this conversation could begin with the epistemological question: how is it that we know and therefore learn?

Debra Dean Murphy, in her work, *Teaching That Transforms*, asks the question, "How do we know what we know?" She then goes on to describe a typical response, observing that we know because someone has taught us. A person or persons with a knowledge we do not have communicates this data or understanding to us. When the transfer of wisdom or knowledge is successful, the recipient can grasp it, utilize it, and or manipulate it. Murphy concludes, "Understood this way, knowledge is conceived as a kind of repository of neutral facts, and the mastery of these facts constitutes the process and ultimate goal of coming to know." [35]

Murphy turns to St. Augustine for an alternative vision of learning, to the "objectivist view" described above. Murphy observes that knowledge, for Augustine, always involves a third party, the reality to which knowledge points; and ultimately that reality is God. The ground of learning is therefore doxological. It is also an educational approach that finds worship as its primary place for learning. It is bodily and physical, it involves more than just our minds; it engages our entire selves. It provides knowledge that can only be known in the doing of it. Relating this to the larger task of Christian education, Murphy concludes, "Any formalized teaching about *any* particular practice or doctrine must concede the primacy of worship for shaping persons to be able in the first place to receive and understand such doctrinal instruction. Worship catechizes, and worship is the matrix and milieu from which all catechesis can take place." [36]

These are bold assertions about the nature of learning and the nature of Christian education in particular. How does one appraise them? The best way is to eavesdrop on a conversation on learning and knowing between Plato, Augustine, and Wittgenstein. Philosopher Peter King created such a conversation, investigating how it is that we learn. [37] The conversation pits three different views of what knowledge and learning is against one another and invites us to consider how our epistemology informs our pedagogy. For example, Plato understood that all knowledge is prenatal. The human soul existing in heaven before its incarnation has knowledge of the eternal forms and eternal truths. The act of learning, therefore, is an act of "un-forgetting" recalling one's prenatal knowledge that was lost at birth. Augustine, responding to the belief that learning comes from prenatal knowing, suggests that not everyone can understand the complexities of geometry, because not everyone was a geometer in their previous

35. Murphy, *Teaching That Transforms*, 97–98.

36. Murphy, *Teaching That Transforms*, 105. The entirety of Murphy's argument is contained in her chapter, "Worship and Catechesis: Knowledge, Desire and Christian Formation," 97–116.

37. King, "Augustine on the Impossibility of Teaching," 179–95.

existence.[38] This sarcastic *reductio ad absurdum* quickly dismisses Plato's approach to learning and knowing.

On the other hand, Wittgenstein (who represents Murphy's "objectivist view") proposed that learning is a matter of mastering a technique of assessment and integration—assimilating neutral data. A teacher presents data, information or a theory, and the student or students process this information. Once they are able to understand well enough, they are able to go on to the next level. For example, in Plato's model, "1+1=2" is knowable because in a prenatal consciousness, this truth was learned and now recovered. In Wittgenstein's model, "1+1=2" is learned once the concept is grasped to the extent that one can apply it and move on to "1+2=3." Those who master this learning technique ("a rule-following behavior") learn more than others, but still the technique and process are public, outside of oneself. It is an objective process.[39]

Augustine offers a third alternative: that learning is an interior process of correlation. Learning is an inspired flash of insight. Learning is a result of human beings having both a fallen nature and divine image. In our sinless state, humans could communicate directly, without mediation, to other human beings or to God. However, because of our fallen state, we necessarily must use signs to communicate. To put it another way, the only way I can get a thought from my mind to your mind is through the use of signs, words, and gestures—in this specific case, I communicate my thoughts to you the reader by the use of words encoded in an alphabet (signs) for which we have agreed-upon meaning. Most importantly, for Augustine and for us, a sign only makes sense if one has knowledge in this world of that to which the sign points. Here we see the distinction with Plato (the referent is of this world) and with Wittgenstein (knowledge is not meaning in itself, but in relationship to the world). For Augustine, signs point to what is known, signs are not the thing known in itself.[40]

Like Helen Keller making the connection between the word "water," the water being pumped out of the well, and the signs being formed in her hand, learning is an illumination. And this illumination is only possible because of our being created in the image of God, and the reality which upholds our world being God. The most important point of this illustra-

---

38. King, "Augustine on the Impossibility of Teaching," 184.

39. King, "Augustine on the Impossibility of Teaching," 182–83.

40. King, "Augustine on the Impossibility of Teaching," 185–87.

tion is that Helen had a knowledge of the thing "water" and only because of that could make the correlation to the word and the sign. But not everyone is able to make these connections. King concludes his essay this way, "For if the teacher doesn't cause the student to understand—and its clear that the teacher cannot literally cause the student to understand, since otherwise everyone in the classroom would get it, or nobody would—then what is it that takes place? What *is* learning if not a mysterious inner episode of awareness?"[41] This illumination requires integration, a holistic process: phronetic learning.

Pedagogy and Proposal

How might the conversation between Plato, Augustine, and Wittgenstein help us understand both the history and the future of the place of common worship in seminary education? If we agree with King and Murphy, that Augustine offers an insight into learning that is particularly relevant to the topic of the relationship of worship and theology, then there is one essential element of Christian learning: to know the belief one must see the belief embodied. Hence the seminary chapel becomes a place where the common meaning of signs is learned and practiced. Worship is one obvious "it" to which the words and signs of the classrooms refer.

Christian educator, Mary Hess, in her essay on seminary education in post-modernity, offers a "trio of triads" to establish a strategy for contemporary theological education.[42] The first set identifies the context, people, and purpose of education of the teaching event. Each seminary will necessarily answer this set of questions differently depending on its current reality. The second set consists of the ideas, feelings, and actions involved in teaching. This will vary from subject to subject, as well as school to school. The last set describes the curricula (either of a course or school) as the explicit, implicit, and null curricula. The purpose of this trio of triads is to raise to a level of consciousness the choices that must be made in theological education today. Not to make such choices places

41. King, "Augustine on the Impossibility of Teaching," 195. There are two places where Augustine deals most directly with the concept of teaching, learning, and signs. The first is *De magistro* (The Teacher) in Augustine, *Concerning the Teacher and On the Immorality of the Soul.* The second is more well known, *De doctrina Christina.*

42. Hess, "Rich Treasure in Jars of Clay," 123–40.

issues in the "null curriculum," or those things that are taught by their absence.

In the current North American liturgical context, we have a variety of liturgical genres and styles that find their way within almost all Protestant seminaries. How do we address this situation? Not to address this reality, is to communicate that this situation is unimportant, or to privilege or dismiss one or some liturgical traditions. There are a variety of approaches seminaries are taking to address this situation, but little work has been done studying these models and assessing their effectiveness.[43] Chapel in this context, in Augustinian terms, functions as a "non-sign" as it has no common agreed-upon referent. Each seminary must find a way to teach theology in a pluralistic Christian context, and part of that process is finding a way of establishing agreed-upon meanings (at least in general) for the rituals that occur in the chapel. This is a situation that did not exist at any other point in the church's history, either because of lack of diversity or lack of tolerance.

Further, from the survey of the history of chapel we have one theme that appears to have run through most of the history of ministry education. There seems to be an agreed-upon "given" that there is some form of common worship—either in the school or at a church—that the students share. Learning took place in the context of prayer. How different this is from the situation I find myself in now, where this year I sat on a faculty panel discussing whether or not seminary students should attend church, at a school whose once-a-week chapel can only accommodate a small percentage of its students. Possibly the starting point of the intersection of past history and future practice is reconsidering the place of corporate prayer in seminary education. This is the thing to which the signs of theological education points—human interaction with God.

43. A singular example of a study of this current situation is Anderson, "Worship and Learning," 117–30. Anderson identifies the multiple issues of diversity facing seminaries today: multiple denominations, ethnic and cultural diversity, diversity of worship practice and style—all of which converge often in conflicted ways in the chapel. He also identifies the lack of attention given to this issue by some schools. Anderson contributes chapter 9, "Worship and Formation for Ministry."

Reflections from History: Benedict and Bonhoeffer

There are two figures that represent this principle of teaching taking place in the greater context of the life of prayer: St. Benedict of Nursia[44] and Dietrich Bonhoeffer.[45] From this unlikely pairing of these two examples from the history of the church, we find a common model of *ora et labora*, or prayer and study working in concert as the historical charism for ministry education and formation.

Almost all western monasticism can be traced–directly or indirectly–to Benedict's Rule. In this short, terse guide for communal religious life, there is a balance of life in the oratory and life doing the work of community. As we saw, the monasteries were the vehicles that carried classical Roman education until developed in the medieval university, so for some their *labora* was *studia*. The corporate prayer of the Rule was not designed to create community and fellowship between the brothers alone. It was designed to draw one closer to God in their personal prayer as well. It was a practice designed to bring the community and individuals into the immediate presence of God, where the monk should remain throughout the day no matter what they were doing. This is the balance of *ora et labora*.[46]

This balance between the corporate and the personal is essential to learning in the Rule. It is of primary importance in the care of souls that disciples of Christ be instructed in prayer. For this reason it is crucial that *Opus Dei* and *oratio*—liturgical prayer and personal prayer—work together in concert. The Rule suggests that one is breathing with both lungs only when one prays privately *and* corporately, and that both feed the other.[47] As this carried over into education, it implied that faith and learning worked together in concert in the same way that the personal and the corporate worked together. It was an ideal of balance and integration.

For Benedict the Hours of Prayer was the embodiment of prayer without ceasing. It was the context in which one learned obedience and humility, the qualities Benedict discusses in the chapters that precede his discussion of the Divine Office in the *Rule*. Submitting one's life of prayer

---

44. See *The Rule of St. Benedict in English*.
45. See especially Bonhoeffer, *Life Together*.
46. Kleiner, *Serving God First*, 206–7.
47. Heufelder, *The Way of God according to the Rule of St. Benedict*, 153–55.

to the rhythms of the Office conformed one's life in the posture of the Cross, the discipline of obedience, and the spirit of humility.[48]

What I offer in this first example is not a philosophy of Christian education that recovers the values of monasticism or asceticism. Instead I suggest that what gives Benedict's *Rule* such an enduring quality is its clearly articulated vision of the integration of prayer with the larger life of the person. It is this belief that leads to the presumption of common worship in the early years of public education in America. It is an ideal that has long since passed in most colleges and universities. And in light of the current liturgical tensions of our day, it is an ideal that seminaries may have gradually backed away from.

It is striking to find an almost identical balance in Dietrich Bonhoeffer's *Life Together* as we find in Benedict's *Rule*. It is even more interesting because of the context of Bonhoeffer's writing. In the Summer of 1935 Dietrich Bonhoeffer began what he describes as his true calling—beginning a preacher's seminary in Finkewalde. A preacher's seminary was a response to the limitations placed on pastoral education by the structures of the State Church system in his conflicted political times. Although Bonhoeffer's curriculum was mostly traditional, he included in it a core program of discipleship. This was unique in that it was an intentional community the likes of which was not known in Germany at the time. This small community of students lived and learned together creating a fertile context for theological discussion and pastoral application. The *Gestapo* closed the small seminary down in the Fall of 1937. It was in response to the demise of this school that Bonhoeffer wrote *Life Together* in 1939, his most popular book during his lifetime. It was his hope that the model he created might be planted elsewhere, and that his students would be encouraged to continue the life of disciplined study they had begun.[49]

Bonhoeffer, in the second chapter of *Life Together*, addresses the corporate life of his school. In Bonhoeffer's model, the day is framed by worship, prayer, and Bible study in a way that is very much like standard Hours of Prayer.[50] Bonhoeffer presents in a self-evident way that each day is God's and should be begun with prayer. The offices of prayer were to

48. De Vogüé, *The Rule of Saint Benedict*, 127–30.

49. Bethge, *Dietrich Bonhoeffer*, 419–72.

50. This observation about Bonhoeffer's seminary prayer life is not a new or uncommon one. See Rakoczy, "The Witness of Community Life," 43–62.

include the recitation of Psalms, scripture reading, offering prayers and the Lord's Supper. Times of prayer were to be repeated at the close of the day, and at Noon if possible. Bonhoeffer then adds, "After the first morning hour the Christian's day until evening belongs to work."[51] He goes on to say that because the day is framed in prayer, "Thus the prayer of the Christian reaches beyond its set time and extends into the heart of his (sic) work. It includes the whole day . . . [t]hus every word, every work, every labor of a Christian becomes a prayer."[52] In so doing, one has achieved a unity to the entire day, a balance of *ora et labora*, faith and learning, prayer and study.[53]

It could be conjectured that though St. Benedict and Dietrich Bonhoeffer are two very different characters in the history of the church, Benedict and his *Rule* are so well known that Bonhoeffer is, consciously or unconsciously, in Benedict's debt, and the pairing of these two examples says little more than how pervasive Benedict's influence is. I would suggest, even if this is true, that the most important common theme that this unlikely couple offer is that theological education and ministry formation require learning that is both theory and praxis. Learning to be a Christian disciple requires reflective learning of the Christian disciplines, not in addition to the core of the curriculum, but at the core of the curriculum. This is what I suggest the lesson that the history of chapel in seminary education offers, a lesson that is becoming more and more difficult to learn and apply in our increasingly diverse church.

Defining Future Success

I began this essay with the disclaimer that this chapter was a failure. It ends with the hope of success. I propose two very basic suggestions that any seminary could do that would help address the deficiencies identified in this study. The first suggestion is historical and the second is curricular. As we saw in the opening sections of this essay, there is a significant lack of data regarding the details of chapel practices in seminaries. Eliminating

---

51. Bonhoeffer, *Life Together*, 69.

52. Bonhoeffer, *Life Together*, 71.

53. For Further exploration of Bonhoeffer's program of prayer and learning see Dan Caldwell, "Bonhoeffer's *Life Together* and the Christian University," 27–38; and, Eberhard Bethge, "Le culte dans un monde séculier tel que l'entendait Bonhoeffer," 42–59.

this lack will require archival research, examining documents of the worship life of the seminary and correlating them with both the description of the worship and preaching curriculum of the same time along with the worship practices of constituent churches of that time. This research could be done within any number of seminaries, each one adding one more puzzle piece to the overall picture of the history of common worship in theological education. At the same time this could be a tremendous asset to a seminary in terms of its own institutional identity.

The second suggestion is not one of application but of conversation. The contexts our seminaries find themselves in today are much too complex to suggest even one or two general practices. Instead the suggestion is for a conversation a seminary faculty and administration could initiate that could bear a great deal of fruit. That is, the question could be posed concerning the place of *phronesis* of that particular seminary's curriculum, and how that relates to the place of chapel in the teaching ministry of the seminary. It would be too easy to say all seminaries simply need to return to the ideal of being a community that balances prayer and study. With the variety of students seminaries are nowadays serving: part-time students, evening and weekend students, on-line students, etc., such a historical recovery seems inappropriate and ill-advised. The answer to this question is neither easy nor will the conversations it instigates always be harmonious or pleasant, but this is where I believe the conversation must start. Such a conversation could well be aided by historical data about the seminary's history of chapel worship, its form, philosophy, and function over the years.

Neither I nor any of my colleagues who contribute to this volume see this task as an easy one. We all have first-hand knowledge of how difficult the issues surrounding the chapel of a seminary can be. But we all have high hopes for chapel, and our contributions are part of our wager on the future of common worship as part of theological education. Success may not come quickly or easily, but we hope and pray it will come. Might we convince you to hope and pray along with us.

Works Cited

Anderson, E. Byron. "Worship and Learning." *Theological Education* 39 (2003) 117–30.
Augustine, *Concerning the Teacher and On the Immorality of the Soul*. Translated by George Leckie. New York: Appleton-Century-Crofts, 1938.

————. *De doctrina Christina* (On Christian Doctrine)/*Teaching Christianity*. Translated by Edmund Hill. Hyde Park, NY: New City, 1996.

Bass, Dorothy C., and Craig Dykstra, eds. *For Life Abundant: Practical Theology, Theological Education, and Christian Ministry*. Grand Rapids, MI: Eerdmans, 2008.

Behle, J. Gregory. "Educating *The Lord's Redeemed and Anointed*: The University of Illinois Chapel Experience 1868–1894." *The Master's Seminary Journal*, 11 (2000) 53–73.

Bethge, Eberhard. *Dietrich Bonhoeffer: A Biography*. Revised edition. Minneapolis: Fortress, 2000.

————. "Le culte dans un monde séculier tel que l'entendait Bonhoeffer." *Communion* 24 (1970) 42–59.

Bonhoeffer, Dietrich. *Life Together*. Translated by John W. Doberstein. New York: Harper and Row, 1954.

Caldwell, Dan. "Bonhoeffer's *Life Together* and the Christian University." *Faculty Dialogue* 17 (1992) 27–38.

Cherry, Conrad. *Hurrying Toward Zion: Universities, Divinity Schools and American Protestantism*. Bloomington, IN: Indiana University Press, 1995.

Cooke, Bernard. *Ministry to Word and Sacraments: History and Theology*. Philadelphia: Fortress, 1976.

Cunningham, Agnes, and John Weborg. *Prayer and Life in the Spirit: Adventure in Academic Excellence and Ecumenical Collaboration*. Chicago: North Park Theological Seminary, 1993.

De Vogüé, Adalbert. *The Rule of Saint Benedict: A Doctrinal and Spiritual Commentary*. Translated by John Baptist Hasbrouk. Kalamazoo, MI: Cistercian, 1983.

Ferré, Nels F. S. *Christian Faith and Higher Education*. New York: Harper, 1953.

Foley, Edward. "Academy Membership: A Case Study in Liturgical Methodology." In *Proceedings of the North American Academy of Liturgy*, 3–16. Valparaiso, IN: North American Academy of Liturgy, 1997.

Foster, Charles, Lisa Dahill, Larry Golemon, and Barbara Wang Tolentino. *Educating Clergy: Teaching Practices and Pastoral Imagination*. San Francisco: Jossey-Bass, 2006.

Fraser, James W. *Schooling the Preachers: The Development of Protestant Theological Education in the United States 1740–1875*. New York: University Press of America, 1988.

Hess, Mary E., "Rich Treasure in Jars of Clay: Christian Graduate Theological Education in a Postmodern Context." In *The Conviction of Things Not Seen: Worship and Ministry in the 21st Century*, edited by Todd E. Johnson, 123–40. Grand Rapids, MI: Brazos, 2002.

Heufelder, Emmanual. *The Way of God according to the Rule of St. Benedict*. Translated by Luke Eberle. Kalamazoo, MI: Cistercian, 1983.

Kleiner, Dom Sighard. *Serving God First: Insights on The Rule of Benedict,* Translated by James Scharinger. Kalamazoo, MI: Cistercian, 1985.

King, Peter, "Augustine on the Impossibility of Teaching." *Metaphilosophy* 29 (1988) 179–95.

Longfield, Bradley, "From Evangelicalism to Liberalism: Public Midwestern Universities in Nineteenth-Century America." In *The Secularization of the Academy*, edited by George Marsden and Bradley Longfield, 46–73. New York: Oxford University Press, 1992.

————. "'For God, Country, and for Yale': Yale, Religion, and Higher Education between the World Wars" In *The Secularization of the Academy*, edited by George Marsden and Bradley Longfield, 146-69. New York: Oxford University Press, 1992.

Maag, Karin. *Seminary or University? The Genevan Academy and Reformed Higher Education, 1560–1620*. Brookfield, VT: Ashgate, 1995.

Marsden, George. *The Soul of the American University: From Protestant Establishment to Established Nonbelief*. New York: Oxford University Press, 1994.

Miller, Glenn T. *Piety and Intellect: The Aims and Purpose of Ante-Bellum Theological Education*. Atlanta, GA: Scholars Press, 1990.

————. *Piety and Profession: American Protestant Theological Education, 1870–1970*. Grand Rapids, MI: Eerdmans, 2007.

Miller-McLemore, Bonnie J. "Practical Theology and Pedagogy." In *For Life Abundant: Practical Theology, Theological Education, and Christian Ministry*, edited by Dorothy C. Bass and Craig Dykstra, 170-90. [Grand Rapids, MI: Eerdmans, 2008.

Murdock, James, *Nature of the Atonement*. Andover, MA: Flagg and Gould, 1823.

Murphy, Debra Dean. *Teaching That Transforms: Worship as the Heart of Christian Education*. Grand Rapids, MI: Brazos, 2004.

Nieman, James R. "Liturgy and Life." In *For Life Abundant: Practical Theology, Theological Education, and Christian Ministry*, edited by Dorothy C. Bass and Craig Dykstra, 150-67. Grand Rapids, MI: Eerdmans, 2008.

Orme, Nicholas. *Medieval Schools: From Roman Britain to Renaissance England*. New Haven, CT: Yale University Press, 2006.

Rakoczy, Susan. "The Witness of Community Life: Bonhoeffer's *Life Together* and the Taizé Community." *Journal of Theology for South Africa* 127 (2007) 43–62.

Redman, Robb, *The Great Worship Awakening: Singing the Lord's Song in the Postmodern Church*. San Francisco: Jossey-Bass, 2003.

Rowe, Henry K. *History of Andover Theological Seminary*. Newton, MA: Thomas Todd, 1933.

The Rule of St. Benedict in English. Edited by Timothy Fry. Collegeville, MN: Liturgical, 1982.

Tripp, Diane Karay. *Daily Prayer in the Reformed Tradition: An Initial Survey* Cambridge, UK: Grove, 1996.

White, James F. *Christian Worship in North America*. Eugene, OR: Wipf and Stock, 2007.

Witvliet, John D. "Teaching Worship as a Christian Practice" In *For Life Abundant: Practical Theology, Theological Education, and Christian Ministry*, edited by Dorothy C. Bass and Craig Dykstra, 117–48. Grand Rapids, MI: Eerdmans, 2008.

2

The Politics of Seminary Chapels

DWIGHT W. VOGEL, OSL

Seminary chapel is not *a* church but it *is* Church, a local embodiment of the Body of Christ—the people of God called out, gathered together, and sent forth. It reflects, embodies, generates, and affirms the nature of the Church.

Whether or not seminary chapels are believed to have a transcendent dimension as well, seminary chapels are human institutions. As with churches, politics are involved in the human dynamics of who they are and what they do. I am not using the word "politics" as a term of negative judgment, although common usage sometimes implies that the word refers to unfair tactics used to gain power or control in a conflict of interests. Rather I am using "politics" here to refer to "the often conflicting interrelationships among people in a society" and how we deal with them.[1]

The politics of seminary chapel could be analyzed in the same way the politics of any other group or institution is analyzed. However, because of the ecclesial nature of seminary chapels, political dynamics in their leadership and life reflect, explicitly and/or implicitly, ecclesiological concerns. Reflecting on the politics of seminary chapels thus involves us in a theological task.

Seminaries and their chapels are not monolithic. Like churches, they embody a wide variety of traditions, practices and contexts. Each is

---

1. Answers.com, "Politics," definition 6, http://www.answers.com/topic/politics (accessed August 24, 2008).

unique, and to understand any one of them demands that we recognize its heritage and the context in which it exists. For example, the seminary where I served as Dean of the Chapel is denominationally affiliated, but it includes many students and faculty from other denominations. Students come from a variety of ethnic and cultural backgrounds. It is located on a university campus, but is independently governed. It is in a large metropolitan area with twelve other seminaries.

A cameo of the nature of the early church tells us that the baptized "devoted themselves to the apostles' teaching and fellowship, to the breaking of bread and the prayers" (Acts 2:42). All these dimensions of the life of the Church are present in a seminary and are embodied in seminary chapel, to a greater or lesser degree.

The body of Christ gathered in a seminary chapel is also the body politic of the seminary community. It is not surprising that chapel becomes the lightening rod for the issues and concerns at stake in the community. If it were not so, participants would not be passionate about either worship or the issues, or both. It was not easy for me to wrestle with these dynamics as Dean of the Chapel, but their absence would signal an irrelevance that would be even more lamentable.

While educational agendas and methods vary from school to school and class to class, a seminary community is gathered together for *teaching and learning.* Every discipline comes with questions to ask about what goes on in chapel. Is it theologically sound? Is it biblically informed? Is it pastorally sensitive? Does it take into account the various ways in which persons learn? Does it have liturgical integrity? And so on and so on. If professors bring their whole selves into worship, they will not park their minds at the door. There are legitimate questions to raise, especially in a community engaged in preparing persons for ministry.

We know that faculty will not always agree with one another. When one faculty member teaching theology is a process theologian, another is a feminist/liberation theologian, a third is deeply influenced by Bonhoeffer, and a fourth by radical orthodoxy, passionate theological dialog is likely to take place. There is another possibility, however: that one stands within a classroom citadel and lobs theological grenades at colleagues, student preachers and church leaders. The temptation is to let chapel become the battleground for warring agendas. As faculty, we bring legitimate questions and concerns with us. However, when the primary purpose of our participation is criticism and critique, our ability to worship is seriously threatened. During a time of confession and forgiveness I heard one of my colleagues say, "I confess that I have great difficulty loving my enemies." While that is true for all of us, in this case what was at stake for my colleague was the difficulty of being at the Eucharistic table with theological opponents.

When I was a seminary student, a guest speaker told us that during the days of the underground seminary at Finkenwald, Dietrich Bonhoeffer was asked how he could cope with the variety of levels of ability and perspective manifested in their worship life together. He answered, "There is only one crucial question: 'What is God saying to us in this service?'" One of the tasks of a Dean of the Chapel is finding ways to invite colleagues to let that happen, so that the inevitable politics involved do not become the dominant voice.

Already, in addressing the politics of teaching and learning, we are involved in the province of "fellowship." Because that word is often interpreted too narrowly and superficially, I prefer to use the original Greek word, *koinonia*, namely, that which makes these people with their often conflicting interrelationships a community. One of my faculty colleagues objected to the use of the term "community" for either the seminary or the chapel. My response then as now is that, as the body of Christ, we have *koinonia* not in spite of our differences but because of it. Our *koinonia* is not uniformity but the connectedness we have in our diversity. "Indeed, the body does not consist of one member but of many" (1 Cor 12:14). It is one body because there is no dissension within the body, "but the members may have the same care for one another. If one member suffers, all suffer together with it; if one member is honored, all rejoice together with it" (1 Cor. 12:25–26).

In our consideration of the politics of seminary chapel that bit about "no dissension" is likely to strike us as extremely unrealistic. Dissension, however, is not the same as disagreement, difference, or diversity. When my colleague Ruth Duck was Dean of the Chapel, one of our students made use of a resource that imagined how the medium at Endor might have spoken (cf. 1 Samuel 28). The words were to be prayed by the congregation. I was among those who could not join in that prayer. It raised considerable discussion and feelings ran high among both students and faculty.

With the cooperation of the student involved, Professor Duck organized an open forum, which was very well attended. She set the stage by indicating that the purpose of the forum was not to assign blame, but to foster understanding. The student talked about what her aim had been and how it had gone wrong. Students and faculty shared their feelings and their theological and liturgical objections. The forum ended with a discussion of the importance of care in designing liturgies and especially what planners put in the mouths of the congregation. The forum created "safe space" for the student and her critics. We all learned much and the student was upheld in understanding even as she recognized the furor she had unwittingly caused. At the next chapel, one of the most vocal faculty critics of the chapel embraced the student during the passing of the peace. The result was not dissension, but disagreement with both passion and compassion.

However, someone in the community sent a report of the chapel (not of the forum, interestingly) to an outside group with a very strong political agenda where it was used (inaccurately) to depict the seminary as encouraging paganism. We do not escape dissension from outside even when we are able to foster understanding within the community. No matter how adept we become at the politics of seminary chapel, we do well to remember that we cannot control the world. We can only be faithful to the ministry with which we are entrusted as best we know how, and commend ourselves and our ministry to God.

Churches and seminary chapels have many members with different functions, even as they did for the New Testament church (cf. 1 Corinthians 12). Students, staff, faculty, and administration may all be active participants in seminary chapels. There are also non-resident groups who have a stake in seminary chapels: trustees, donors, judicatories, and/or local congregations among them.

Seminaries frequently talk about chapel as central to their mission in their public relations materials, but then conceive of it as peripheral in discussion of curriculum or funding. Neal Fisher, the president of the seminary who twice appointed me Dean of the Chapel, did not follow that pattern. Unless he was out of town on a chapel day, he was in attendance. He took no appointments during chapel time, and terminated the previous appointment in time to arrive before chapel began, often bringing his last guest with him. His commitment to the importance of chapel in the seminary and in his own life did not go unnoticed by students, faculty, and staff. When he encouraged us to make chapel participation a priority, we knew he was sharing his own conviction.

In earlier years, the chapel program had been coordinated by various faculty and staff members, among them a church historian and the seminary librarian. Like many other seminaries up until the 1970s, there were faculty positions in homiletics, but none in liturgy or worship itself. That changed when, after the appointment of Ruth Duck to teach worship, she became Dean of the Chapel. By the time I was appointed Dean of the Chapel, I was splitting my time in teaching both theology and worship. My focus on liturgical and sacramental theology was a bridge between the two fields.

When full-time faculty members with other teaching responsibilities are appointed to be Deans of the chapel, they already have a recognized seat at the table in faculty discussions. When a person is appointed primarily to coordinate the chapel program (whether with faculty rank or not), that is not necessarily the case. There are advantages and disadvantages both ways. A person whose primary responsibility is the chapel program will be able to devote more time to the task, but not have the same access to faculty discussions. A faculty person who also oversees chapels will have an entrée to the faculty, but will need additional staff in order to handle the program. President Fisher recognized that a commitment to chapel required budgetary investment. In times of financial restrictions, we scaled back budget for guest speakers and musicians, but not for the personnel needed to coordinate the program.

While attending to the "apostles' teaching" and aware of the importance of nourishing *koinonia*, the focus of seminary chapel is on *the breaking of bread and the prayers*. While Services of Word and Table are normative for United Methodists, there is also a legacy of non-Eucharistic Services of the Word, as well as prayer services (in both the Daily Office tradition and more informal structures). Prayer cells and prayer meetings of various sorts would be born, flourish, and pass from the scene according to the changing levels of interest and natural leadership. In our setting, the prayers of the Daily Office were available from the Episcopal seminary across the street and in the offices and services sponsored by the seminary chapter of the Order of Saint Luke. It was the services centering in the Sacrament of the Table and/or the Sacrament of the Word that were the responsibility of the "chapel program."

Reflecting on the needs of our seminary community led us to the recognition that we were *saying* that our chapel program was for the whole community, but *in fact* those included in our evening classes were being excluded. Since this included a large number of African-American students, racial inclusivity was also at stake. While there was considerable freedom in the design of Tuesday and Thursday chapels, they tended to follow a rather traditional pattern, albeit in a variety of creative ways. And so, we instituted a Wednesday evening Gospel service.

In recent years, discussions about the pattern of worship in countless churches across America make clear that decisions about the nature and style of Christian worship are political—reflecting the definition of politics cited above as "the often conflicting interrelationships among people in a society." Because worship is so important for many persons, discussions about it are often quite passionate. While there was no organized protest about the current state of worship at our seminary, there were rumblings. As in many churches, they reflected concern for the politics of style and the politics of music. In both, the heart language of the worshipper is at stake, and that is not something to be taken lightly. When what we choose to do in worship becomes a bottleneck rather than a channel in one's relationship with God, it is very serious business. And here the designer of worship runs into a political challenge: it is impossible to design any service that meets the needs of each person in attendance and even more impossible to do so at every service.

Our default is usually to design worship that either meets our own needs or meets needs and expectations in the way we have experienced or were taught to meet them. In a setting where that responsibility lies primarily with the Dean of the Chapel, political realism demands that one's vision of these needs and expectations be expanded. A team approach brings its own advantages and frustrations, but it usually broadens the number of perspectives being heard. I realize that talking about "designing worship" means something quite different to a "prayer book" tradition than to a "free church" one. In every setting, however, there is a scale of options from informal to highly formal, and significantly different styles of music available.

In our situation, as in many churches, we opted for a different approach in each of the services. The Tuesday chapel would be a Service of Word and Table (usually using the resources of *The United Methodist Book of Worship*, but also including patterns from ecumenical sources). The seminary choir would sing, the organ would be the primary musical instrument, and *The United Methodist Hymnal* would be the primary source of congregational song. The Wednesday evening service would be a more informal Gospel service. We secured the services of an African-American student who was an outstanding pianist to form a gospel choir. The Thursday chapel would attempt to provide a "blended service" using a variety of creative approaches. The music would be provided by a praise ensemble.

Qualified master's level and doctoral students were appointed as assistant to the Dean of the Chapel (a "Dean's verger," if you will), as coordinators for each of the three weekly chapels, and as a sexton (a position added when we recognized that Dean and coordinators were spending a lot of time moving chairs!). At a retreat at the beginning of the year, the Dean of the Chapel met with these coordinators and the key musicians for each of the services to worship, pray, and reflect together on the purpose and shape of worship for the seminary community. We recognized the danger of becoming so absorbed in our own responsibilities that we forgot the larger picture. We covenanted to support each other, including being present at chapels other than the ones for which we were responsible, and making ourselves available to other coordinators to help plug any unforeseen cracks. We met weekly to assess how the various chapels were going, to share frustrations and note how we might address problems and make improvements. This team meeting became both my primary way of coordinating the chapel program from week to week and creating a community of learning liturgical praxes.

The politics of worship is a messy business and it is difficult to predict what the outcomes of change will be. Services of Word and Table on Tuesdays had a head start; we were building on years of experience and could concentrate on "fine tuning" the service. This chapel had the most participants of students, faculty, and staff. The "traditional" ordo and the consistent celebration of the Eucharist were hallmarks of this service. Leadership included a Eucharistic presider, a preacher (who was sometimes also the presider), and a liturgist. Since we had a significant number of persons in our seminary community who were preparing for ordination as permanent deacons, the liturgist often took on a "deacon role."

The Gospel service on Wednesday evening quickly developed its own sense of identity and developed a faithful core of participants. The outstanding gifts (both musical and spiritual) of the musician we had asked to work with this service was a tremendous asset; although no longer a student, she continues to give leadership to this chapel a decade later.

Most of the singers in the gospel choir, interestingly, were not African-American, so they were learning to sing a new kind of choral music. Early on, we decided that the coordinator should function as a kind of "host pastor" to begin the service each week, welcoming the community, and providing a sense of continuity. Musician and "pastor" carried this service, supported by a preacher and worship leader.

The Thursday chapel had the most trouble finding its direction. Part of the problem was the lack of experience by the Dean of the Chapel in planning "blended" or "contemporary" services, although our praise ensemble leader had both gifts and experience for the task. Our attempt to use both organ and the praise ensemble never seemed to work very well—both organist and ensemble leader would need to have more knowledge of the "other side of the street" than they had. (I later had a graduate student in music ministry who was both an excellent organist and played keyboard with the praise ensemble in his church.) We did not make adequate use of "bridge music"—that is, music that can be adapted and appropriated in different styles of worship services. Hymns "with a beat" (provided by guitar and/or percussion), gospel songs (especially from the African-American tradition), and songs from Hispanic/Latino composers are examples of this kind of music. Bridge music enables worshippers whose primary experience is in another genre to have a point of contact with a different kind of service.

The students who made up the praise ensemble had their own ideas about what the role of such a group should be, and the music frequently used by such groups was often dissonant with the school's commitments to inclusive language and social justice concerns. The praise ensemble and I had some very fruitful discussions along the way. As the seminary choir director, I noted that the most important function the choir had was to enable congregational song. This shift from performance to congregational support was further encouraged by thinking of the musicians as prompters in the wings rather than performers on the stage—the congregation being seen as the chief actors. That resonated with the members of the ensemble and led them to decide to move the location of the praise ensemble from center stage to off-center. Change of location and primary function were followed by an expansion of repertoire as they were introduced to the music of Jim Manley, the Strathdees, and Christopher Grundy, music consonant with the style they used but with content that fit our theological context more adequately. These changes did not take place overnight; rather they took several years. I used invitation, suggestion, and mutual reflection rather than direct edict. Meanwhile, however, the Thursday chapel lurched along.

While the style of music used at the Gospel service bonded with that community, the same was not true for the Thursday chapel. In retrospect, I believe I misread the politics of the situation. There were some who were yearning for a more "contemporary" service, it's true. What we discovered was that a rethinking of what that kind of a service could and should be was in order, and that takes time. The "performance" demands on a new musical group were very heavy—something I should have foreseen. What was really wanted (and needed), I now believe, was a more informal service making use of a wider variety of resources in worship arts. A praise ensemble could have been one of those resources. How that would have worked, I don't know. But as with many churches, leaping into a very different style of worship without taking into account the nature of the base community involved, and without doing carefully reflection and planning in advance, was not wise. The politics of worship is more complex than we often assume.

So also is the ecclesiology reflected in it. To what extent is the Church incarnated in individual worshipping communities? To what extent are they, or should they be, autonomous? In what way are they related to other such communities? How can they be helped to recognize that the Church embraces more than the stylistic preferences of a specific community? In what ways can they incarnate the reality of the Church universal embracing many times, cultures, traditions, styles and patterns of worship? There are no certain answers applicable in all situations. The important thing is to be asking the questions and engaging in an ongoing search for answers to them.

Deans of the Chapel, like pastors and priests, are "servants of Christ and stewards of God's mysteries" (1 Cor 4:1). How we go about that servant leadership reflects both our ecclesiology and our sense of the politics of chapel. One of the ways I sought to carry out that ministry was to design a "Shape of Worship" for the seminary for the academic year. As with a local congregation, this had to take into account the local calendar, special events, vacations, and the basic pattern of the Church year. Unlike a local parish, however, we were not in session during some of the "high holy days" such as Christmas, Easter, and sometimes Pentecost. One of my colleagues strongly supported keeping liturgical time *with* the

Church. The only decision then, would have been whether to take the lections from the previous Lord's Day, the following Lord's Day, or a daily lectionary.

Recognizing our identity as both a teaching/learning institution and a *koinonia*—a faith community—I choose to see the Church year as both a liturgical and mystagogical gift. Whether or not seminary was *the* primary worshipping community for students and faculty, it was *a* significant *koinoia* for us. To share Advent together and next meet after Epiphany would mean that we would not share a celebration of the feast of the Incarnation together and benefit from the experiential learning that went with it. Instead, we assigned one of the Sundays in Advent to each of the services preceding the last chapel of the term and then celebrated the incarnation at that chapel, usually led by the seminary choir. It would not be the Christmas cycle in all its fullness, but we would not be ignoring it. Rather it could prepare us for the celebration in our local church communities, not only that year but in the future as well.

Likewise, I would consult with the team about how to celebrate Epiphany and the Baptism of our Lord after the holidays. One year, when the calendar brought us together late in the cycle, we were ready for the marriage at Cana lections the following Lord's Day. I suggested we start with an Epiphany celebration (complete with brass) in the tower room outside the chapel, move to a renewal of baptism at the font near the doors, and then continue with a Service of Word and Table based on the Cana lections. It was a way of learning how the visit of the magi, the baptism of Jesus, and the turning of water into wine were all epiphanies, thus breaking open the deep meaning of the word.

Such a practice reflects a liturgical ecclesiology (the Church year as servant of the community's faith and worship) and affirms the seminary community as part of the Church by keeping time with it. That is both an ecclesiological and a political act, but it is a political act that recognizes there are also divergent views.

Schools never seem to figure out what their expectations of chapel really are, maintaining multiple and often contradictory expectations of it. Some of these expectations will be explicit and publicly stated. The extent to which the seminary and its administration really believes what it says and is willing to act on it is something a new Dean of the Chapel will have to discern gradually. Frequently, however, the stated purpose is a goal to be lived into rather than a description of what is. If the plans and values of the Dean are consistent with it, the statement can provide a certain amount of leverage in bringing about a commonly hoped-for outcome. One should expect neither too much nor too little from the statement.

One of the places such statements are tested is in who is entrusted with actually leading worship services and how those persons are chosen. In some schools, chapel leadership is a faculty prerogative. At others, it provides the setting for the graduating student's "senior sermon." Sometimes it is a matter of who volunteers.

We decided that designing, leading, and preaching at chapels was not a right, nor was volunteering the best way to discern who should lead. Rather we sought to identify who had the gifts to design services that would enable us to worship "in spirit and in truth" and who was best able to "break open God's Word" for the gathered community. We asked a variety of persons to identify such students, giving preference to those who would be graduating at the following commencement. Those asked to help us discern included faculty in homiletics and worship, the directors of the various ethnic centers, the women in ministry, and peace and justice centers, and the worship team members. We tabulated the results and noted the number of times a student's gifts were identified.

Faculty and administration were asked if they were willing to preside, preach, and/or design a service. Staff who were regular participants were also surveyed. With this list in hand, I sat down with the Dean's verger to chart out chapel leadership for the year, with special attention to the upcoming semester. With three chapels a week plus some special chapels (e.g., Ash Wednesday), we had some seventy-five chapel services to cover. For each Tuesday and Thursday chapel, we named a design team coordinator to work with two or three other persons. This person could be the preacher or presider (whom we also named), but often was not. We left some spots open to provide adaptability later on but tried to chart out the shape of upcoming chapel leadership. We shared this list at the weekly worship team meeting, asking for input. Where did we have people in the wrong place, or on a team that might not be productive? The collective wisdom of the team saved me from many pitfalls and more than a few embarrassing situations. Almost everyone on the list was known by one or more persons on the team. Our aim, as "servants of Christ and stewards of the mysteries of God" was to identify the students and faculty most able to lead the seminary in its worship life.

The letters of invitation provided the lections for the service and suggestions regarding resources. For the Tuesday Eucharist, we recommended a Great Thanksgiving from our denomination's Book of Worship and a musical setting of Eucharistic music, or requested that the presider use a pattern from his or her own tradition, or encouraged the team to identify and use some other resource. Once these requests were made, the design team (in the free church tradition) had the responsibility and freedom to design and lead the service. Almost always they used the recommendations we had made. When they didn't, they usually checked it out with me. We reviewed the liturgy when it came in for printing and noted any problems we saw (usually having to do with the length of the service!).

This approach served us well. We avoided micro-managing the content of each chapel while still providing vision and direction. The response of the seminary community was affirming. The price of providing this freedom is that twice in six years I was embarrassed at the result. One was when a student who could be an excellent preacher heeded the advice of someone to "trust the Spirit" for her sermon. Evidently the Spirit had to work with little previous preparation on the part of the student.

We had a wide variety of styles of preaching (something fostered by our homiletics faculty). The quality of presiding at Table was more uneven. Most of our faculty (who served as presiders most of the time) came through seminary in the days when there was no worship faculty. Interestingly, as time went on, those who were good presiders provided good modeling for the others and the quality of presiding improved. We met the political question of who could preside by adopting the policy that those who had sacramental rights in their own tradition could preside in our chapel. The few problems we had usually resulted from persons trying to preside in a pattern and style that was not their own.

Such a procedure for the design and leadership of chapels did, however, have political repercussions, particularly from faculty who did not share the views of the Dean and his team. Some of my colleagues were convinced we should use only those forms found in our Book of Worship (and they interpreted even those much more narrowly than I did). There were demands that only "vetted" prayers be put in the mouth of the congregation (that is, prayers from some approved resource).

Indeed, another Dean of the Chapel sought to enforce these requirements. To put this in context, I should note that one of our colleagues on

COMMON WORSHIP IN THEOLOGICAL EDUCATION

the faculty in worship is widely known and respected for her expertise in helping students write resources for worship that have both integrity and creativity. My position had been to encourage the use of both the traditional resources and creative, newly written ones. An ordained woman staff member from an ethnic minority on one of the teams wrote a prayer of confession for the community to use. The Dean said it could not be used. Another faculty member on the team protested that this was denying her the right to her own voice in the service. The Dean countered that it was the community's voice that was at stake. It should be noted that the content of the prayer was not in question as such. The prayer was finally used, but here is a clear example of divergent views and values.

The most embarrassing confrontation came when one of our Presbyterian colleagues followed his tradition in indicating when the community was to be seated during the Eucharistic liturgy. A chief administrative officer and some faculty refused to be seated. Students didn't know what to do; some sat, some didn't. Quite apart from who was right and who was wrong about when to stand, we might reflect theologically on the way in which Paul, after talking about the various members of the body and how they are complimentary in working together, notes the "more excellent way" of love (1 Corinthians 12 and 13). Or we might consider discerning that which builds up the unity of the body with that which destroys it. The politics of chapel here was not merely dissension, but involved that other definition of politics we discarded above, namely using questionable tactics to gain power and control.

The seminary chapel can be seen as a platform for the promotion of various political agendas. This is true for individuals, design teams, and "centers" devoted to various social and theological concerns. For example, our rota of services included chapels designed and led by Women in Ministry, Center for Peace and Justice, the Ethics Center, Church and the Black Experience, Asian American Ministries, Hispanic American Ministries, Sacred Worth (supporters of GLBTQ), and the Wesley Institute. Each of these had important concerns to bring to the attention of the seminary community. The problem was that the resulting chapel might become primarily a vehicle for calling attention to certain issues and concerns rather than a service of worship. Individuals also have their political agendas and may succumb to the same temptation.

We were helped in this regard by our commitment to follow the Sunday lectionary at Tuesday and Thursday chapels. We tried to foster an understanding that the primary concern of those designing the service should be to provide a significant and meaningful worship experience for the seminary community. I shared with them my conviction that the best way for each of them to make their concerns visible in the chapel setting was to think about how they would like other students and faculty to be aware of their particular concerns when planning their own chapels. We encouraged them to let the lectionary and the Church year provide the focus of their planning, recognizing that their own commitments and values would be implicit in what they did.

We intentionally scheduled them for some of the important seasons, holy days, and festivals. The Church year and lectionary became the dominant context in which they were to do their planning. Most of the time this worked well. Sometimes it did not. It would not be true to say that everyone felt equally supportive of all these chapel services. If one believes that inclusive language automatically threatens orthodoxy, or that the music of another culture cannot become the means by which we worship, or that a particular sexual orientation may disqualify those persons from being worship leaders, the fact that they are preaching from the lectionary and observing the rhythms of the Church year are not likely to make a decisive difference.

There are difficult challenges involved: Do you honor or dishonor a specific culture when persons not of that culture use forms and patterns that come from that heritage? One has to take into account that neither Native Americans nor African Americans all feel the same way about the answer to that question. One tries to make the most sensitive decision one can to provide the community with significant worship, and then goes forward, knowing that not everyone will be pleased.

Reflecting on the theology of chapel politics leads us to ecclesiological, Christological, and anthropological concerns. Up to this point I have primarily noted the way in which chapel politics are related to ecclesiological dynamics. While in most cases seminary chapel is not *a* church, we cannot understand seminary chapels apart from their being part of *the* Church. Those who participate in seminary chapels are the people of God, but they are also many peoples. Just as in the Church, this has implications for *koinonia*. It is instructive for us to remember that on the day of Pentecost, the gift of the Spirit was that the variety of peoples there could hear the testimony of the disciples, *each in their own native language* (Acts 2:8).

This ecclesiological principle of unity with diversity (rather than unity as uniformity) has clear implications for the politics of seminary chapels. So too does the principle of the Church universal and concern for the unity, rather than fragmentation, of the Body of Christ. While there will be different dynamics in each seminary, the commitment to honor unity with diversity while avoiding fragmentation will be an ongoing challenge. The importance of faithfulness to a tradition will frequently intersect with ecumenical hospitality for many seminaries. Being conscious of both a commitment to one's own tradition and to the ecumenical Church (not only beyond it but within the worshipping community itself), will provide ecclesiological foundations for coming to terms with the politics of seminary chapels. Being Dean of the Chapel involves an ongoing learning process and calls for a leadership style characterized by humility, patience, and charity, as well as vision and integrity.

Christological dynamics must also be taken into account. For me, the celebration of the paschal mystery is at the heart of seminary chapel. I refer not only to the death-and-resurrection theme of the Triduum, but to the wider Christological understanding reaching from creation through incarnation to consummation. Furthermore, in our setting, this focus on the paschal mystery was by its very nature Trinitarian. We were primarily concerned with ritual events through which we could engender, experience, and celebrate our participation in these mysteries of faith. This celebration is not insular, for learning to "do a redeemed world" through sacramental living blends the sacred and secular aspects of our lives.[2]

Incarnational theology has important implications for the politics of seminary chapels. On the one hand, the incarnation teaches us to recognize and honor a specific context. Christ is always incarnate in particular places with particular characteristics. To ignore context is theologically invalid and politically unwise. On the other hand, every particular context (whether theological or cultural) will be dissonant with the fullness of the gospel of Jesus Christ. Thus, seminary chapels must be not only contextual but also counter-cultural. Our given context is not all of the Church there is. Just as the Church is multicultural, so too seminary chapels are called to recognize the multicultural nature of the Church's worship. This is particularly true because seminary is often a microcosm of the rich

2. See Nathan D. Mitchell, "Ritual as Reading," in *Source and Summit: Commemorating Josef A. Jungmann, S.J.*, ed. Joanne M. Pierce and Michael Downey (Collegeville, MN: Liturgical, 1999) 161–82, see specifically 180.

cultural fabric of the Church, with all the frustration and potential that brings.

The politics of seminary chapels will also involve dynamics of theological anthropology. What it means to be human from a Christian point of view will be reflected in the dynamics of the disagreements within, and the divisions among, those who participate. One of the realities of human nature (some would say a mark of our fallen state) is the perpetual tendency to see everything from one's own perspective. This is as true of the Dean of the Chapel as it is of his or her critics. The ability to really listen to what is being said beneath the words that are being used is a skill to be learned but never perfected.

Another mark of our humanness is our propensity to let little things that are not central to our values, goals, and basic beliefs become issues that engulf the important matters. We treat the peripheral with an urgency that belies our deeper sense of priorities. As a result we find ourselves out of relation with ourselves, others, and God. Sin is a part of the landscape of chapel politics. The problem is that we are much more adept at seeing the specks of sin in our brothers' and sisters' eye than the mote that is blocking our own vision. On the other hand, guilt over our shortcomings can immobilize us or cause us to overcompensate, so that the last state is worse than the first.

Dealing with the politics of seminary chapel can be very draining. A Dean of the Chapel needs a survival guide. How does one deal with all the criticisms that come? To dismiss them all would keep us from reaping the harvest of that which would help us make seminary chapel a richer, fuller, more adequate worship event. To accept them all would involve carrying a burden greater than we can bear, rendering us unproductive by diverting our attention to a multiplicity of problems rather than our basic ministry.

To separate the "wheat from the chaff" I have found it helpful to separate criticism and emerging problems into one of three types:

1) *A problem that emerges or a criticism that is valid and to which an appropriate solution can be found.* Here one can express appreciation and implement change. As our Wednesday evening Gospel service got under way, it was pointed out that students coming only for evening classes never had an opportunity to share in the Lord's Supper at the seminary. We adopted the requested practice of "once a month" com-

munion, calling it the "Lord's Supper" as those who had called it to our attention suggested. We also decided to let the use of the lectionary at that service be optional. The preacher chose the scripture for the evening in keeping with the "Gospel service" tradition.

2) *Problems or criticism, whether valid or not, about which nothing can be done.* One of the biggest controversies during my time as Dean of the Chapel was with a group of students from one of the ethnic centers. They saw the first week of November as their "domain." As I was planning the Spring before, I interpreted this to be the first full week of November and scheduled them for that week. None of the team noted anything amiss. I sent out the schedule; no one (including the faculty advisor of that center) objected. The next Fall, however, there were new student leaders who asserted their right to the week in which November began. By then, other commitments involving an outside speaker had been made for that week. I was charged with being racist. Indeed, it may have been a cultural difference in understanding what the first week of the month was. The controversy divided the ethnic group itself. I apologized, said I would learn from my mistake, and tried to make amends. Nothing seemed to help. I was unwilling to compound the problem by un-inviting the other group that had planned for the week according to the earlier schedule. I had to live with the judgment of a vocal group of students that I was unresponsive to their rights and needs. I was helped by recognizing that there was no way I could have known of the problem sooner.

3) *Criticism that arises out of a difference of values or perspectives.* Questions about the appropriate use of the deacon in the Eucharist surfaced during my tenure. Some of my colleagues believed in a restrictive understanding of that role. I was committed to a broad interpretation of what it means to "assist the elder at the Table." I was unwilling to follow their interpretation, believing that the Eucharistic Prayer was not the property of the presider but of the Church, that it was the congregation that stood "in the place of Christ" as his body, and that a deacon as a representative of the bridge between the Church and the world had an important contribution to make in the leadership of parts of the prayer. The guideline we adopted was that "the presider presides." That is, the presider could determine what role the deacon would play, as well as the rubrics regarding the Eucharist itself.

For me "presiding" did not imply saying everything the congregation didn't say, but having the responsibility for the integrity of the nature and content of the prayer, and what voices are heard in it.

When I was in seminary during the turbulent sixties, a wise African-American pastor in Chicago told us, "If there's nothing you'd be willing to go to the mat for, even if it ended your ministry in a given place, you'll lack a sense of integrity. And if you make every issue something in which you have to have your own way, you'll be ineffective." Knowing when to give in and when to stand firm calls for the gift of discernment, a gift for which Deans of the chapel need to pray continually.

Another key to survival is what we might call the pastoral norm. I learned it from the senior pastor with whom I first worked. "Love the people," he said, "especially the ones you find difficult to work with. Pray for them—not that they will come to see things your way, but that you will understand them, and even when you don't, will be able to love and serve them anyway." It has been good advice in both local church and seminary. That kind of praying enables one to dare to be vulnerable—knowing that we don't have all the answers, while remaining aware that our critics don't have all the answers either.

Finally, I believe that in dealing with the politics of seminary chapel, we must recognize a pneumatological principle: The chief actor in our worship is the Holy Spirit. I would encourage our worship teams to prepare as carefully as possible, as if the smallest detail were of importance (for, I believe, God is in the details). Then when we have done all that we can do in preparation and come to the service itself, it is time to let go and offer it up to God, confident that the Holy Spirit will receive what we offer, work with it and return it to us with blessings we cannot imagine, and about which we may never know. Beyond the politics of seminary chapel, but not apart from them, is the One who calls us out, gathers us together, meets us in Word and Table, and sends us forth. "Unless the Lord builds the house, They labor in vain who build it" (Ps 127:1 NKJV).

3

My Cup Runneth Over?
Seminary Chapel As A Laboratory

MARK W. STAMM

Placing the words chapel and laboratory in the same title may seem odd. "Laboratory" evokes memories of my high school chemistry lab, with its beakers, flasks, and Bunsen burners, along with stern warnings to measure carefully and not mix and heat chemicals contrary to directions. This memory is not altogether pleasant. "Chapel" brings to mind a more recent event, with a flagon of port wine, a cruet of water, and a chalice in which the wine and water would be mixed, but exactly how much of each? Two bishops, a United Methodist on my left hand and an Episcopalian at my right, watched me do the mixing, along with a bemused Episcopal sub-deacon. This memory comes from the first service in Perkins Chapel (Southern Methodist University) that used the "Common Guidelines for Bishops, Clergy, and Laity for the Implementation of Interim Eucharistic Sharing Between The Episcopal Church and The United Methodist Church."[1] It is a more pleasant memory, yet not without its conflicts. In its own way, it, too, was a laboratory experience. In spite of the seemingly odd juxtaposition of chapel and laboratory, all good schools contain the

---

1. "Common Guidelines for Bishops, Clergy, and Laity for the Implementation of Interim Eucharistic Sharing Between The Episcopal Church and The United Methodist Church," Episcopal–United Methodist dialogue, September 2006, http://www.episcopal church.org/documents/Common_Guidelines(1).pdf. (Our service was held on Thursday, April 26, 2007.)

laboratory function within them, that is, some place where received practices are honed and new ones are proposed and attempted.

We worked hard on the United Methodist-Episcopal Church shared Eucharist. We had read the recently adopted agreement but we had not developed a liturgy using it. I was charged with drafting the service and I did so using classical liturgical units. The greeting, from Psalm 134, was delivered by the two bishops while standing at the baptismal font, which we placed at the entrance to the chancel. This ritual move reminded us that our ecumenical fellowship is rooted in our common baptism. The rest of the service was a standard Word and Table service with a slight but significant alteration on the performance of the Great Thanksgiving. Under normal circumstances, one elder (or bishop) speaks the entire prayer and makes the appropriate presidential gestures. On this occasion, we did the Words of Institution and epiclesis differently. At the words for the bread, "On the night . . . ," the United Methodist bishop spoke and the Episcopal Church bishop raised the bread. For the words for the cup, "When the supper was over . . . ," the roles were reversed, with the Episcopal bishop speaking and the United Methodist raising the cup. At the epiclesis, each made the gesture specified in his church's rubrics. As an expression of ecumenical hospitality from the United Methodist side, we decided to use wine in each of two chalices. We would, of course, normally use grape juice. The fact that we were using wine was duly noted in the order of worship. I was pleased by the plan that we developed, and by the fact that both bishops agreed to it.

I briefed the leaders before the liturgy began and all went well as we moved through it, including the unusual choreography within the Great Thanksgiving. I neglected, however, to see the two chalices and their contents as a potential problem. Since most within our predominately United Methodist congregation communed by intinction, they drank very little of the wine. In the midst of the service I realized that I had put too much port in the chalices and had thereby caused a problem. The guidelines insist that "Any and all of the consecrated elements should be reverently consumed," and we had decided to do so within the service itself. After communing the congregation, the two bishops retired to their respective chairs while I, ever the good ecumenist and not wanting to cause offense, consumed the contents of both chalices in full view of the congregation. I led a worship practicum session about an hour later, and my student assistant claims that I was more garrulous than usual, although I have consistently disputed his claim.

We may think of an experimental liturgy as something odd or radical, but that is not necessarily the case. As noted, the Episcopal-United Methodist liturgy was an experiment that taught us much, including important lessons about how much wine to pour in the chalice, yet depending on one's perspective and experience, almost any seminary chapel worship service can feel like a laboratory experiment. I am reminded of one of our students who, having experienced another Episcopal Church liturgy led out of *The Book of Common Prayer*, said, "I've never experienced that kind of liturgy before." In ecumenical communities we learn that one person's heart language is another person's experiment or foreign language. Part of the experimental function of seminary chapel worship is simply its ecumenical character; indeed, there is no other community quite like it. Commitment to regular chapel attendance in such an authentically ecumenical setting will challenge and stretch most people. Even using classical United Methodist ritual texts (say for Word and Table or for the Baptismal Covenant) may seem odd or experimental to students whose congregations have used them only in abbreviated form, or outright ignored them.

Bearing in mind this perspective on the experimental nature of seminary liturgical life, in the remainder of this essay I will address the following specific matters:

- The Tradition of Experimentation at Perkins Chapel, Southern Methodist University.

- Possibilities and Procedures for Liturgical Experiments

- Limits and Safeguards on Liturgical Experiments

In the latter two sections, I will demonstrate how these principles were applied to a Service of the Word in Hip Hop style, and to a Bluegrass Eucharist, both of which have been done at Perkins Chapel within the past several years. I will also discuss how these principles might apply to a controversial (or failed) experiment.

The Tradition of Experimentation at Perkins Chapel, Southern Methodist University.

Perkins Chapel at Southern Methodist University has been the regular venue for worship at Perkins School of Theology since 1951 and, like many seminary chapels it has a history of liturgical experimentation. Commenting on the Protestant vocation in general, former Perkins Professor James F. White noted that Protestant denominations have often functioned as laboratories for the wider Christian church. A greater freedom within their rubrics allows it. White wrote, "The role of Protestant worship in the general context of all Christian worship is that of pioneer," while he also reminded his readers that "Pioneering is dangerous business."[2] Perkins Chapel functioned as a laboratory even before White began work there in 1960.

A service of Morning Prayer accompanied by a nine-piece jazz ensemble from the music school at North Texas State College (now the University of North Texas) was held in 1959 and received widespread local publicity, some of it with controversial undertones. In a report broadcast on Dallas Channel 8, correspondent Dick Wheeler observed, "The religious syncopation by the nine-member combo led by (North Texas student Ed) Summerlin moved some of the worshipers, left others wondering."[3] One wonders what, exactly, these unnamed "others" were wondering about, and why? Wheeler did not say.

The service followed a classic order of Morning Prayer printed in a 1957 volume titled *The Wesley Orders of Common Prayer*.[4] The service text was essentially Morning Prayer according to the sixteenth-century versions of *The Book of Common Prayer*, including the Elizabethan language. The jazz ensemble accompanied the reading of the various prayer texts and canticles, attempting to interpret them musically. The anthem, which followed the sermon, was a free-form jazz selection played by the

---

2. White, *Protestant Worship*, 215.

3. "Wesley Order of Morning Prayer, Perkins Chapel, May 20, 1959." Recording held in Bridwell Library archives, Perkins School of Theology, Southern Methodist University. Track 11, beginning at minute 19:45.

4. "The Order for Morning Prayer (With Music)," 24–31. The designation "with music" meant that the order indicated places at which hymns might be sung. No musical score was actually provided within the text itself. Thus, the jazz ensemble prepared its music independently.

ensemble. The two scripture readings, the Apostles Creed, and the sermon were spoken without accompaniment. One might argue with the various accompaniment schemes. Why, for instance, was a percussion riff, and not piano and saxophone, used to accompany the *Benedictus*?[5] During the versicle that began The Service of the Word, tones moved up the scale at the beginning of each response, along with an increase in volume, and the tones descended quickly after the congregation said, "The Lord's name be praised."[6] Why so? At times, accompaniment seemed too loud, overcoming the text. Was this intentional? Such questions address matters rooted in personal taste; although interesting, they were not the most significant issues.

The more interesting arguments were theoretical ones about holding such an experimental service in the first place; they will likely seem familiar to those of us who have endured the so-called worship wars, and they remain significant. According to Summerlin, the jazz accompaniment would serve as a liturgical alternative, taking "the role usually carried by an organ in church." It was not, he argued, "a revolt against conventional church music, but an experiment with a new form."[7] One could substitute the word "traditional" for "conventional" and recognize a statement that could have been made at last week's worship committee meeting, complete with missing definition of "conventional." What exactly did "conventional" mean? Summerlin did not say. He justified the experiment in terms of its potential evangelistic appeal: "We hope through this music to draw some young people to church who might not be in the habit of going."[8] Again, the evangelistic argument is like some that we might hear today. His most compelling argument, however, is rooted in a robust theology of creation and culture: "our jazz movement is so much a part of our culture and everyday lives, we cannot ignore it. Jazz music is part of our

5. Ibid., 28–29.
"Wesley Order of Morning Prayer, Perkins Chapel, May 20, 1959." Recording, Track 6, beginning at minute 6:00 and continuing through 7:06

6. "The Order for Morning Prayer (With Music)," 26.
"Wesley Order of Morning Prayer, Perkins Chapel, May 20, 1959." Recording, Track 5, beginning at minute 0:00 and continuing through 0:27.

7. Helen Bullock, "Jazz to Get Try in Church," *The Dallas Morning News*, 17 May 1959, sec. 3, p. 1.

8. Ibid.

lives and should be part of our religion."[9] In other words, everything God has given, including music, should be offered to God in thanksgiving. If we find that we cannot offer it, then any use of such music is called into question, and repentance is needed.[10] Such thinking continues to shape our experiments in liturgical enculturation, and such discussions should be a significant part of a seminary's work.

A set of experiments conducted within Perkins Chapel from 1970 through 1972 drew little media attention but proved deeply influential within the United Methodist Church. According Robert Brian Peiffer, drafts that led to publication of *The Lord's Supper, An Alternate Text* were tested in Perkins Chapel, with some of the laboratory work also occurring in Cox Chapel at nearby Highland Park United Methodist Church.[11] During that time, White and H. Grady Hardin were professors at Perkins and served as members of the drafting committee. Hardin occasionally ministered at Cox Chapel. Thus, laboratory use of the two venues was natural. As they were used, various problems within the text were worked out and improvements made. According to White, the experimentation raised vigorous conversations within the community, some of which directly affected phrases within the rite. For instance, a sermon by Professor William Farmer on the scandal caused by Jesus's seemingly indiscriminate choice of dinner companions (e.g., Mark 2:15–17) led to White's adding the phrase "ate with sinners" to the Great Thanksgiving.[12]

Experiments with other classical rites have been done at Perkins Chapel. The first United Methodist version of the Easter Vigil appeared in *From Ashes to Fire* in 1979,[13] although an Easter Vigil was conducted in Perkins Chapel in the mid-1970s. A student from that era tells me that

---

9. Ibid.

10. I am reminded of Vincent Donovan's description of Masai dancers who discerned that they could not bring some of their dances into their eucharistic liturgy a realization that pointed out a need for repentance. They realized that which they could not dance within their eucharistic assembly should not be danced at all. See: Donovan, *Christianity Rediscovered*, 125.

11. Peiffer, "How Contemporary Liturgies Evolve," 26, 320.

12. James F. White, "Word and Table I: An Historical and Theological Commentary." DVD recording of White's keynote address delivered on October 16, 2000 at the Convocation of the Order of Saint Luke, Saint Joseph Retreat Center, Greensburg, Pennsylvania. Minute 1:23.35 through 1:24.02. See also Stamm, *Let Every Soul*, 51; *The United Methodist Hymnal*, 9; *The Sacrament of the Lord's Supper*, 3.

13. *From Ashes to Fire*, 165–201.

an aluminum saucer sled was used as a baptismal font during that service and that an infant born to a seminary couple was presented in the classic ancient style—that is, in the nude—and then baptized in that font. Larger fonts and naked candidates were radical ideas at the time and, in many ways, they remain so; but, such practices are part of the larger liturgical studies conversation, and seminary chapels are ideal places to test them.

Seminary chapels are also good places to experiment with official denominational rites that receive but little use in parishes. For example, various mainline denominational texts now contain rubrics for the foot washing ritual,[14] yet they are not widely practiced, perhaps because performing them can be complicated. Seminary chapel can become a proving ground that allows students to gain a sense about how they might introduce such rites in their congregations. In planning for a recent foot washing service at Perkins Chapel, we considered the following issues:

- Where, within the worship space, will the foot washing occur?

- How shall we protect the floor against water damage?

- Who will wash whose feet, and how shall people wait their turn? Where shall they wait?

- What vessels will be used?

- Should the water be heated, and to what temperature?

- After feet are washed, how shall we dry them? With what?

- Who will change out water and towels?

- What, if anything, shall we say or sing while the foot washing is occurring?

- How shall the worship leaders instruct persons regarding their participation in the rite?

These questions came to mind even before the scriptures, prayers, and other hymns and songs were chosen, and the homily written. The chapel provided a relatively safe place where students could learn to plan, execute, and evaluate such a powerful but potentially complicated set of ritual actions. The liturgists in training were encouraged to develop the following habits of mind:

14. *The United Methodist Book of Worship*, 351, 353; and *Book of Common Worship*, 273.

- Effective liturgical planners always keep the *telos* of a liturgy in mind, and they never lose sight of that goal. For instance, embodiment of servant leadership is the *telos* for a foot washing service. They allow nothing to obstruct that goal.

- Effective liturgical planners learn to think through and plan for the intricate details of a particular liturgy in service of that overarching goal. They make checklists.

These two dispositions may at first glance seem contradictory. However, leaders were encouraged, if you will, to see both the forest and the trees.

In this section, we have seen how Perkins Chapel has functioned as a laboratory on a number of levels, in the creation of new ritual practices, in the testing and developing of rituals and ritual texts for the wider church, and in learning how to implement official rituals that may be underused in the church. I trust that similar experimental dynamics have been experienced at other schools. Now, I will turn to a discussion of the essential guidelines for conducting such laboratory work in seminary chapels.

Possibilities and Procedures

"Professor Stamm," asked one of my best students, "Can we do a Hip Hop Service this year?" She asked that question on August 25, 2004, at the first meeting of the chapel committee for the 2004–2005 school year. How should a faculty leader respond to such a question, especially one whose knowledge of Hip Hop was quite limited? Responding well requires having a clear set of liturgical and pedagogical values in place.

As I have noted, good schools include the laboratory—function as places where ideas and processes can be tested. Seminaries do laboratory work, although they also form persons in classical traditions and practices. Inevitable tensions will arise between these experimental and formational vocations, yet they do not necessarily contradict. The Christian tradition continues developing, and it must do so. In the medical field, prospective physicians study accumulated knowledge and learn well-developed practices, yet teaching hospitals also take part in developing theories and experimental procedures. Then they actually carry out those experiments in a well-regulated manner. Assuming chapel as part of the curriculum, seminaries will want to discuss the boundaries and limits of experimentation, as well as its possibilities.

When my student inquired about the possibility of doing a Hip Hop Service, I responded affirmatively, on the condition that it be Christian corporate worship and that she and others do the hard work of developing it. Thus began an eight months' journey that culminated in a Hip Hop Service of the Word on April 21, 2005. We rarely simply say "no" when a project is proposed; indeed, we want to encourage creative thought and risk-taking. That is what schools should do in their laboratories. Nevertheless, we insist that planners do serious liturgical-theological work on their project. What are the characteristics of such work?

First of all, serious liturgical-theological reflection is not done in a hurry. Professors often remind their students that they cannot expect to write a good term paper if their research and writing process is but several days (or hours!) long. In like manner, one cannot expect to do a quality liturgical experiment without proper time for research, reflection, and problem solving. We have found that the best projects allow for a process of at least two months development. Of course, anyone who has tried to administer a seminary chapel program knows that cancellations and other scheduling problems arise. When services must be organized on short notice, it is best to fall back on classical patterns. Because I already know the pattern, I can lead a reasonably nourishing service of midday prayer on about ten minutes notice.[15] Insistence on an extended reflective process means that we do only a limited number of liturgical experiments in any given year. It provides a caution light against innovation run amok.

Taking time to plan well is essential. For instance, we have done a Bluegrass Eucharist on three separate occasions and have developed a good sense of how one executes such a liturgy, but we have also discovered that this service is a more fulfilling participative experience when we use a pickup ensemble drawn from our own Perkins/SMU community. Forming the band requires ample time for recruitment and rehearsal.

15. Having taken this stance against liturgical planning done quickly, I will confess to a major exception. On September 11, 2001, I led a service of lament about three hours after convening a short brainstorming session among our liturgical studies faculty. After the meeting, I prepared a service unlike any we had ever held before. It was, in a sense, experimental, but the exception proved the rule. Previous conversations about liturgical theology and practice allowed faculty members to work from an existent consensus and the liturgy that we designed borrowed classical monastic rhythms of readings, silence, and prayers.

Second, when doing an enculturation experiment we respect the piety of others and take it seriously. As my colleague Michael Hawn insists, to use music and ritual forms from another culture is to pray with them and for them.[16] By receiving texts respectfully, one learns to love those who sing them.

Taking culture seriously is a function of the reflective stance described above. In my case, that meant reading about hip-hop and learning about its roots as an indigenous protest movement.[17] I also consulted with colleagues who had some expertise on its traditions and practices. Although I was not about to take the lead in planning the service—I simply did not know enough to do so—I wanted to gain enough knowledge to ask intelligent questions and then experience the event with some understanding. In order to help persons within our community arrive at a similar place, my student and I planned and hosted a one-hour orientation event entitled "Hip Hop 101." Although only about fifteen people attended the session, it widened the circle of those with greater understanding. One could also justify having such sessions at some point following an experimental service, working from something like a mystagogical perspective. In the case of the Hip Hop Service, its history as an out-of-doors, urban phenomenon led us to hold the service on the chapel plaza, outside the pew-ridden confines of our Perkins Chapel nave. This move required another level of planning, as we had to obtain the University permits needed for an out-of-doors event.

Third, we insist that all of our experimental services be genuinely Christian worship, reflecting sound principles of liturgical theology. They must not be mere demonstrations of a practice, or worse, Christian concerts. For us, that means expressing the classical liturgical movement value of "full, conscious, and active participation."[18] Participation can, of course, take a variety of forms, but planners should be challenged on this question and they must articulate how persons will be invited into active participation. As to whether it is genuinely Christian worship, we look for fairly classic marks of the church and its worship such as the reading of Scripture and contemporary witness related to it, as well as praise of the Triune God. And so, the Hip Hop service included both a Christian

16. Hawn, *Gather Into One*, 27, 70.

17. George, 66, 212.

18. *Constitution on the Sacred Liturgy*, 14. http://www.adoremus.org/Sacrosanctum Concilium.html (accessed August 8, 2008).

rap and a sermon. We also look for the intercessory work that should mark Christian gatherings. Thus we insist that every service develop intercessory prayers that are adequate to the style of the service. They must follow an intercessory agenda that reflects catholic consensus while also responding to the particularities of the occasion. In some ways, the challenge to plan adequate intercessions becomes the test that must be passed in order to move the event from demonstration to Christian liturgy.

For the Hip Hop service, student Robert R. Davis prepared and led intercessions that drew upon Psalm 130, a prayer "For The World and Its Peoples," printed in *The United Methodist Book of Worship,*[19] and lyrics from rap artist Tupac Shakur. Classical intercessions were offered for the nations of the world and for the churches, but also for these particular concerns related to hip hop culture:

- "For all men disregarded by the Church, denied justice by the legal system . . . "

- "For all women defined by their bodily features, baby momma status, brash dealings with insensitive, irresponsible and immature men . . . "

- "So that You might . . . enable us to acknowledge and accept the good, redeeming, and creative work You are doing in Hip Hop culture and all cultures whose expressions and norms seem foreign or frightening to us . . . "[20]

Congregational responses included the more classic "Hear our cry" as well as "Holla Back"[21] a cultural phrase that can mean, among other things, "Pay attention, and don't forget us."[22] Constructing such prayer requires reflection on both cultural particularities and classical liturgical traditions.

Adequate liturgical planning should facilitate freedom in performance, and so, having planned well, we expect to enjoy our laboratory experiences. As I reported in our Perkins alumni magazine regarding our

19. *The United Methodist Book of Worship,* 526–27.

20. Davis, unpublished.

21. Ibid.

22. Definition confirmed via e-mail exchange with Robert R. Davis, September 4, 2008. I also consulted http://www.urbandictionary.com/define.php?term=hollaback (accessed September 4, 2008).

October 2007 Bluegrass liturgy, "For my money, (it) was about as much fun as a United Methodist elder can legally enjoy."[23] Nevertheless, enjoyment must not be mistaken for frivolity, and apparent ease in performance must not be interpreted as lack of preparation or liturgical-theological rigor. In order to maintain a high quality of performance and reflection, faculties and administers must establish some limits and safeguards.

Limits and Safeguards

Administrative oversight of the seminary chapel program should be assigned to tenured (or tenure-track) professors in liturgical studies. Why so? If seminaries understand that chapel worship is part of their curriculum— that is, a central part of their pedagogical and formational work–then a liturgical studies professor should oversee the chapel planning committee. Moreover, that worship professor should have significant influence in shaping the calendar along with well-defined veto power that may be judiciously exercised when necessary. Such a veto is not unlike that which a pastor normally holds in a congregation. Again, if chapel work is part of the curriculum, then its operation should not stand entirely at the whim of a student and faculty committee, any more than the contents of a syllabus for a New Testament class would be decided by the students or, for that matter, by the Christian Education faculty. While the nature of liturgy as common prayer requires consultation among the wider community, and thus a planning committee, such committees should exist in dialog with a hierarchical function that exists both to guard and to administer accumulated wisdom.

My claim that chapel oversight should be given to a tenured (or tenure-track) professor means that it should not be delegated to a chaplain or Dean of the Chapel hired specifically for that task. Presumably, such a chaplain would be a presbyter in good standing within a particular denomination. As such, his/her qualifications for leading congregational worship would not be in dispute. However, if we are to consider chapel worship as part of the seminary's pedagogical and scholarly work, then the vast majority of ordained persons do not possess the qualifications and expertise in liturgical theology needed to lead that discussion on a level adequate to graduate academic work.

23. Stamm, "Blue Grass Liturgy," 17.

In like manner, since the best liturgical theology and practice is done in gathered communities of discernment, the chapel oversight should not be given to an adjunct professor, whose relationship to the seminary community would be tenuous. These are not simply theoretical ramblings. In recent years, some Boards of Ordained Ministry (i.e., review boards for ministry candidates) within my denomination (The United Methodist Church) have been reluctant to ordain persons who identify an academic vocation. Such reluctance, if taken to its ridiculous extreme, could leave theological seminaries with faculties of all laypersons. If they were to have any sort of sacramental life, such schools would need to import guest presbyters with neither expertise in liturgical theology nor an organic relationship with the seminary community. That would be a serious deficit.

In like manner, oversight of the chapel program should not be assigned to faculty members in other fields who may have a strong interest in worship. One can imagine that such persons might possess a well-formed sense of liturgical piety, perhaps of an Anglo-Catholic type, or even one rooted in the contemporary Christian worship movement. Such persons should be included in the community's conversation regarding chapel worship, and thus should be on the planning committee. One should not assume, however, that such faculty persons would have sufficient expertise in the liturgical studies field to lead the broadest possible conversation about worship.

Having expert leadership within the community assists and deepens the evaluative process. Many times, evaluation will assume a predominately celebrative tone. Persons will realize that they can plan and carry out a foot washing service or perform a classic Eucharistic prayer to a Bluegrass setting. It is especially important, however, that leaders are accountable to the community when an experiment becomes controversial or when it appears to fail. All laboratories will have failed experiments. Seminary communities can learn from failed (or less than successful) experiments in chapel, but only if they are committed to disciplined reflection on their liturgical work.

As part of a recent Lenten Taizé service held at Perkins in March 2008, Eucharist was celebrated without using words. That is, in lieu of a spoken Great Thanksgiving, the celebrant used gestures only. At the place where the *sursum corda* would have occurred, he stretched his hands toward the congregation in place of "The Lord be with you," paused, and then raised his arms for "Lift up your hearts." In like manner, he lifted up the bread and cup at the place where the Words of Institution normally would have occurred and then he made gestures of blessing for the epiclesis. Then after another short pause, bread was broken in silence and a hand signal was given inviting persons to come forward and receive communion. We had done such a silent consecration in previous years and without controversy, yet in 2008 the practice was challenged, both by members of the worship committee and by some in the wider community. Since no one said the Words of Institution, had we really celebrated the Eucharist? In departing from the classical practice, had we violated ecumenical sensibilities? On a deeper level, what had changed from one year to the next?

Our committee's decision to conduct the silent Eucharist experiment was rooted in a variety of positive commitments. Perhaps first among these is a commitment to weekly Eucharist, an ecumenical and Wesleyan commitment that is widely held by the community at large. John Wesley's well-known sermon "The Duty of Constant Communion" motivates this commitment among Methodists. Since the other service that week was the aforementioned foot washing service, which did not include Eucharist, it was argued that the Taizé service should include it. That decision, however, potentially put us at odds with another of our central values, that classic forms should be maintained in their integrity. Indeed, Taizé worship reflects a unique hybrid of the daily office tradition, combining corporate ("cathedral") forms of prayer and praise with the long periods of silence characteristic of the monastic daily office.[24] By that logic, the silent Eucharistic prayer made sense, but the daily office is by definition not usually the setting for the Eucharist. Classic Taizé practice includes no Great Thanksgiving during the weekday daily office and when communion is offered on those days they use pre-consecrated communion elements from the reserved sacrament.[25] We did not consider pre-consecration a viable option because the Methodist Articles of Religion, consistent with our Anglican forbears, forbid reservation of the sacrament.[26] Recent United Methodist documents have reaffirmed this

24. For a discussion of the characteristics of cathedral and monastic forms see Bradshaw, *Two Ways of Praying*, 1995.

25. I am grateful to my colleague Michael Hawn, a frequent pilgrim to Taizé, for this report on their practice.

26. Article XVIII: "Of the Lord's Supper," *The United Methodist Book of Discipline*

prohibition.[27] Thus, pre-consecration was not a viable option within our predominately United Methodist context. As a strictly practical matter, we have no adequate place to house a reserved sacrament, even if we were to begin the practice. Our intent is ecumenical, but Perkins Chapel is clearly a mainline Protestant worship space.

Worship planners thought that our Perkins congregation would see silent consecration as a one-time exception to our normal practice, and not as a challenge to the long-standing consensus that valid sacraments must meet the criteria of adequate matter, verbal form, and intention. Through the exception, we intended to critique the Western Church's long-standing preoccupation with the proper words said at the proper time by the proper person, yet we may have underestimated the weight of that so-called preoccupation, which might better be called *a commitment*. We thought that such an unorthodox consecration would make sense in an academic community that knows the classic Great Thanksgiving well, and that it would encourage us to pay greater attention to gesture. Nevertheless, in the eyes of some, we ended up failing the validity standards (1) on proper form—obviously, there were no words; and (2) on intention to do what the church does. For some, what we did was simply not the Eucharist. Some might also argue that, given our use of grape juice in the cup, we had also failed on the criterion of proper matter. Three strikes and you're out?

What went wrong with our experiment? On the one hand, perhaps nothing at all. If our experiment led to lively argument about the nature of the Eucharist and its performance, then perhaps it was a successful pedagogical exercise. On the other hand, there were problems, perhaps foremost being the presence of a significant number of guests that day. Indeed

---

2004, par. 103, p. 64. *The Book of Common Prayer*, Article XXVIII, 873.

In Anglican practice since the Oxford Movement (mid-nineteenth century), there has been an occasional gap between the Articles of Religion and parish practice of Eucharistic reservation, with some parishes practicing reservation and, in some cases, even adoration of the reserved sacrament. No such gap exists in United Methodism, although the developing practice of lay home communion serving ministries at times leads to a somewhat casual reservation of a day or two before elements are taken to homebound members and others. On a more serious level, some have proposed using pre-consecrated elements to meet the sacramental needs of parishes without pastors. I have written a strong caution against these practices in my book *Extending the Table*.

27. "This Holy Mystery, A United Methodist Understanding of Holy Communion," *The Book of Resolutions of the United Methodist Church*, 921–22.

our Executive Board was in session. Our chapel is a public worship space, and more often than not, we have at least a few guests present. The laboratory metaphor fails at that point, for scientific laboratories are by nature closed and controlled environments and seminary chapels are neither closed nor controlled. One might hope that visitors will make allowances knowing that they are participating in a unique liturgical milieu, but it cannot be assumed. Perhaps schools could provide some type of brochure for visitors detailing the unique mission of the chapel, including its need for occasional experiments.[28] When experimental practices are planned, some type of service notes might be placed in the bulletin giving a short explanation of their intent. Planners should, however, avoid scripting the experience of the congregation. We do, in fact, provide such notes when introducing classic practices that may prove new for some worshipers. For instance, when using wine for communion instead of grape juice, we inform people that we are doing so and tell them that they may receive the wine by sipping from the cup or by intinction, and that they may also invoke the doctrine of concomitance and receive by the host alone. When we do foot-washing liturgies, we remind persons to dress appropriately, particularly that they be able to remove their footwear. We could advertise when experimental practices are planned, and thereby help persons avoid crises of conscience, but such warnings might unwisely segregate the community and they would contradict our conviction that "liturgical shock"[29] is helpful pedagogically.

As noted above, we had done a similar service on several occasions in previous years without significant negative feedback. We assumed that

---

28. Indeed, I have developed the following statement of purpose for Perkins Chapel:

1) Worship at Perkins celebrates the Gospel and forms us in that mystery.
2) Worship at Perkins addresses the ritual needs presented by this particular academic community.
3) Worship at Perkins celebrates our ecumenical diversity and embodies the same.
4) Worship at Perkins is part of our teaching ministry. Thus, we attempt to model an exemplary liturgical praxis.
5) Worship at Perkins allows for ritual experimentation and innovation while encouraging theological-liturgical assessment of the same. I note that different persons may experience the same worship service at different points on this grid.

29. Hawn, *One Bread, One Body*, 184. See especially his "Observing Rituals in Corporate Worship in New Cultural Situations: Guidelines for Participant-Observers" (184–86).

we could do so again.[30] What happened this time? We may have lost sight of the fact that our community continues changing. Given the dynamics of matriculation and graduation, our student body changes from one quarter to one third every year, and thus, an explanation made in one year does not necessarily carry over to the next. Given the transient nature of our congregation, we must continue making what to some of us may seem like elementary explanations.

The negative response that we received may also indicate success in related realms. For instance, it may indicate that we have made significant progress in forming a community where the Eucharist is taken seriously, both theologically and as liturgical action. Although painful, causing offense is one way to discern the shape of a community's piety. Such clashes of commitment may be the inevitable result of worship in an ecumenical milieu. They also provide persons with an opportunity to describe both liturgical problems and possible remedies in specific, yet charitable, terms. Learning to make such descriptions is a helpful skill for parish ministry.

In the final analysis, it may be that we simply tried to accommodate too many commitments within one service, that we could not accommodate our commitment to the integrity of Taizé, our commitment to weekly Eucharist, and our commitment to the Methodist Articles of Religion within the same liturgy. A relaxing of any one of those three commitments might have solved our dilemma. We could have added a spoken Great Thanksgiving, compromising Taizé somewhat, or we could have used a pre-consecrated or reserved sacrament, calling upon our Anglo-Catholic Episcopalians to do what United Methodists could not do. Easiest, and less problematic of all would have been simply not to offer communion in that service. We were, to some extent, victims of our own perfectionism, and perfectionism is rarely a helpful trait for liturgists. Attempting to do too much in one liturgy is a temptation well documented in the history of liturgy and invariably such overloading causes the deletion of important things.[31]

30. Indeed, while I was a chapel assistant at Boston University in 1992, we held a clown Eucharist in which the Great Thanksgiving was done in pantomime. As we prepared for that event, I remember similar discussions about validity, about pre-consecration and reservation, and the need to emphasize gesture. The service itself was completed without significant controversy.

31. Baumstark, *Comparative Liturgy*, 16–30.

As to our worthy desire about emphasizing strong ritual gestures, we might have worked on that in other venues. For instance, in a practicum session on the Great Thanksgiving, a professor could demonstrate the gestures in pantomime and then ask the students to stand and do the same, followed by a discussion of the experience. One might also actually do a pantomime of the Great Thanksgiving gestures within a liturgy itself, but in a different way, as something like a liturgical dance. One would probably not add dance to a Taizé service, but such a dance could occur somewhere else on the chapel calendar. The dancers would do the offertory procession, bringing the bread and cup to the altar and then pantomiming the central Eucharistic gestures around the altar. Following the dance, the celebrant would then lead a spoken Great Thanksgiving, taking care to do the gestures with the appropriately full range of motion pantomimed by the dancers.

Conclusions

Theological educators should remember that everything done in their schools is educational. It is not just what one teaches, but also how one teaches it; not just what one publishes, but also how one conducts the research; not just how one interacts with students and professional colleagues, but also how one treats the support staff. By such logic, it should be obvious that seminary chapel is a pedagogical setting. How one handles the cup (and its contents) is significant, and perhaps especially when it is a bit too full.

When considering chapel as a laboratory where liturgical experiments might be conducted, the following values should be remembered:

1. There is a long tradition of using seminary chapel as a laboratory, and such experiments have covered a wide range of liturgical styles and theologies. To speak of seminary chapel as laboratory is not simply to speak of the *avant-garde*.

2. That seminary chapel is a liturgical laboratory should be acknowledged and affirmed by the faculty and the school administration, along with protection of the academic freedoms that one rightly finds in other pedagogical settings.

3. As with other educational settings, effective oversight should be administered by qualified faculty members, in this case by persons who are recognized members of the liturgical studies guild. Such oversight would include the setting of appropriate goals and the enforcing of boundaries.

4. As with all laboratory work in academic settings, liturgical experiments in seminary chapels should be subject to appropriate review, both within the specific seminary community and beyond, particularly within the liturgical studies guild.

Works Cited

Baumstark, Anton. *Comparative Liturgy.* Revised by Bernard Botte. Translated from the 3rd French ed. by F. L. Cross. Westminster, MD: Newman, 1958.

Bradshaw, Paul. *Two Ways of Praying.* Nashville: Abingdon, 1995.

Davis, Robert R. "Hip Hop Worship Prayers of the People." Unpublished prayers from Perkins Chapel service, April 21, 2005. Reprinted with permission of the author.

Donovan, Vincent J. *Christianity Rediscovered.* Maryknoll, NY: Orbis, 1978.

Hawn, C. Michael. *Gather Into One: Praying and Singing Globally.* Calvin Institute of Christian Worship Liturgical Studies Series. Grand Rapids: Eerdmans, 2003.

———. *One Bread, One Body: Exploring Cultural Diversity in Worship.* Foreword by Justo L. González. Bethesda, MD: The Alban Institute, 2003.

George, Nelson. *Hip Hop America.* New York: Penguin, 2005.

Peiffer, Robert Brian. "How Contemporary Liturgies Evolve: The Revision of United Methodist Liturgical Texts (1968–1988)." PhD diss., University of Notre Dame, 1993.

Stamm, Mark W. "Blue Grass Liturgy: A Window on Teaching Liturgy." *Perspective* (Perkins School of Theology; Spring 2008) 17.

———. *Extending the Table: A Guide for a Lay Ministry of Home Communion Serving.* Nashville: Discipleship Resources, 2009.

———. *Let Every Soul Be Jesus' Guest: A Theology of the Open Table.* Nashville: Abingdon, 2006.

Wesley, John. "The Duty of Constant Communion." In *The Works of John Wesley.* Vol. 3, *Sermons III: 71–114,* edited by Albert C. Outler, 427–39. Nashville: Abingdon, 1986.

White, James F. *Protestant Worship: Traditions in Transition* Louisville: Westminster John Knox, 1989.

Liturgical Resources Cited

The Book of Common Prayer. New York: The Church Hymnal Corporation, 1979.

Book of Common Worship. Louisville, KY: Westminster John Knox, 1993.

The Book of Resolutions of the United Methodist Church. Nashville: The United Methodist Publishing House, 2004.

From Ashes to Fire, Services of Worship for the Seasons of Lent and Easter with Introduction and Commentary. Supplemental Worship Resources 8. Nashville: Abingdon, 1979.

"The Order for Morning Prayer (With Music)." In *The Wesley Orders of Common Prayer.* Nashville: National Methodist Student Movement, 1957.

The Sacrament of the Lord's Supper, An Alternate Text. Nashville: The United Methodist Publishing House, 1972.

The United Methodist Book of Discipline 2004. Nashville: The United Methodist Publishing House, 2004.

The United Methodist Book of Worship. Nashville: The United Methodist Publishing House, 1992.

The United Methodist Hymnal. Nashville: The United Methodist Publishing House, 1989.

4

Musical Formation in Seminary Chapel Worship

PATRICK EVANS

Much has been said and written about the ways we sing in Christian faith communities in the United States. The rancor and division in the so-called worship wars often find their most public touchstone in the hymns and songs the congregation will be invited into. Although the nominal categories of traditional, contemporary, emergent, alt-, global, etc., mark much more than patterns of congregational song, at the local level it's not usually ways of praying, meditating, or proclaiming that seem to be the most contentious, but what we sing and how we sing it.

These same conversations and concerns about faithful ways of worshiping are present when the assembly gathers in our seminary chapels, and appropriately so, since most students preparing for the practice of ministry have come *from* these same churches, and bring to our academic communities the richness of their particular experiences in congregations with regard to worship. Since they largely intend to return *to* the churches, or to study and write about matters of great import to the churches, it is essential that their seminary education explore questions of practical importance to ecclesial communities.

We who work in seminary chapel worship find ourselves in a bit of a paradox. The worship life of the community is often central to the institution, and in many cases it is also vital to its proper functioning, because of its role in both building community and consolidating all the various aspects of the curriculum. At the same time, the worship in seminary chapels is usually considered extra-, co-, or para-curricular. There are good reasons for this—student preachers offering homiletic reflections shouldn't fear the red pens of homiletics professors jotting down flaws on the service leaflet any more than those professors should feel the need to critique instead of simply responding to the Word proclaimed.

Still, it is all too easy to underestimate the educational and formational value of the seminary community regularly coming together for worship. Formation occurs, certainly, in learning about various doctrines, practices, and modes of praying, singing, and proclaiming, but also in experiencing the movement of the Spirit in worship, a profound sense of meditative prayer, or the abiding presence of the divine wherever two or more are gathered. The planning and enacting of worship in seminary chapels offers the richest opportunity, if we fully utilize it, to help the leaders of the church—ministers, musicians, artists, lay worship leaders— to hear and understand each other. If we can help future clergy think more artistically, and artists and musicians think more theologically, the worshiping church will be all the better for it. If we are able to traverse barriers, labels, and categories within and outside denominational structures, we will draw closer to the will of Christ, who prayed that we may be one.

The gathered assembly raising many voices in a wide range of congregational song—from saints of every time and place—will be, in addition to a glorious act of praise to an ever-creating God, a useful tool for moving beyond human-constructed boundaries. In order to enable the assemblies in our seminary worshiping communities (as well as the congregations they will eventually serve) to join their voices in such an act of worship, however, we need to imagine new ways of encouraging the people's song. The principles set forth in this article are drawn from my experience as a practicing church musician working in several denominations over twenty-five years, as well as my collaborative work as Director of Chapel Music at Yale Divinity School (YDS).

Seminarians Should Recognize the Power of Song: Deep Memory

In almost all forms of Christian worship, music—particularly communal song—is central. Encouraging the full development of musical skill and love of singing in seminarians (many of whom have been disenfranchised from their own participation in the song of the church) is essential, and the most effective place for that to happen is in the worshipping life of the seminary chapel. It is, of course, of great benefit if there are courses in the curriculum which also expand this facility and knowledge, but the repertoire of congregational song in our common worship, and the ways in which we introduce and invite it, will have by far the greater impact, for good or ill, on the attitudes and aptitudes of the future church leaders with whom we worship and work.

I believe in the transformational power of communal singing and that the theological language that is deepest within us—which we call on in the time of trouble—is drawn more from what we have sung than what we have spoken, studied, or heard preached. As most of us know from personal experience, music has a powerful effect on memory, because that which is sung and repeated goes in deep, and remains accessible to us for many years to come.[1] When looking for a file on the computer, especially one beginning with a letter in a less-often-traversed section of the alphabet, see if you don't find yourself humming, either aloud or internally, the familiar tune which helped you learn the order of letters in your younger days.

My beloved grandmother Rosemary spent the last years of her life in declining states of dementia. When I would visit her in the final year or so of her life, she would begin a statement, get to the third or fourth word, and repeat it, unable to complete the thought she was trying to communicate to me. She seemed to understand what I said to her, and certainly she responded to non-verbal and emotional cues like hand-holding, hugging, smiling, and laughing. But the most direct communication we had in those days was when I began singing something like, "It's very clear" to which she responded with the consequent phrase, "our love is here to stay," as surely as the presider and assembly converse in the *sursum corda*. The lyric by Ira and tune by George Gershwin from her youth had gone so deep that even now she knew (often better than I could recall) that it was the Rockies that might eventually crumble and Gibraltar that may tumble. The specifics of those words mingled to that tune communicated those brothers' clever and heartfelt way of saying what Big Rosy, as her fourteen grandchildren affectionately called her, had taught us all from as

---

1. For recent relevant discoveries in the field of brain science and music, see Levitin, *This is Your Brain on Music*; and Sacks, *Musicophilia*.

early as I could remember—that our love was here to stay—that there was nothing in life or in death that could shake it.[2]

In New York City on September 11, 2001, we were not gathered on street corners quoting the best sermon we'd ever heard or the most enlightening article we'd read. We were at the Strawberry Fields Memorial in Central Park, singing "Imagine"; we were in Greenwich Village, just south of St. Vincent's Hospital, where hundreds of wheelchairs and gurneys were lined up outside as medical personnel waited for droves of survivors who never came, singing "Amazing Grace" with whoever walked up to the circle and joined in the song; we sang "Ain't Gonna Let Nobody Turn Me Around" on the side of the West Side Highway a few days later, cheering the heroic rescue workers as their trucks emerged, covered in ash; and in Union Square Park, we sang, among many other songs, the Jewish Shabbat greeting "Shalom Aleichem," as several musicians had set up multiple stands, with copies of the tune in transposition for every instrument, enabling a continuously reconfiguring orchestra and choir of strangers to join and leave the song over the course of a few minutes or many hours. "May your coming be in peace. Bless me with peace. May your going be in peace." In those days, we were constantly reminded of the deep power of communal singing to form bonds across every kind of barrier, to provide comfort, and to rehearse the songs of hope and faith which have sustained humanity from generation to generation. But in contemporary American society, both inside and outside the church, more and more people find themselves alienated from the sustaining act of communal singing.

Seminarians Should Understand the Problem in the Pews: Vocal Disempowerment

It is essential for students who will be involved in the practice of engaging parishioners in song to be aware that the people we are inviting are not neutral in their attitudes toward music or their participation in it as part of the assembly.

The people in the pews (or chairs) in our seminary chapels or Sunday morning congregations bring a significantly different set of previous musical experiences, cultural fluencies, and self-understandings about their

2. Ira Gershwin and George Gershwin, "Love is Here to Stay," 1939.

role in the music-making of the community than the people occupying those pews forty or even twenty years ago. John Bell notes that as many as one in four people nowadays has had some formational experience in which they were told outright that their singing voice was not good enough to be heard in public.[3] The bearer of bad tidings is usually someone with an emotional connection (a family member or love interest) or some perceived authority (a school teacher or church choir director). Bell reports the testimony of numerous people for whom this is a devastating experience and who, as a result, literally become voiceless regarding singing, both alone and in the company of others. Most of us likely know someone with such an experience.

Even those people who have not been told outright that their individual voice is substandard and is best not heard have received the subtle, yet powerful message of contemporary performance culture. That message insists that only the highly skilled, trained, and/or gifted singers should sing, and that they should be well-paid to do so. Everyone else is now audience, whether in the concert hall or on television, the web, or any manner of digital media currently available. Most people in contemporary culture are conditioned to lend only ears, not voice to music.

Since the spring of 2002, an enormous media message about individual vocal ability has been communicated widely and powerfully through the *American Idol* reality television show. A talent search contest, the program follows thousands of pop/rock star hopefuls through several rounds of auditions, with the final twenty-four singers competing on live television, with a combination of judges' decisions and popular voting by the nationwide audience constantly narrowing the pool until one contestant is finally declared the American Idol. I was initially heartened to hear so much interest from so many people of all age groups talking about which contestant offered a soaring rendition of a power ballad the night before, or which one connected with so much heart and musicality in the Beatles tune they were assigned. However, as each successive season began a new search, the producers increasingly sought to highlight the wishful dreamers who sang poorly, not beautifully. As seasons have progressed, they have interviewed hundreds of the thousands of people in line for auditions, inviting them to go on record with their deepest hopes and dreams. In earlier seasons, auditions by the hopeful but tune-

3. Bell, *The Singing Thing*, 95.

less would have been ended after a brief time, with some judges offering sympathetic comments, others snide and demeaning remarks. But in the most recent seasons, those who offer terrible auditions (especially those who are least aware of how they are being judged) have been invited by the judges to offer a second song. Everyone knows that the second song will be no better than the first, but the producers do it in order to have that much more footage to find the most awful (and unaware) moment to air for the quick, intense, cringe-inducing commercials promoting the new season. For anyone who watches only occasionally, or even just catches a commercial while flipping through the channels, an unequivocal and powerful cultural message is transmitted: "Unless you have a recording-contract-worthy ability to sing, do not ever attempt it, especially in front of others, lest you humiliate yourself like these poor souls."

Further, the increasing perfection of digitally recorded music allows exceptional fidelity of sound and absolute perfection of performance. Multiple takes are easily spliced together, from the rock band to the symphony orchestra or Broadway's music. The ability to digitally tune and splice only the most perfect takes into a seemingly effortless, seamless track means that the recordings we hear are so perfect in every controllable way that they aren't actually repeatable at that level in live performance, except by artists of the absolute highest levels of skill and discipline. As a result, controversies over lip-synching in live concerts and television performances have brought attention to the disconnect between what consumers of music are hearing, and what performers of music are actually able to do in a live setting without digital tunings and extra takes. A recent example of this was the revelation that at the opening of the 2000 Olympics, the Sydney Orchestra mimed while a recording of the Melbourne Symphony played.[4]

Additionally, people are not only listening to music while driving to work or school, or on a shabby clock radio in the office. With the advent of mp3 players and other digital technology, our world has been quickly transformed into a vast market of consumers of absolutely perfect vocal and instrumental performances, available at any time. And our playlists are available for a much larger percentage of our waking and even our sleeping hours than ever (I have several friends who fall asleep with their mp3 players set to "shuffle" and earphones in both ears). This means that

---

4. Gelineau, "Orchestra Admits Miming at Sydney Olympics."

people are nearly surrounded by digitally perfect, humanly unattainable music, and the gap between what they hear and what they believe they can do has consequently become wider than ever.

Finally, the advent and explosive growth of online music purchasing has changed the ways we learn to love and appreciate new songs. In the past, with vinyl records, 8-tracks, cassettes, and even compact discs, a few of the most popular songs would be released as singles. For the most part, however, the musical consumer would usually purchase an entire album to hear those one or two songs that had been released as singles and encountered on the radio or video channels. This resulted in the other ten to twelve songs being heard repeatedly, and many times one or more of these songs would become more beloved than the hit tune the consumer was originally seeking with the purchase.

In purchasing music digitally from online sources, full albums are still available, but the format strongly favors the $.99 download of one track. The economic impact on artists of this relatively quick but powerful shift in purchasing habits toward single downloads has led some (Kid Rock among them) to boycott iTunes.[5] The argument is that it "pushes the *a la carte* music track system instead of allowing artists to sell music in album-only format."[6] And the anticipated result will be an entire generation that encounters music primarily as a commodity from which it is easy to choose only that which immediately appeals.

Because the cultural forces of digital technology and *American Idol* are relatively recent, these powerful overt and covert influences are more likely to have the strongest impact on younger generations. While they may marginally impact second-career seminary students, these trends will have the most effect on those who are pursuing theological education immediately or shortly after their undergraduate studies. Given the likelihood that many have additionally been advised that they should not sing, it is clear that the people who gather for worship in our communities are not picking up their hymnals in a neutral frame of mind. These powerful trends will no doubt be informing the relationship of congregants to corporate song for decades, and the students in our seminaries will be the ministers, worship leaders, and musicians who are working counterculturally to encourage the people's song.

5. As of this writing, iTunes is the largest single retailer of music in the U.S.
6. Cheng, "Album-loving," para. 2.

For these reasons, those of us who are teaching and inviting people into the act of communal singing in our worshipping communities must respond pastorally to the particular vulnerabilities among our congregations, while resisting the negative effects of the market forces influencing musical preferences.

It is no longer enough that the only way congregational song is invited or encouraged is for the hymn to be played through once on the organ, or for the praise band to sing, expecting folks to join in on the chorus. Such standard methods would likely be sufficient for those among us who have always loved to sing and who feel comfortable raising their voices in the presence of others, but the ranks of those who consider themselves secure singers are thinning, and the numbers of the unsure in our midst are rising.

Modeling The Singing Church in Seminary Chapels

John Bell often remarks that people who feel disenfranchised from their voices are unlikely to take the risk to join in singing unless they hear a strong voice within three feet of them.[7] The reality is that for folks who don't feel relatively confident in their singing, a choir in a loft or balcony far away, or a praise band whose sound is mixed and coming through speakers as a wall of sound instead of acoustically recognizable individual voices and instruments, don't encourage singing, but, instead, discourage it. If the unsure singer gains enough courage to attempt to join the singing, the gorgeous sound of the faraway choir or the monolithic speaker sound of the amplified leaders is heard by the congregant as a distant background against which her or his individual voice, with all its flaws, is drawn into auditory contrast. This happens largely because of the human physique: the singer hears her or his own voice mostly internally, with only a small perception of its sound in the room. Our vocal mechanisms are such that the internal hearing of our own singing is more prominent than the external, because the vibrations are resonating in the open chambers of the pharynx, nasal passages, and the mouth, and the aural sensors are internal and linked to both the vocal folds making the initial vibration and the chambers in which that vibration resonates. So it is that our internal hearing magnifies our speaking or singing voices in the foreground

7. Bell, *The Singing Thing*, 22.

of aural perception, while simultaneous externally produced sounds tend to take a back seat. There also usually tends to be a mis-hearing of one's own voice as it actually sounds in the room for the same reason. One is likely to believe one's speaking or singing voice sounds one way, only to find, when listening to the recording of your own voice (in a voicemail greeting, or the *YouTube* posting of your karaoke performance) that it sounds quite another way in the room.

Consider what happens *physically* in the act of singing. If a cantor is humming a drone, vibrations are being formed within that singer's body, and anyone who is hearing the cantor hum has those vibrations touching their skin, engaging their eardrum, then being interpreted for pitch, timbre, and other aspects by their brain.[8] Imagine then, that instead of one person singing and the others listening, that you're standing in the midst of an Orthodox service of worship, and the assembly is humming a drone, while the cantor is intoning over it. This means that vibrations created in the bodies of each member of the assembly are touching the skin and engaging the ear drum of every other person in the room. When one member of the assembly gets to the end of her breath, she is able to breathe in deeply, knowing that the sound will be sustained by the other singers around her, and that she will in turn maintain the sound when others need to rest. The individuals in that worship service are *physically* connected by the mutual sound they are making, and it supports the *spiritual* and *theological* connections being formed by the enacting of the liturgy. The physical connection of the act of communal singing embodies so much of what we claim theologically in worship—that we are gathered into one.

The Placement of Bodies:
Supporting the People's Song in a "Traditional" Space

For ten years I was Minister of Music at the Hanover Street Presbyterian Church in Wilmington, Delaware. This congregation was like none I had ever experienced in their understanding of radical hospitality and being the gospel in the world. Hanover church was a downtown, urban, intentionally inter-racial, social justice-minded, LGBT-affirming congregation. It had a food pantry, a clothing closet, a Head Start program, and

8. Levitin, *This is Your Brain on Music*, 114.

a true passion for being Christ's light in a challenging neighborhood. A neighborhood that included half-million-dollar houses on one side and government public housing on the other, including a halfway house for women transitioning back into society from the Delaware State Mental hospital right next door. One of their major concerns was that, although this was a diverse, dynamic, inter-racial, globally–concerned community six days per week, on Sunday morning, the worship, and the music especially, had been almost exclusively "traditional Presbyterian" in the ways it described God and God's people. Consequently, the repertoire the congregation sang on Sunday did not fully bear witness to the richness of the faith they enacted and believed every other day of the week. So we began to journey together, to draw on the multicultural riches of the relatively new 1990 hymnal, and to expand the ways in which we praised an ever-creating God who had called and sustained us for the work of ministry in Wilmington. But it was not just a matter of expanding the repertoire. If we were to expand *what* we sang, we would need to also expand *how* we sang.

The congregation numbered approximately 150 and were spread across a forward-facing space which could hold 400 or more. In order to better support the singing of the people in the pews, the choir sang the *introit* from the ground-level loft in the back, and then began to process during the first hymn, down the side aisles, meeting in the center, and coming back up the central aisle. By this movement, we made sure that all worshippers were supported in their singing by having a strong voice singing somewhere physically close by. Some in the congregation were concerned that a procession was too "high church" or "not Presbyterian," but others commented that they felt much more comfortable singing the opening hymn, which was usually a familiar hymn of praise.

Then, after that became familiar, we altered the procession so that we stopped and turned to face forward in the center aisle, allowing the choir to stay in the midst of the congregation for the *Kyrie* and the *Gloria*, which made it much easier for the congregation to join in when we sang new responses in those places. After the passing of the peace, the choir would either go to the forward loft if they were singing a gospel anthem with piano, or to the back loft if they were singing Mendelssohn with organ. As our journey together progressed, if the sermon hymn was new and in Spanish, they might be seated in the congregation for the sermon, robes and all, to lend their voices as a cantor succinctly and clearly taught the Spanish hymn phrase by phrase as an act of worship. Finally, we often processed down the side aisles and stood there for the final hymn, singing a choral benediction, usually unaccompanied, surrounding the congregation.

The faithful people in the choir literally put their bodies on the line so that the gathered community would be better able to sing a new song to the Lord, and thus faithfully name, learn, and embody a much richer repertoire of memorized theology to call upon in either time of trouble or during the working week. There were benefits and challenges, of course—Irene and Mary Frances, who were some days less mobile, might simply stay in the back loft, or meet us in the front after the passing of the peace. Gigi, after a dangerous car accident, processed in her wheelchair for a while, which meant the tenors in front and behind needed to give her a little extra space for cornering! But the musicianship in this volunteer choir increased exponentially as they stood, three feet apart each other, surrounding the congregation, singing in time and in tune across space. Their flexibility and willingness to try new ways enabled that congregation to sing a wide range of African-American spirituals and gospel songs, music from global church, and the best of new hymnody from Shirley Erena Murray, Tom Troeger and others who offered new insights into a historic faith at that time.

In my last year at Hanover, we finally had the right boy soprano at the right time of year to present Menotti's opera *Amahl and the Night Visitors* for Epiphany. The chancel choir would take the roles of the shepherd's chorus, who come running from the hills greeting each other, singing vibrantly and calling each other's names across the fields "Emily, Emily, Michael, Bartholomew, how are your children and how are your sheep?"[9] During one particularly energetic dress rehearsal, we stopped to fix a staging detail and one of my more sardonic basses remarked, "You know, this isn't really much more running around than you have us doing on any given Sunday." We all had a great laugh at that, and realized that except for the colorful scarves, shepherds cloaks, and baskets of hazelnuts and chamomile, it might not actually be more locomotion than usual. Reflecting on that scene more fully, I have come to realize that these shepherds had taken on this very pastoral role every Sunday, although wear-

9. Gian Carlo Menotti, "Amahl and the Night Visitors," copyright 1951, 1952 (renewed) by G. Schirmer, Inc. (ASCAP), New York, NY (International copyright secured. All rights reserved) 33.

ing different cloaks, calling out across the space, greeting and welcoming, and enabling the communal praise of a people who might otherwise be unsure of the song, and their place in it.

The need for the twenty-first-century church to learn by heart an expanded repertoire of song naming God and God's people in ways both historic and contemporary, "Western" and "non-Western," will require an expansion of our methods of inviting the assembly into it. The church needs leaders who have considered these challenges.

Seminarians Should Be Invited to Think Carefully About What We Sing

The church universal has an extensive repertoire of songs of praise, lament, narrative, and testimony, spanning thousands of years, various theological and liturgical movements, and a wide variety of vocal and instrumental genres. Although denominational differences may mean that some seminary chapels emphasize certain traditions rather than others, it seems sensible to me that those who gather to worship a creating, redeeming, and inspiring God should be interested in singing from as wide a range as is available to a particular worshiping community. Hymnals in the past twenty years have become ever more ecumenical in their scope, and there is every reason to believe such a trend will continue, offering a rich diversity of congregational song.

Seminary communities in particular need to explore these riches more fully, and I would argue this is especially true in the song of the global church. If we humbly approach the songs of Christians throughout the world, seeking to learn from the testimonies of faith and struggle in their prayers, texts, tunes, and movements, we will be better prepared to be the church in the world in our globalized time and place.

Neuroscientist and musician Daniel Levitin points to a fascinating discovery in brain science that I believe has implications for congregational song, especially for cross-cultural singing. There seems to be a strong response of delight when our expectations are set up by certain familiar melodic, rhythmic, and harmonic patterns, then upended when one or more of those factors moves in an unexpected and surprising way.[10] This not only builds interest but is more likely to embed itself in memory

10. Levitin, *This is Your Brain on Music,* 114–19

than a song that follows expected patterns of anticipation. Consider, for example, a very popular exuberant "Alleluia" by Abraham Mairare from Zimbabwe:

Fig 1. "Alleluia," Abraham Mairare, Words and music (c) Zimbabwe East Annual Conference. Used by permission.

Recognizing that western singers of this song would be treading on thin ice to imagine what these harmonic and rhythmic patterns might mean to singers from its culture of origin, we tend to be greatly surprised when singing it for the first time by the movement of the bass part on the last chord. Western classical expectations of harmony would dictate that the last phrase move strongly from c to f—the "root" or "tonic" of the expected cadence. Here, however, the bass line moves from c only one step up to d—in the music theory we learn in conservatory, that's a "deceptive" cadence—moving to the sixth scale degree instead of to the strongly resolved first scale degree. Many North American singers of this alleluia describe it as being both a joyful song of praise, and one that does not feel as if it is completed—that it seems to hang in the air. The worship experience of singing an alleluia like this as opposed to one that strongly resolves is different, inviting other understandings—praises that hang in the air, unresolved. It opens up possibilities that our other alleluias might not invite.

We are often prone to imagining the theology of a hymn to be found in its text, and the musical setting to be a means to enable the proclamation of that text. One is hopeful that the musical setting will support and amplify the meaning of the poem, and that it wouldn't undermine it. However, rarely is the tune imagined to have its own theology. Interchanging suitable tunes with appropriate texts is a practice that is more common in some traditions than others (indeed, the idea that one tune is wed to one text is foreign to much of the church, but relatively unquestioned by other parts of it). When a familiar text is sung to an unexpected tune, the tune's interpretation of the theology of the text sometimes becomes more apparent.

Robert Grant's text "O Worship the King" is known to most in a setting of the tune LYONS, a triumphal, energetic, angular hymn of praise. Daud Kosasih from Indonesia, however, has a beautiful tune for this text, with an accompaniment written to evoke an Indonesian *gamelan*. When our seminary community first sang this text to this tune—a much more flexible rhythm, with half-steps and leaps in the melody in places the western ear might not expect—I was flooded with comments from people who heard certain parts of the text in new ways—"Thy mercies, how tender, how firm to the end!" and "Frail children of dust, and feeble as frail."[11] A hymn text that had always been about God's triumphant majesty was now additionally about a God who is an intimate, tender companion, full of mystery and wonder. We were singing the same text—with a few alterations for gender inclusivity—but the tune implied a very different theological interpretation of the text, at least to these singers of it, whose expectations of the meaning of this hymn were delightfully and surprisingly redirected by an unexpected tune.

I am not claiming that Kosasih's tune is superior to LYONS or that an alleluia with a deceptive cadence is more faithful or even more interesting than one with a full cadence. Their addition to the repertoire of the songs we sing together in the seminary chapel, however, have allowed for a wider range of experiences of the presence of God, and have formed prayerful experiences which go into deep places of memory and meaning. Additionally, they and other songs from the global church are a constant reminder that not only are we but one small part of the body of Christ, but that the worldwide church is vast: different to us, and related to us. When we join our voices with the saints from the global church, we are more likely to pray with them, be mindful of them, and learn new insights from their testimonies.

11. "O Worship the King," words by Robert Grant (1779–1838); music by Daud Kosasih (Chicago: Christian Conference of Asia, GIA Publications, 1990), http://www .giamusic.com. All rights reserved. Used by permission.

The earth with its store of won-der un - told, al - might-y Thy pow'r has

found - ed of old. Es - tab - lished it fast by a change-less de -

cree, and round it has cast, like a___ man - tle, the sea.

Fig 2. Verse 3 of "O Worship the King," words by Robert Grant (1779–1838); music by Daud Kosasih (Chicago: Christian Conference of Asia, GIA Publications, 1990), http://www.giamusic.com. All rights reserved. Used by permission.

Seminarians Should Be Invited to Think in New Ways About How We Sing

In Marquand Chapel we now have the benefit of flexible seating, which allows us on most days to be facing toward a central space with curved rows. This greatly encourages the people's song, not only because the sound of the worshipers opposite you comes towards you instead moving away from you, but because you are also able to see the faces of people joining their voices in song. It is a great encouragement when one can both see and hear other singers nearby. Following the methods I learned in the Hanover church, the Chapel Choir, the Gospel Choir, and the cantors all sit in the midst of the assembly, and in designing the liturgy we plan with those choirs' directors a way for them to go to the area of the space where they might sing an anthem together when that time comes, often moving into place on the last verse of a hymn.

In addition to the re-thinking of the choir's role as ministers of congregational song, the role of the *enlivener* or *animateur* will play an essential part in inviting the person in the pew into new ways of singing (or even daring to attempt the old ways!). Both John Bell and C. Michael Hawn discuss the role of the *enlivener*, and in many of our worshiping traditions, there is already something akin to it.[12] Many congregations are accustomed to having a cantor chant the psalm, a priest intone the liturgy,

---

12. In *The Singing Thing*, Bell is concerned in its entirety with the role of the *enlivener*. See also Hawn, *Gather into One*, 241–70.

a worship-leader announce the song and set the tempo, or a pastor or musician engage the people in improvisational call and response, either as part of the sermon, in a time of prayer, or in shouting their praises. If we are to sing from a wide range of repertoire from the worldwide church, draw on ancient traditions of chant, and raise our voices in a time of praise and worship, most of us will need to be invited into it and led by a fellow worshiper. In *The Singing Thing*, Bell describes key techniques for teaching and inviting congregational song. The most important are that the leader should be: a pastoral presence (someone the community trusts): someone with a clear but not overwhelming voice: someone who will know the song they are inviting from memory; an someone who can gently give the assembly just enough vocal and gestural leadership, with a concise theological/musical invitation. The *enlivener*, just as a leader of bidding prayers, should offer reliable leadership, leadership that is present when needed and in the background once the assembly has fully assumed its role.

Drawing further on Levitin's understandings of musical expectation and surprise, it is important that we vary the ways in which congregational song is accompanied. In the same way that it becomes easy to recite prayers by rote, not fully engaging with the words we say, it becomes easy to set our voices to automatic pilot if everything we sing is accompanied in one way, be it organ, piano, praise band, or drumming, with the same pattern of introduction every time. Additionally, fidelity to a wide range of traditions requires whatever is closest to an original instrumentation and available to the gathered assembly. For example, we try to sing dispersed harmony from *The Sacred Harp* unaccompanied where possible, or a psalm setting based on a Brazilian dance tune with guitar, percussion, and perhaps piano or accordion. Beyond our humble attempts to remain faithful to the sending culture of a hymn or chant, varying the instrumentation provides a wider opportunity for experiential learning—such as the likelihood that the wailing of the saxophone will send someone's heart soaring more than if only a piano were used.

Finally, the community is not invited into a Taizé chant by a clarinet line and a soprano melody. They are invited by Rebecca, the clarinetist, and Greta, the soprano, whom they know from previous leadership in chapel, from their prayer requests, from having lunch with them, or from struggling through a difficult exegesis exercise in an Old Testament section with them. When Rebecca blows breath into the instrument and applies her skill and musical expertise to the phrase, she is presiding and inviting the people's worship every bit as much as the person who offered the collect or led the prayers. When Greta gently raises her hands, looks at the members of the assembly, and leads them with her clear but not dominant soprano voice, she is serving in a ministerial role, not as a concert artist. These ways of presiding should be fully cultivated, and theologians, musicians, dancers, poets, and artists should collaborate in shared planning and leadership, as each will preside and invite in a different manner, and the other will benefit from it.

Seminary Worship Can Model Variety and Repetition

In order for a congregation to deeply internalize the theology of both a text and a tune, a hymn must be sung repeatedly, over time. "How Great Thou Art" would not be the important anchor it is to so many worshipers today if it had only been sung once or twice a year. If songs from the global church and newly-written hymn texts and tunes are going to join the canon of deeply-beloved songs of the faith, we will need to sing them often, not as rarities. Seminary communities, especially those who gather for worship more than once a week, have the opportunity to systematically enable the familiarity that only comes with repeated singing.

In Marquand Chapel, we gather for worship five days a week, Monday through Friday. There has been a long tradition at YDS that Wednesday mornings are Sung Morning Prayer, and Friday mornings are community Eucharist, with various other forms of worship the other three days of the school week. In recent years, we have followed a slightly abstracted *ordo* for Sung Morning Prayer, engaging various styles of psalmody, sung prayer, hymnody, and other service music. Because the other worship services are different every day, we repeat the same service of Sung Morning Prayer for three or four Wednesdays, with only the spoken scripture readings changing from week to week. This gives the community one day when they know when they walk through the door what worship will sound and feel like, after the initial week of the particular form.

If there is a hymn, psalm, or response we hope the entire community will eventually learn by heart, we make sure it finds its way into one of the forms of Sung Morning Prayer. This has enabled many unforeseen blessings. One of our student chapel organists, an Episcopalian, introduced us to the beautiful Calvin Hampton setting of Frederick W. Faber's text "There's a Wideness in God's Mercy." Hampton's tune, ST. HELENA, weaves through several changing meters and unexpected harmonic shifts, with a beautiful yearning solo line, often played on the oboe. This tune, in my opinion, expresses the boundless nature of God's mercy described in the text in a much more visceral way than other tunes which stay in one meter, with strong beats and expected melodic and harmonic cadences—boundaries—clearly proscribed. I believe Levitin's principle of the delight of surprise is at play here. Because we sang it weekly in Sung Morning Prayer over the course of a month or so, any time thereafter when the community heard the oboe begin the introduction, the majority of them were able to sing, nearly for memory, not only the three verses published in *The Hymnal 1982 (Episcopal)*, but another of Faber's verses, our organist's favorite, which says in part: "But we make this love too narrow by false limits of our own; and we magnify its strictness with a zeal God will not own."[13] This is an amazing theology from 1854 which has an especially powerful impact when sung from the heart by not only Episcopalians, but Catholics, Baptists, Pentecostals, and those from at least twenty other traditions in an ecumenical community in which the denominational divisions often loom large. This heartsong, I'm convinced, has had a deeply formative effect on the ways we interact outside the chapel doors—in community life, in the classroom, in difficult conversations. That meaningful impact on the living of our days would not be possible without the opportunity for repetition and deep experiential learning provided by regularly gathering for worship, nor without the opportunity for the adventure of a new tune or text. What we sing, how we sing it, and how often we sing it, matters.

It should be noted that there are certainly limits on what we are able to do musically in seminary chapel worship. Limits of time, resources, faculty input, student interest, available musicians and singers—these will vary from community to community. Most of our seminary worshiping communities, however, have room to grow with regard to the range of what we sing and the ways the assembly is invited to sing it. A collaborative process of planning, mutual listening, and good faith on the part of all the participants will be necessary to expand the musical formational

---

13. Frederick W. Faber, "There's a Wideness in God's Mercy," in *Evangelical Lutheran Worship*, Evangelical Lutheran Church in America (Minneapolis: Augsburg Fortress Press). Original written in 1854.

opportunities available to our assemblies, and the range of experiential learning available to the future leaders of the church. The seminary chapel needs to be the place where those who have been rendered voiceless are relentlessly invited to rejoin the community of song—so that they and their future parishioners will be empowered to develop a deep well of theologies to call on when no Bible or pastor is nearby. But also so that they will constantly be reminded of the wideness of God's mercy and that nothing in life or death can separate them from the love of God in Christ Jesus.

Works Cited

Bell, John. *The Singing Thing: A Case for Congregational Song*. Chicago: GIA, 2000.

Cheng, Jacqui. "Album-loving artists blame iTunes for changed music tastes." *ars technica* (August 28, 2008). No pages. Online: http://arstechnica.com/old/content/2008/08/album-loving-artists-blame-itunes-for-changed-music-tastes.

Gelineau, Kristen. "Orchestra Admits Miming at Sydney Olympics." Associated Press (August 29, 2008). No pages. Online: http://abcnews.go.com/International/wireStory?id=5682906.

Hawn, C. Michael. *Gather into One: Praying and Singing Globally*. Grand Rapids: Eerdmans 2003.

Levitin, Daniel. *This is Your Brain on Music: The Science of a Human*. New York: Dutton/Penguin, 2006.

Sacks, Oliver. *Musicophilia: Tales of Music and the Brain*. New York: Knopf, 2007.

5

Seminary Chapel in a Prayer Book Context

LIZETTE LARSON-MILLER

It is right and a good and joyful thing, to give thanks to You, Creator of all things . . .

Ecclesial, Academic and Physical Contexts

The Church Divinity School of the Pacific (CDSP) is a major seminary of the Episcopal Church in the United States, particularly supported by Province VIII of the Episcopal Church,[1] but drawing students from dioceses beyond the western United States and from member churches of the Anglican Communion.[2] In addition to the MDiv students who make up the majority of the student body,[3] there are certificate students coming

1. Province VIII is made up of 15 dioceses in the Western United States, Alaska, Hawaii, and Taiwan.

2. For example, in the academic year 2008–2009, there were students representing Anglican dioceses from Canada, England, Cameroon, Brazil, and Korea.

3. Most, but not all, of the Master of Divinity students are on an "ordination track," with a few lay students working toward lay ministries. The majority of Episcopal and Anglican dioceses prefer that their MDiv students be in "the process" before going to seminary. This means that most of the MDiv students have been sent by their diocese, having already done a number of initial steps toward ordination, including parish discernment, and diocesan approval to the point of making the students "Postulants" for their diocese toward ordination. A few students come (and finish) seminary before arriving at postulancy either because they were rejected by their diocese or are still in discernment about ordination. Ordination is not an individual undertaking in Anglicanism, but rather a common discernment between the individual, God, the local parish, the diocese,

for a year or two for a variety of reasons, DMin students, MTS students, and the General Theological Union-affiliated MA and PhD students. The latter represent the ecumenical and interfaith consortium to which CDSP belongs, The Graduate Theological Union (GTU) in Berkeley, California.[4] The seminary itself is a small school, with generally between 90 to 110 students, and approximately ten full-time faculty, but the consortium, with its constant presence and interaction, gives the impression that the school is bigger and busier.

The chapel sits in the middle of the campus, both physically and emotionally. It is not an attractive space in the eyes of the majority of beholders, dating back to the early days of CDSP's move to Berkeley.[5] Liturgy takes place in a building that was originally designed to house the chapel and the library, but the dividing wall between the two was removed in 1960 leaving a very long narrow room with a raised platform dividing two unequal spaces. For the last ten years, the chapel has been separated into two uses, on the smaller side it is set up choir-style (pews facing inward in two long rows) for the daily offices of morning and evening prayer. The seating arrangement allows for the normative practice of antiphonal psalmody with room for a maximum of fifty people.

On the other side of the chapel, in a longer and therefore larger space, the daily Eucharist is celebrated, and the space alternates between a quasi-circular set-up with the altar an ambo in the middle of pews radiating out, and a set-up with the middle platform as an altar area and the pews all facing the same direction. The seating arrangements allow for approximately 90–120 people to attend the Eucharist. The raised platform contains the two-manual organ console (the pipes are housed above two closets leading off of the platform opposite the console) and a grand piano, as well as either the liturgical furniture for the Eucharist (if

---

and the seminary.

4. The Graduate Theological Union, founded in 1962, is comprised of nine seminaries and five centers or programs representing Christian groups such as Eastern Orthodox, Roman Catholic, Anglican, Lutheran, Presbyterian, and several other Protestant groups, as well as Buddhist, Jewish, and Muslim interests.

5. CDSP was founded in 1893, on the feast day of St. Luke, in the city of San Mateo. It moved to a property in front of Grace Cathedral, San Francisco, following the 1906 earthquake, and finally settled in the current location in Berkeley in 1930. The present chapel was consecrated in 1937. For an in-depth history of CDSP, see Morgan, *From Ocean's Farthest Coast.*

arranged that way) or rows of chairs if the Eucharistic side of the chapel is arranged in a circle.

The Shape of Liturgy

For approximately fourteen years, the *cursus* of liturgies at CDSP has remained fundamentally the same. Monday through Friday there are three liturgies a day, morning prayer five days a week at 7:30am, evening prayer four nights a week (excluding Thursday) at 5:30pm, and the Holy Eucharist celebrated daily at 11:30am Monday, Tuesday, Wednesday and Friday, and at 5:45pm on Thursdays. Midday Thursdays have seen a variety of other common prayer options including midday prayer (according to the *Book of Common Prayer)*, centering prayer, the rosary, stations of the cross, Episcopal Peace Fellowship prayers, or other patterns. Many semesters there have also been weekly or even daily celebrations of compline, but that is student-led and in addition to the regular (and official) *cursus* of fifteen liturgies a week. There are no school liturgies on the weekends, students are encouraged to visit a variety of parishes in their first year, and generally are busy in field education parishes their second year (and increasingly, in their third year also).

Attendance at all the liturgies varies by day of the week, by season, and by the rhythms of the academic calendar: morning prayer attendance averages fifteen on a daily basis, evening prayer averages twenty-three, and attendance at the Holy Eucharist averages sixty on a daily basis. Students are not required to attend a particular number of liturgies each day or week, but MDiv students are to develop "a pattern of worship attendance that is sufficiently full to be a real and necessary part of their formation in a ministerial and professional degree program."[6] They are required to honor their rota assignments, which generally number about eight per semester. Other students (in other degree programs) are invited to be part of the rota. Faculty members are required to preside and/or preach depending on their ordained status, other members of the community (staff, family members) are invited to participate. All, of course, are welcome to attend any liturgy, and there are usually some children at every Eucharistic celebration. Often members of other GTU schools, and neighbors, friends, alumni, or others are present every week.

6. *The Customary for Chapel Worship,* CDSP (2008–2009) 4.

Within this general pattern, there are both consistencies and deliberate exceptions. Morning prayer is led by volunteer officiants,[7] who are almost always students. Volunteer means that they are not scheduled and required to appear when on the rota, but may instead sign up for the mornings they wish to oversee this rite. At the beginning of the year, the volunteers are usually students who know morning prayer well from parish experience or attendance at CDSP morning prayer. As the academic year unfolds, more students feel confident to sign up to lead morning prayer, but overall, the numbers remain quite small. For several years, the ritual pattern has had variety built into it in order to expose students to different language and musical options. Until the Spring semester of 2009, the pattern was Rite I once a week, Rite II twice a week, sung morning prayer (Rite II) once a week, and Spanish language morning prayer once a week.[8] After a request and survey of the regular attendees in the Fall of 2009, the community dropped Rite I morning prayer and uses only Rite II, with its optional additions of expansive and inclusive language gathered in volume one of *Enriching Our Worship*.[9] The other mornings continue as noted above, and the Spanish language morning prayer often draws Spanish-speaking staff members in addition to students and family members. The volunteer officiant selects the optional elements of morning prayer, asks for a volunteer lector, and presides over the service, which is generally about twenty to twenty-five minutes long, depending on prayer choices made and whether there is music.

Evening prayer, observed four nights a week, is generally celebrated using Rite I one night of the week, Rite II two nights a week, and the *EOW*

7. Officiant is the title given to one who presides at non-eucharistic liturgy, particularly used for the daily office.

8. The terms Rite I and Rite II refer to rites in the *Book of Common Prayer* 1979 (hereafter *BCP*). Rite I is generally understood to be the traditional language version of daily office, Eucharist, the burial rite, and virtually all the public prayers in the *BCP*. But in some rites, the differences are more than linguistic; there are also structural differences that reflect the 1928 *BCP*, and generations of prayer books before that, including the 1662 prayer book. In morning and evening prayer, however, the differences are basically linguistic, not structural.

9. *Enriching Our Worship* (hereafter *EOW*) is a series of supplementary texts to the *BCP*. Volume I (1998) contains additional prayers and texts for Holy Eucharist and morning and evening prayer, *EOW* II (2000), contains the additional liturgies for Ministry with the Sick or Dying and the Burial of a Child, *EOW* III (2007) contains Burial Rites for Adults (with the Burial of a Child repeated). The latter two also contain, for the first time, the theological *praenotandae* for these rites.

expansion of Rite II usually once a week. Evening prayer is not volunteer, but assigned primarily to MDiv students according to the rota. Two students are scheduled, one as officiant, the other as lector. The officiant usually takes the initiative to choose the optional parts of evening prayer according to the rite assigned,[10] learning the shape of evening prayer by attending evening prayer, participating in a mandatory workshop at the beginning of the academic year, reading the customary, thinking through the choices ahead of time, and rehearsing at 5pm (with a paid student sacristan running the rehearsal) for a half hour prior to the 5:30pm liturgy.

The Holy Eucharist is celebrated on a daily basis with several cycles of diversity built into the pattern. The primary cycle is that governed by the liturgical year, which adds its own pattern to the celebrations. In the Spring semester, the major liturgical seasons of Lent and Easter dominate the style and choices made for the Eucharist, as well as for morning and evening prayer to a lesser extent. In the Fall semester, the week is shaped by observance of most of the lesser feasts and fasts,[11] and of the major feasts,[12] with the last two or three weeks of the semester falling in Advent. The secondary cycle is that of the school itself, with its own "feasts," such as the Alumni Convocation, arrivals and departures of new students, the beginning of the year, and other observations of a local nature. Additionally, there is the rhythm of the week both by intention and by reality of academic scheduling. The Thursday Eucharist is in the evening to allow more family members to attend, and attendance is twice as large as most other days. The children of the community are invited to attend *Godly Play* during the Liturgy of the Word, joining their parents at the Peace for the Liturgy of the Eucharist. There are visitors, prospective students, members of the local religious order (Anglican Franciscans), neighbors, and others who swell the community gathering, which is fol-

10. The scripture readings and psalms are appointed for each day of the office in the *BCP*, but can be grouped in different ways. For the past academic year, CDSP has used the Old Testament and Gospel readings at morning prayer, and the epistle and a reading from hagiography at evening prayer. The officiant also chooses which prayers and music to be used at any given liturgy.

11. *Lesser Feasts and Fasts* (2006) contains the daily Eucharistic lectionary for Advent and Christmas, and for Lent, as well as proper collects for the Easter season. It also contains the lesser feasts that fall throughout the liturgical year, each with a biography, a collect, a preface, and the appointed scripture readings.

12. The major feasts (so-called "red letter days"), are obligatory feasts grouped into principal feasts, Sundays, and major holy days. See *BCP* 15–18.

lowed by a social hour and community dinner (and often by a talk or presentation). Thursday night Eucharist is therefore the high point of the weekly cycle for the CDSP community in most weeks.

Tuesday Eucharist, at 11:30am, is the weekly occasion of a senior sermon, a required rite of passage for all graduating MDiv seniors. Next to Thursdays, it is the largest liturgy, and like Thursdays, it has full music and ceremonial appropriate to the season. Fridays are generally the next smallest gathering at Eucharist, without music, but monthly they also include the celebration of the anointing of the sick, which draws about forty-five people. Mondays and Wednesdays alternate between different music patterns. Attendance is generally the smallest on Wednesdays because there are few classes at the GTU held on that day and it is the day students go off to their field education parishes. Once a month the Wednesday Eucharist is bilingual (Spanish-English) which affords an opportunity to introduce students to the Spanish language *BCP* and related music repertoire.

In addition to the regular *cursus* of liturgies described above, each semester has room for a number of experimental liturgies. The term "experimental" may be unfortunate, but it describes the ten to fifteen liturgies (both eucharistic and non-eucharistic) per semester which are not on the rota, and emerge from ideas and designs submitted by students to the worship committee the semester prior to the liturgical celebration. Sometimes the proposed liturgies are thematic, sometimes they highlight a particular culture, sometimes they use rites from other Anglican churches, sometimes they are focused on a saint, and sometimes on an issue of social justice.

The resources on which the students and others are dependent for fulfilling these liturgical ministries include liturgical courses (most MDiv students take four liturgy courses in a full three-year MDiv program), the training sessions and rehearsals, workshops, an extended introduction to the chapel during orientation week for new students (held the week prior to the beginning of the Fall academic term), and the *Customary*, a thirty-page booklet given to all community members, which describes expectations for students and faculty, each of the liturgies done at CDSP in detail, the differences between daily liturgies, a glossary of liturgical terms, a question and answer section on particular issues, and the training available. The *Customary* is edited each year to remain current and reflect changes in the pattern of liturgies. Above all, there is the person of the Dean of Chapel, a faculty appointment that works out to about half-time classroom teaching and half-time directly overseeing the chapel and the student sacristans, who are interviewed, hired, and paid to assist in the coordination of the chapel and the training of students through workshops and rehearsals. Their office in the seminary sacristy is often a gathering place for students, who come by to volunteer for various tasks (including polishing brass, washing liturgical linens, baking the bread for the Eucharist) and to soak up the ethos by learning what goes on behind the set-up and planning for liturgies.

Most classes at the GTU are twice weekly (Monday-Thursday or Tuesday-Friday) or once a week for three hours. About forty percent of CDSP students are fully residential, the remaining sixty percent commute, so patterns of attendance are tied to class and commute schedules, as well as work and family obligations. In light of the busyness of life for graduate students, an amazing number of students attend at least one liturgy every single day, which is still a source of surprise to many people.

The elements of background described above will assist in setting the context for the theological, formational, catechetical, and ministerial categories that follow and which help address the multifaceted understanding of the role and place the seminary chapel plays in a specific liturgical tradition.

Interpreting the Meaning and Role of the Chapel

"Concerning the Service of the Church"[13]

The chapel and, more to the point, the liturgies that take place in the chapel at an Episcopal seminary, always live in several tensions, including being both a place of worship and a laboratory for future leaders. Theologically, it is the former that concerns us here. Ecclesiology and liturgy are inextricably linked in Anglicanism, as they are in other ecclesial traditions. Without a Magisterium or a set of Augsburg Confessions, however, Anglicanism has often put a tremendous weight on the *Book of Common Prayer* as the means of self-identity and of doctrinal articulation. Because of the ambiguous nature of liturgical language, the spectrum of practices

13. This is the title given to the 1979 introduction to the *Book of Common Prayer,* summarizing the contents and intentions of the revised prayer book (*BCP* 13).

and interpretations does not allow for precision and clarity, a reality that has both shaped the image of Anglicanism as a *via media,* and left open room for continual and dueling differences of opinions as to what it all means. All of this is daily expressed and created in the liturgies of a seminary chapel. The outwardly homogeneous gathering (majority Anglican) often masks real differences in piety and presumption. The doing of liturgy takes up a tremendous amount of time at CDSP, and for most of the community it can be agreed upon that chapel is important, but theological and devotional differences often lurk beneath the surface.

Ecclesiologically there is institutionalized the presumption that liturgy is what the church does. Often assuming the essence of Henri de Lubac's famous saying, "the eucharist makes the church and the church makes the eucharist,"[14] the 1979 prayer book restored, returned, or turned to (depending on one's perspective) a eucharistically centered church rooted in a baptismal ecclesiology. Older American Episcopalians often express amazement at how fast the church has changed (in this country and elsewhere) from a "morning prayer church" to a "eucharistic church."[15] In the course of the last fifteen to twenty years, that shift has reshaped the liturgical life of the seminary too, replacing the daily office with the Eucharist as the primary daily liturgy. Fewer students come to seminary with a comfortable familiarity of the daily office, but all know the Eucharist well. The daily office, morning and evening prayer, is often a new discovery, and whether the students pray the office in their dorm room, at home, or in the chapel, by the end of their seminary career they have grown to appreciate the rhythm of this monastic prayer which still reveals the roots of Anglicanism in the English Benedictine tradition. The balance between the daily office and the Eucharist is a mark of cathedral

14. De Lubac, *The Splendor of the Church,* 134.

15. This is generally understood to mean that in the 1928 prayer book, the most common, or primary service on Sunday morning was Morning Prayer—distinctively Anglican—whereas leading up to the 1979 prayer book and after its publication, the overwhelming majority of Episcopal Churches now have the Holy Eucharist as their primary service on Sunday morning. This shift, a product of the ecumenical and liturgical movements of the 20th century, as well as the many contributions of those movements within Anglicanism, is readily seen in the opening sentence of the 1979 prayer book introduction: "The Holy Eucharist, the principal act of Christian worship on the Lord's Day and other major Feasts, and Daily Morning and Evening Prayer, as set forth in this Book, are the regular service appointed for public worship in this Church" (*BCP* 13). Thanks to John Kater for pointing out the generational shift in Anglicanism.

churches, monasteries, and seminaries, and the recitation of the daily office is also an important part of the link between theology of church and liturgy.

Aside from this historical shaping of a particular ecclesial identity, there is the deeper and more profound link between the church (understood to be a multi-layered reality of a particular community, the diocese, the national church, the Anglican communion, and all of Christianity) and how it prays. Whether it be a particular facet of polity (the smallest unit of the church is the diocese),[16] a sociological sense of being a global church, a canonical and liturgical reality that Anglicanism is not a denomination, or a theological statement about the communion of saints, church means much more than who is gathered in a room at a particular time.

Perhaps the best reminder of this came from an American Baptist colleague, who helped me see what it is by what it is not. He frequently railed against the almost obsessive focus on chapel, complaining that too much time, money, and attention was given to liturgical events. What was most unsettling for him was why we had so many liturgies with so few people in attendance. He asked, "why not just have one liturgy a week where everyone will come, and be done with it?" He could not understand what was behind our daily practice, and I couldn't understand why he didn't get it. After talking for a while, especially about the service of the church, it became clear. For him church equaled everyone who belonged to a particular community being in the room at the same time. But the ecclesial ethos that was the foundation of the liturgical system in which he found himself saw it very differently. It is the work of the church to pray everyday for the church and for the world, and where "two or three are gathered together" not only is Christ present, but the church as the body of Christ has gathered.[17] Whether it was two or twenty or two hundred, it was still the church gathered to do the office. This *officium divinum,* or divine office, is the official and "regular service appointed for public worship in this Church."[18]

---

16. Preamble, *Constitutions and Canons of the Episcopal Church* (2006) 1.

17. Cf. Matthew 18:20. Acknowledging the common misuse of this verse does not negate its meaning for the presence of Christ in liturgical gatherings.

18. See above n. 15.

The ordination vows to the priesthood in almost every Anglican member church require the clergy to do this daily office,[19] and while it would be artificial to claim that the present-day service is what has been prayed for centuries, it is the case that a version of these daily prayers has been practiced since the earliest centuries of Christianity, and became a hallmark of Anglicanism in the mid-sixteenth century. The daily Eucharist, along with the theological circle articulated by de Lubac above, also structurally reflects the life of the church and individuals within the church. We gather, we listen to the word of God, we respond by offering thanks, and commune, with God and one another, so that we can be the body and blood of Christ for the world. This is an outline of Christian life, not only of the liturgy. Centuries of trying to articulate that we are what we eat is still open to many personal interpretations, but the daily doing of communion, along with its interpretive words, shapes the church by shaping its present and future leaders:

> Almighty and everliving God, we thank you for feeding us with the spiritual food of the most precious Body and Blood of your Son our Savior Jesus Christ; and for assuring us in these holy mysteries that we are living members of the Body of your Son, and heirs of your eternal kingdom. And now, Father, send us out to do the work you have given us to do, to love and serve you as faithful witnesses of Christ our Lord, To him, to you, and to the Holy Spirit, be honor and glory, now and for ever. Amen.[20]

While different rites (Rite I, Rite II, the language of *EOW*, and of other Anglican rites) will use different phrases, the omnipresent "us" and "we" seeps into every body gathered there; from gathering, to praise, to confession, to offering ("Recalling his death, resurrection, and ascension, we offer you these gifts") as much as the embodied reality of gathering with the community, standing, kneeling, sitting and walking, exchanging the peace, and receiving communion reinforce the ecclesiological message that the church is a corporate reality.

19. The questions presented to the ordinand in the ordination rites are all based on the 1662 Ordinal, and ask for a vow to persevere in prayer. For example, the proposed contemporary Church of England version asks: "Will you be diligent in prayer, in reading Holy Scripture, and in all studies that will deepen your faith and fit you to bear witness to the truth of the Gospel? By the help of God, I will."

20. Post-communion prayer, Rite II Holy Eucharist (*BCP* 366).

"We offer and present unto Thee, O Lord, ourselves, our souls and bodies"

The emphasis on being formed through the liturgy is at the heart of this second lens through which we can view the role of a seminary chapel. I begin with another story that portrays the difficulty of getting hold of something as intangible as formation.

The periodic assessments for the purposes of accreditation were almost always bogged down when it came to liturgy. The non-theological assessment groups particularly found it difficult to understand why there was so much chapel with so little in the way of tangible outcomes—what is all this liturgy doing for the students? The faculty finally got better at describing the catechetical dimensions of liturgical formation, but the description by means of hard evidence for spiritual formation was more difficult. The accreditation teams looked for quantifiable checklists; we looked for growth in spiritual maturity. They could not understand why something that was not measurable could be so central to the curriculum; we showed them the questions that we had to answer for every student in their second year of the MDiv—a review that was to be sent to each student's bishop.[21] The second question of the canonical middler evaluation asked us to evaluate the student in light of "their faith in God as revealed in Jesus Christ, nourished and expressed by participation in the seminary's liturgical life and in an intentional pattern of personal spiritual discipline and a commitment to promote peace and justice among all people."[22] We tried to explain why bishops sent students educated at non-Anglican seminaries to CDSP for a final year, often derogatorily referring to it as "Anglican finishing school." Our response was so that they could learn Anglican, be steeped in Anglican liturgy and tradition, and learn the ethos of the community they would be called to lead. When pushed on how this happened, we could point to a few classes that specifically addressed Anglican issues, and then to the chapel.

The participation in the rota, the training in various liturgical ministries, the study of liturgy, the preparation groups for liturgy, and above all, the doing of liturgy was to form them. We drew from liturgical theology that in recent years has reminded all who work with and in liturgy that we

21. In their second year of MDiv studies, each student is to be reviewed by means of six categories, using standardized form evaluated by the faculty and forwarded to the bishop. See the *Constitutions and Canons*, 71.

22. Ibid, 2.

may have spent too much time being concerned about what we are doing to the liturgy, how we are shaping it and expressing ourselves in it, and not enough time on how God is working on us in the liturgy. The repetition, the pattern of daily liturgy, and the patterning within each liturgy, especially alternating speaking and silence, work together to teach all members of the worshipping community that God is not only speaking to us in liturgy, but shaping and forming us. This insight,[23] coupled with the regular *cursus* of liturgy which kept a consistency from day to day, allowed many communities to resist the temptation to form liturgy in their own image. Such a rota of prayer enables us to learn from, be inspired by, and be led into something beyond ourselves by the liturgy of the church. The subtitle of this section is a quote from the second Eucharistic prayer of Rite I and articulates a formational cornerstone. We are formed to be emptied of ourselves, to allow room for God to work in and on us, we are formed to serve others with all that we have, we are formed for ministry, not for careers. At the ordination of a priest, the presenters of the candidate to the bishop are asked "Has she been selected in accordance with the canons of this Church? And do you believe her manner of life to be suitable to the exercise of this ministry?"[24] The suitable "manner of life" is ethical (action) and contemplative (prayer), both realities formed in the crucible of liturgy.

"A carefully constructed liturgical apprenticeship"[25]

The third lens through which we might understand the role of chapel in a liturgical tradition is catechetical. Unlike the seemingly intangible dimensions of spiritual formation through chapel mentioned above, the catechetical intention of the liturgical practice has not only been noted by outsiders, such as the Carnegie Foundation for the Advancement of Teaching (quoted in the subtitle above), but has been better articulated by the faculty for quantifiable outcomes such as required for accreditation. In describing the overall program of liturgical practice and complementary coursework as an "apprenticeship," the Carnegie Foundation study right-

---

23. Articulated in several liturgical writings in recent years, a good example being the two-part article, Aune, "Liturgy and Theology."

24. "The Ordination of a Priest," (*BCP* 526).

25. Foster, Dahill, Golemon, and Tolentino, *Educating Clergy*, 276.

fully articulated a program that transcends the usual in-the-classroom, out-of-the-classroom divisions, and by doing so functions as the heart of the pedagogical enterprise.

> The offices surrounding the atrium of one of the campus buildings may function as the administrative center of the campus. The dining hall and adjoining courtyard may function as the social center of the campus. Classrooms are scattered across the campus. However, the chapel, which sits off to the edge of the campus, is not only its liturgical center; it may also be its pedagogical center. In this place, the secular rhythms of the academic calendar are transformed as the seminary community moves through the liturgical events of the Christian year, and the liturgies of each week.[26]

At the heart of the teaching role of the chapel is the hope that the academic studies of the tradition, of history, of theology, of scripture, will be put into practice in the liturgy. In ecumenical conversations, this is a perspective that often catches other schools and traditions by surprise because from their perspective, worship belongs solely in practical or functional theology courses. In a prayer book tradition, it cannot be a matter of learning only *how* to do the liturgy, it must always be growing in the understanding of *why* we do what we do, which puts the study of liturgy and the doing of liturgy right at the intersection of theology and praxis.

The "program" by which this is accomplished is a combination of classes, workshops, rehearsals, liturgies, and post-liturgical critiques or reflections. MDiv students begin their seminary career with a workshop course titled *Fundamentals of Worship* that walks them through the eucharistic liturgy of the *BCP*, looking at each element of the rite and asking "Where did it come from?"; "What are its theological meanings throughout history?"; and "How do we do it and why?" In this same first semester, each student is required to take a workshop on specific liturgical roles before being put on the rota for those ministries, including officiant at evening prayer, lay assistant at the eucharist (which includes being a eucharistic minister), and thurifer. In addition, every eucharistic liturgy and every evening prayer is preceded by a rehearsal for all liturgical ministers, and these rehearsals provide a context for questions to be asked, while teaching the importance of learning with one's body. They are not op-

26. Foster, Dahill, Golemon, and Tolentino, *Educating Clergy*, 276–77.

portunities to talk through the liturgy, but to walk through the liturgy, generally with any objects being used and with the liturgical vestments already put on. In watching these rehearsals for a week, the Carnegie Foundation study observed, "prior to each worship service, the Dean of the Chapel physically models and then guides the students and faculty members involved in its leadership through each movement in the liturgy in what is undoubtedly the most consistent pedagogical activity students experience."[27] This practice, common to many liturgical traditions, is based on the presumption that kinesthetic knowledge is what stays with us. Liturgy is multi-sensory; it is not an intellectual exercise alone, and should not be taught as such. This first semester (and for many, this first year) approach is deliberate. It is intended to help the students learn, in their head and in their bodies, a way to do the liturgy. In the second year, when students go out to field education parishes and assist in liturgies with slightly different liturgical practices and patterns, they have a default position that they can adapt and accommodate to a different community's practice. Without this, there is no starting place for them as developing liturgical leaders. The differences between seminary chapel practice and field education parish practices present wonderful opportunities for re-visiting why we do what we do, and for seeing the spectrum of liturgical practices as reflecting nuances in theological understandings.

At the end of the MDiv program, after having studied homiletics, liturgical history, and sacramental theology, the students return for a course in liturgical leadership in which they will preside at a "Eucharist" (either in class or on a video) as well as celebrate baptisms, marriage, hearing confessions, anointing, and presiding at a funeral. These class-room liturgies are video-taped, and followed by a discussion and critique by the whole class, which allows them to function as a way to reflect on the integration of all the academic study as it shapes the students' shaping of a given liturgy. They are asked to give a reason for each choice they make, not as a criticism, but to encourage them to reflect on what they believe the liturgy is doing, how and what it is communicating, and how it is transformative. At the heart of these classes is the chapel experience— it is the place that students keep returning to in order to observe and learn from the classroom discussions (chapel as lab) and the place they return to in order to pray and to move deeper into their understanding

27. Foster, Dahill, Golemon, and Tolentino, *Educating Clergy*, 277.

of what is being done (chapel as place of worship). The conclusion of the Carnegie study summed this up well: "This shared liturgical life enhances and deepens their formation in the communal spiritual practices of that religious tradition.[28]

Another important dimension of the catechetical role of chapel will serve as a bridge to our final lens, the ministerial. The Thursday liturgies are prepared two weeks in advance in a group session by all the liturgical ministers assigned to that particular liturgy. This is one of the few places where faculty, students, and often staff work on a common project together. We are not only fellow Christians, but fellow liturgical ministers. The format for the planning session is based on materials sent out to all participants a week before, and begins with the scripture readings assigned for the day being proclaimed and discussed. The bible study generally takes about half of the planning meeting, but is key to keep the liturgy planning from falling into picking a few pieces of favorite music and seeing that as sufficient. Following the scripture reflection, the group then moves onto a form which may contain some seasonal elements, but is understood to be quite flexible. Some groups follow the format fairly closely; others change a number of elements because of what emerged in the scripture study or because of something that is going on in the world or the community at the time of planning. When the liturgy has been celebrated, the same group meets briefly after the liturgy to reflect on how their planning and the actual liturgy aligned, how they thought it went (often technical issues), but more importantly, how it nourished the faith of the gathered community. The format and the forms, based in the life of the seminary chapel, have now been carried out to many parishes by alumni, and with some adaptation, have proved helpful in developing greater understanding in parish worship committees. At the seminary itself, the process of preparation, celebration, and reflection represents a way that the chapel reaches beyond not only the academic-pastoral divide, but also the faculty-student divide, by allowing us to transcend those particular roles and remember that we are first and foremost Christians who worship together.

28. Foster, Dahill, Golemon, and Tolentino, *Educating Clergy*, 278.

Liturgical leadership as privilege and responsibility

A final approach to understanding the role of the chapel at a seminary in the liturgical tradition is through the training of ministers who will be leaders in the church. CDSP, as with most seminaries in liturgical traditions, educates and trains both lay ministers and those preparing for ordination. While the majority of students at CDSP are either already ordained (in the advanced degree programs) or preparing for ordination (in the MDiv program), the renewed stress in the past forty years on baptism as the foundational sacrament for ministry has been remembered and raised up as a way to encourage laity to remind the church that ministry is not solely a clerical domain. One of the ways that the chapel encourages people to remember and celebrate lay ministry is by encouraging lay students to take on the liturgical roles which do not require ordination, such as lector, lay assistant, intercessor, and officiant. Another way the liturgies of the chapel contribute to this ecclesial reality is to counter the cultural assumption that fairness implies everyone getting to do everything all together all the time. Hierarchy is often thought of as solely a negative aspect of the church, but in a tradition called "Episcopal," and based not only on bishops, but on the threefold ordained ministry of bishop, priest, and deacon, the liturgical teaching and practice provides a way to understand all the ranks of ministry in positive and related ways.

Using the analogy of the Apostle Paul's description of the church as the body of Christ,[29] with Christ as the head, the liturgy provides a way to readily understand that diversity is the point of the church. Just as a human body cannot be all ankles or spleens—otherwise there is no body—so the church cannot be all presiders, or all lectors, or all bishops; it must have all the parts in order to make the whole, and the sum of the parts is far greater than the individual parts. The liturgy is the manifestation of the body, that is the body of Christ, the Church. And, the liturgy recalls that manifestation by its differentiation of roles. The presider does things appropriate to the presidential role; the deacon does things appropriate to the diaconal role; the lector, the intercessor, the assembled community, the musicians, etc., all contribute their part. The result is liturgy, often described using Anselm of Canterbury's idea as both the glorification of God and our sanctification.

29. See 1 Cor 12:20.

Whether it takes place as a constant reminder to those leading liturgy not to say the people's part, or a reminder to the congregation to engage in the dialogue that is theirs, the training in and the doing of liturgy remind us of the corporate nature of the church and the essential diversity that makes for unity. These lessons from the chapel hopefully spill over into other areas of community life, and help contemporary Americans in particular understand hierarchy, difference, and dialogue in more positive ways. With regard to training seminarians for ordained leadership, liturgy is often the most obvious arena of priestly leadership, and the chapel program both highlights that reality and helps to put it into context. Unlike many ecclesial communities, Anglicanism does not ordain people to be youth ministers, or pastoral counselors, or education leaders, it ordains people as bishops, priests, and deacons. In other words, one is ordained to do all of it, with, one hopes, the understanding that collaborative ministry recognizing individual charisms is the only way this will actually work. In the Examination part of the ordination liturgy for a priest, the bishop addresses the ordinand by rehearsing the multiple duties one is being called to—beginning with the statement that ministry begins with baptism, moving through the larger categories of being called as pastor, priest, and teacher, and then to share in the councils of the Church with the bishop and the presbyterate. The list of specific ministerial tasks then follows:

> As a priest, it will be your task to proclaim by word and deed the Gospel of Jesus Christ, and to fashion your life in accordance with its precepts. You are to love and serve the people among whom you work, caring alike for young and old, strong and weak, rich and poor. You are to preach, to declare God's forgiveness to penitent sinners, to pronounce
> God's blessing, to share in the administration of Holy Baptism and in the celebration of the mysteries of Christ's Body and Blood, and to perform the other ministrations entrusted to you. In all that you do, you are to nourish Christ's people from the riches of his grace, and strengthen them to glorify God in this life and in the life to come. Do you believe that you are truly called by God and his Church to this priesthood?[30]

While the ministerial obligations are contextualized in the primary challenge to live what one preaches, the bulk of the tasks fall into the sac-

30. Ordination of a Priest (*BCP* 531).

ramental and liturgical realm. All that a priest does and is flows into and out of these sacramental ministerial acts. Because of this ecclesial stance, the role of the chapel in a liturgical tradition does stand at the heart of what that seminary is about, forming and informing ministers for the church. Finally, the chapel program of a seminary, in any tradition, needs to do more than maintain the *status quo* of liturgical practice. No liturgy this side of the eternal banquet is perfect, no prayer book is perfect, no particular style of liturgy is perfect. Learning the tradition of the church is essential in order to be grounded and confident as a liturgical leader, but also because from that grounded place one can learn to adapt and be creative within an ecclesial tradition. The final paragraph of the introduction to the seminary chapel *Customary* summarizes this hope:

> As a seminary of the Episcopal Church, CDSP is a place and a community that both reflects and influences the liturgical life of the Church. To that end, we hope that the careful liturgical experimentation and inculturation practiced here will influence parish practices in the coming years. We are a seminary committed to diversity and hospitality in all that we undertake, including our worship. CDSP's practice of gender-inclusive language is one aspect of our commitment, another is our use of languages other than English and cultural forms from other parts of the Anglican Communion in our chapel services. Please join us as a worshipping community and a place where good liturgy is grown for the sake of the whole church.[31]

Conclusion

In a collection of essays on the role of common worship in theological education, there will be differences in emphasis on how the chapel functions as part of the formational and educational plan of an individual school. But in the worship programs of seminaries belonging to particular ecclesial groups, and especially those where the liturgical tradition and the resources are not only presumed, but expected, the questions are not so much about what resources will be used as how they will be used, what lessons will they teach us, and how will the doing of these liturgies

---

31. *The Customary for Chapel Worship*, 3. Ministry rooted in both memory and hope, and rehearsed and expressed in the liturgy is part of the role the chapel plays in the overall mission of the seminary.

SEMINARY CHAPEL IN A PRAYER BOOK CONTEXT

be the point of integration of a variety of different disciplines and skills. The questions are about being rooted in a tradition where training leaders for the future is a balancing act between static and organic, between looking back and looking forward. But while tradition is always an act of passing on what has been received, each hand that passes on the tradition is slightly different; each community sees new insights in that tradition. Every liturgy celebrated is both traditional and contemporary; to make a distinction is to falsify the reality. Every liturgy is based on aspects of the tradition handed on; every liturgy is contemporary; it is being celebrated here and now by actual people. Liturgy is not the text on the page, but the doing of the rite, the orchestration of the rite that is word, music, people, gesture, things, intent, and above all, God. The role of common worship is to create a place and a time where all of what the seminary does can come together and be offered, soul and body, to be transformed and revitalized into the next class, the next assignment, the next meeting. "It is very meet, right, and our bounden duty, that we should at all times, and in all places, give thanks unto thee, O Lord, holy Father, almighty, everlasting God."[32]

Works Cited:

Aune, Michael, "Liturgy and Theology: Rethinking the Relationship." *Worship* 81 (2007) 46–68, 141–69.
Church Divinity School of the Pacific, *The Customary for Chapel Worship* (2008–2009)
Foster, Charles, Lisa Dahill, Larry Golemon, and Barbara Wang Tolentino. *Educating Clergy: Teaching Practices and Pastoral Imagination.* San Francisco: Jossey-Bass, 2006.
Lubac, Henri de. *The Splendor of the Church.* San Fancisco: Ignatius, 1986.
Morgan, Aida Marsh, *From Ocean's Farthest Coast.* Berkeley, CA: Church Divinity School of the Pacific, 1993.

32. "The Great Thanksgiving," Rite I (*BCP*, 333).

6

Naming the Elephant: Leading Chapel in a Multi-Denominational Seminary Context

MICHELLE K. BAKER-WRIGHT

Introduction

How does one lead a multi-denominational seminary community in worship when it seems that there are no norms? There are no collective texts or prayer books that can function as standards to be embraced or challenged. Multi-denominational seminaries often have institutional norms that are tacit, that do not reside in particular liturgical texts or ecclesiologies but in sets of experiences and oral histories. Additionally, students often arrive at multi-denominational seminaries having been shaped by a myriad of ecclesial influences, so their own assumptions may be deeply held yet ill-defined. Consequently, worship patterns for chapel are often determined by a combination of issues connected to institutional, denominational, and personal identities of staff and students. As a result, decisions about chapel leadership and worship can come from the "gut," and can stem from perceptions of what "feels right" or "wrong" that have unclear origins that are difficult to translate. But translation is exactly the skill needed to discern community norms that, while not always obvious, do indeed exist.

In this essay, I will propose that chapel leadership in a multi-denominational seminary context requires a constant search for the historical subtexts of the institution as well as the current stories within the community. To this end, I offer paradigms that I have found useful in unearthing these subtexts and stories, and subsequently explore the need for chapel leadership to articulate these narratives back to the community. In order to do this with clear vision, leaders must also discern the stories that inform their own personal and collective outlooks as well. Without this process, decisions that form the worship life of a multi-denominational seminary community may largely be implemented strictly on the basis of pragmatics—either in terms of "continuing with what works" or "reacting to what didn't work." In conclusion, I will offer some suggestions as to how to make informed and aware choices that respect seminary norms while simultaneously challenging the community to broaden the ways in which it worships.

Unearthing the Subtexts and Stories

In seeking to describe and explain chapel leadership at Fuller Theological Seminary, I often find myself telling stories, cumulatively drawing upon those of many students, faculty, and staff that I have encountered in my different roles as a PhD student in Christian Worship, as a former Financial Aid Counselor who advised Fuller students for over four years, and as the current Assistant Director of Chapel. Why is this? I believe that it is because stories are often the only way to make connections—to explain the inexplicable or the ambiguous about institutional and student life.[1] Through learning about Fuller's history as an institution, and hearing many stories of past and current students navigating their educational journeys, I have begun to see patterns and issues that reveal the extent to which we stand in continuity with the traditions that have shaped us, whether we know it or not. Multi-denominational seminaries and the chapels that express their common life bring these tensions to the foreground.

Fuller Seminary's own origins and development arise out of an engaged critique of fundamentalism and evangelicalism, which has resulted in a continued articulation of a form of evangelicalism that seeks to positively engage culture rather than retreat from it. This ethos often forms

1. Herbert Anderson and Edward Foley observe that, "the narrative mode, more than other forms of self-reporting, serves to foster the sense of movement and process in individual and communal life. In that sense, the narrative framework is a human necessity. Stories hold us together and keep us apart. We tell stories in order to live" (*Mighty Stories*, 4).

Fuller students into "bridge people" who learn to navigate suspicion from other more conservative evangelicals on the one hand, and other mainline institutions on the other. The following analysis by George Marsden highlights some ways that these origins are particularly relevant to a discussion of the nature of chapel at Fuller, as he especially examines Fuller's relationship to denominationalism and ecclesial authority:

> The most distinctive institutions of American evangelicalism have often . . . been parts of the personal empires of successful evangelists. Usually these institutions have been run autocratically or by an oligarchy; in any case, they have typically been regarded virtually as private property. They were designed for a special purpose, which could be defined by the people in immediate command, with no need to answer to ecclesiastical authority. These institutions were thus extraordinarily shaped by the personalities of the individuals who founded and controlled them. Fuller Seminary was such an institution. Its history also illustrates how an institution bound neither by any formal precedents nor by ties to an organized church is shaped by the individuals who control it. The key question in such institutions is the question of authority: To what authorities or traditions can individuals appeal?[2]

Marsden's description encapsulates the liturgical issues that are faced in planning chapel worship at Fuller. To what authorities and traditions can individuals—in this case, chapel leaders—appeal, indeed? In some ways, this analysis would seem to indicate that Fuller's chapel is simply an extension of an institutional ecology—maybe even ecclesiology, of sorts—not defined by any denominational tendencies except those constructed by institutional authorities themselves. Or, at best, the denominational tendencies would simply reflect the ones of those in leadership, which in turn arise from the traditions with which they individually identify. Indeed, much of Fuller's history would seem to indicate a self-definition that is *over and against* denominationalism, in favor of a more individualistic or personality driven approach.[3] This raises a number of questions.

2. Marsden, *Reforming Fundamentalism*, 2.

3. Marsden provides ample documentation of Fuller's sometimes stormy attempts to work with mainline denominations, but these relationships took a significant turn for the better in the mid to late 1960s. According to Marsden, "in the past, the realities of Fuller's character and the relationship of fundamentalist-evangelicalism to mainline churches had forced the seminary on a more independent course. Now, as it was becoming alienated from the fundamentalist side of evangelicalism, it was beginning to take

How does seminary chapel function in a setting of this nature? What traditions of worship and of worship leadership has it reflected, does it reflect, and *should* it reflect? Who makes these decisions and by what rationales? What does it mean to facilitate worship that builds up the seminary community, and prepare students to lead worship in the church? For what type of churches and traditions are we preparing them? The fact is there are few guidelines for chapel, and often one only discovers the boundaries of the chapel once they have been crossed.

At this point, it is helpful to turn to a consideration of Fuller's current institutional life, and the stories that lie within it. At present, Fuller is among the largest multi-denominational seminaries in the world, with a student body of over 2700, representing over 100 denominations.[4] Chapel is intended to be for the entire community, including students in masters and doctoral programs, faculty, and staff from Fuller's three constituent schools of Psychology, Intercultural Studies, and Theology. Thus, those leading chapel must attend to a very wide range of traditions and perspectives. For example, some students arrive straight from their undergraduate education, having committed to five or six years of study to complete a doctorate in Clinical Psychology. Others are students of a broad age range, returning to school in response to experiencing a call to ministry as a second career, but having very little prior theological background. Still others are considering or returning from international service as missionaries in a variety of capacities. Students pursuing Masters of Theology or Divinity degrees have often changed denominational traditions, claim no denominational tradition, or are searching for one.[5] They often come to seminary desiring more theological education, but uncertain as to how

---

up the slack with a new, more moderate evangelical constituency." Marsden, *Reforming Fundamentalism,* 255. This dynamic continues to be essential in considering how to both engage a variety of liturgical traditions in a chapel context and help students form a liturgical ethos *vis à vis* their own tradition.

4. See Fuller Theological Seminary, *Final Enrollment Report*; idem, *Demographic Report*.

5. Fuller's top five Denominational affiliations as of Fall, 2008 were Nondenominational (622 students), Presbyterian Church (USA) (369), Unknown—possibly, but not always, meaning that the student did not indicate a denomination (210), Presbyterian Church of Korea (199), and Assemblies of God (114) (Fuller Theological Seminary, *Demographic Report*). While these statistics are for the seminary as a whole, and not exclusively the School of Theology, they do reflect the trend that I am anecdotally describing in the sense of the high proportion of students who do not identify with a tradition or do not know which one they are claiming.

they will apply it. Some students discover during the course of their seminary training that they wish to pursue ordination, while others change their mind about their ordination goals.

I highlight these points about Fuller's history and current demographic in order to draw out some characteristics that may be broadly applicable. Multi-denominational seminaries have varied, ambiguous, or sometimes ambivalent ties to different denominations; hence, students have not gone through a single process to arrive there in terms of their denominational polity. They do not have this common experience as a unifying point of connection. An institution that may have a collaborative relationship with polity requirements of their respective denominations, therefore, shapes students, but there can often be a gap between the seminary and their church tradition. Many may also have been more profoundly shaped by parachurch traditions than the denominational tradition that they claim.[6] In sum: *students are often uncertain about their relationship with their own church tradition, the broader church, and uncertain about how their seminary education relates to either.* They also may not always consciously identify in practice with a given tradition as such, but rather with what "feels right" from their own church experience. While what I am describing may initially appear to be a negative characteristic, it is rich with opportunity pedagogically, in the sense that students at multi-denominational seminaries have often deliberately chosen such an environment because they desire to be conversant across traditions. There are opportunities to help students discern where they "fit" in relation to various church traditions, while simultaneously encouraging students' desires to be innovative and ecumenical.

These stories and experiences are relevant to chapel planning in that they highlight the wide range of perceptions about what seminary worship—and worship leadership—"should" be. Many of these assumptions will not have roots in prayer books or explicit theological formulations, but rather in an *ethos* that is largely oral and often more assumed

6. I am indebted to Ron Anderson for this observation. Anderson is describing seminary life at Garrett-Evangelical Theological Seminary, but his description is quite apropos to Fuller students as well. He states, "seminary students are relatively unformed by the life of the church, unformed by the church's liturgical practices and they don't know the church's repertoire. I have found the primary locus for spiritual formation for many of our students is parachurch organizations on undergraduate campuses." Anderson's comment is quoted on the website for the Calvin Institute for Christian Worship. See Calvin Institute for Christian Worship, "Encouragement."

than articulated. Much of this ethos can begin to be discerned in the frequencies of chapel services, the degree to which services are for the entire community or for portions of it, and the priorities by which the overall annual structure is set. As institutions, seminaries—both multi-denominational and denominational—have their own rhythm, their own "liturgical year." The narrative of quarters or semesters may come into conflict with the liturgical year due to placement of Christmas, Spring and Summer breaks, when the community disperses rather than gathers. At multi-denominational seminaries that stand independently from any denominational requirements, the extent to which the lectionary is used, the types of *ordos* that are assumed, and the very manner in which chapel is structured will thus predominately reflect institutional values of the seminary. For example, while there are denominationally based chapels at Fuller during other times of the week, "All-Seminary Chapel" is the central, primary locus of community worship. This structure makes a number of tacit statements, some of which are helpful and some of which need careful consideration. On one hand, there is the implication that our common identity as the Body of Christ takes precedence over denominational differences. On the other hand, the nature of this worship structure can communicate a misguided assumption that All-Seminary Chapel is able to innately transcend the influence of tradition, or somehow be "a-traditional."

Because chapel is often subject to other festivities or anniversaries pertinent to the life of the seminary, the question arises as to what kind of overarching narrative will shape the nature of the community's worship on an annual basis. An annual, seminary-wide theme based on a scripture text is sometimes determined by departments and entities outside of the chapel office, and the chapel staff may be given the task of implementing themes and aspects of the seminary's history into chapel services. Combine these things with the denominational diversity of the student body, staff, and faculty, and there is a broad range of stories that interact and potentially conflict with each other. Questions arise as to how chapel leadership should assess which stories are dominant norms for chapel worship, the extent to which these stories are in conflict with others present in the community, and how to move forward intentionally in response to these assessments.

An important step towards gaining some clarity is simply recognizing that naming the stories is important. They may be stories that are patently obvious to anyone who is a part of the institution, or they may be influential but unarticulated. I have highlighted the importance of understanding one's own institutional history, particularly as it pertains to denominational identity and leadership. However, additional elements to consider include how current students relate to their tradition, and possible generational tensions that are at play in the community. For example, at Fuller, students and staff face the current, complex identity of maintaining—or, in the opinion of some, restoring—evangelical identity in the face of increasingly polarized definitions of "evangelical."[7] Many students are interested in the emerging church, in search of ancient forms, and interested in liturgical traditions, while simultaneously trying to understand what this means beyond a simple change in aesthetic sensibilities (e.g., more candles?) or nomenclature (what does "emerging" mean besides a critique of what we don't want?).

These varying stories highlight the fact that engaging in forms of worship that are reflective of Fuller's past may hearken to a brand of evangelicalism that is not congruent with the worship experience of current students. What evokes nostalgia for some may evoke nausea for others. Celebrating Fuller's historical roots may bring memories of God's faithfulness to the fore for some, while for others, those early years evoke associations with a time when their gifts would not have been fully welcomed or cultivated.[8] On the other hand, experimenting with different liturgical forms can often awaken concern among those who value greater emphasis upon didactic, word-centered approaches to worship. At Fuller, understanding the stories behind different generational movements of Evangelicalism is key to assessing what forms of chapel worship will be with or against the grain of particular constituencies, and allows for informed and mindful choices about when to go with or against these grains.

Additionally, the importance of *reactivity* in multi-denominational contexts cannot be underestimated. Students, faculty, and staff may hold liturgical preferences as an expression of breaking from rather than continuing with their own past—be it more "conservative" or "liberal"—and

7. See, for example, George Marsden's account of Fuller's own history and tensions with evangelicalism in *Reforming Fundamentalism* and compare this with Lisa Sharon Harper's recent discussion of conflict among evangelicals with regard to race, gender, and political affiliation in Harper, *Evangelical Does Not Equal Republican*.

8. Marsden, *Reforming Fundamentalism*, 123–24.

thus not so much dislike specific liturgical forms as the memories and fears associated with them. This can be an important factor in discussing issues as simple as whether or not votive candles should be lit during a prayer service, which hearkens back to a Catholic past that some associate with "idolatry," or the use of certain groan-eliciting praise choruses that remind others of "cheesy" songs sung in church during their high school years. The manner in which worship leaders dress, the relative formality or informality of a service, can all reference memory in such a way as to make it difficult to discern the nature of criticisms that arise—are they related to actual practice or merely the memories evoked? Reactivity informs the larger rubric of the interacting stories and narratives in the seminary, but is often a dynamic of conflict that gets overlooked.

In Search of an *Ordo*

How, then, do these varied and sometimes conflicting stories specifically inform chapel worship and a specific grain of liturgical expression? Often the seminary's defining norms can be seen in the default pattern that characterizes the shape of chapel worship itself and that is most readily supported by institutional authorities. In other words, *not* choosing this form requires intentional consideration and an assessment of what institutional values are being affirmed or challenged. For example, typically, the pattern of Fuller's weekly fifty-minute chapel service has been a general welcome and prayer, two or three praise choruses, scripture reading followed by a twenty- to twenty-five-minute sermon, and a concluding praise chorus. Sometimes hymns are used, either in traditional form or in new arrangements suitable for a smaller praise band rather than a choral version.[9]

I have identified this structure as being "default" because it is the guiding structure around which chapel is planned—in other words, when a projection for the coming year's chapel services is drawn up, the first determinant is most often the *preacher*. It is therefore most likely that all other elements are structured around the sermon, because those who preach are secured the furthest in advance and require the most input

9. For an outsider's view of Fuller's chapel see Foster, Dahill, Golemon, and Tolentino, *Educating Clergy*, 275–80. At the time of these observations there were two weekly chapels, one in a local church and one on campus in its present location.

from a variety of institutional sources. Additionally, the guiding assumption that the person of the preacher is the locus of the *ordo* extends into the permission given to the preacher to choose the text upon which she or he will preach. It is a speaker-based, rather than a lectionary-based system, which would subordinate the preferences of the individual preacher to a larger scriptural catalogue. This is in keeping with many of the tacit values upon which Fuller was founded—individualism, independence from denominationally imposed structures, and a central emphasis upon didactic presentation of Scripture.

Another manifestation of Fuller's subtexts in liturgical form is a bent towards pragmatism and innovation. Again, these features are in keeping with Fuller's roots as a "transdenominational, evangelical" institution that is shaped by "individualism . . . combined with the Spirit of American free enterprise."[10] The emphasis upon "what works" can be seen in the general attraction on the part of the student body to musical and oral forms of expression that are understood to be accessible, be it current praise music, spontaneous forms of prayer, or the use of film clips, Power Point, and other media. Even the use of ancient forms and practices, such as *lectio divina* or excerpts from prayer books, have an underlying goal of relevance to a culture understood to be moving away from modernity. In other words, the desire is for something to "work" and be responsive to new cultural trends, because it is perceived that older forms of worship, be it "seeker services" or more traditional church forms, have "ceased to work."

I use these examples in order to illustrate larger points that may be applied to the chapel worship of multi-denominational seminaries in a broader sense. Understanding "default" patterns in chapel worship—the ones that happen almost without question—in the context of the institution's history provides a starting point for engaging or challenging these norms with intentionality. On the one hand, articulating the stories and assessing whether there have been default "*ordos*" in chapel does not always imply critique or change, but rather a basic understanding of one's starting points. On the other, sometimes articulating the default *ordo* is akin to naming an elephant in the room, because so many tacit but strongly held values are attached to it. In "naming the elephant," however, a decision to continue worship patterns as they have been inherited becomes

10. Marsden, *Reforming Fundamentalism*, 2.

as much of a choice as a decision to change them, and provides greater understanding of the values that inform such choices. Furthermore, unearthing a seminary's default *ordo* helps to provide a context in which resistances to change can be understood and anticipated. If in a given year there are more chapel services that represent alternate *ordos*—such as more services with a shortened sermon and an emphasis upon the Lord's Supper, for example—the concerns that arise over emphasis upon Scripture can be understood within the broader context of the seminary's own history and values.

Framing the Stories

The larger purpose behind surfacing the seminary's stories and of discerning a default *ordo* is to understand the ecclesial and institutional origins of the community's values. This form of discernment better helps chapel leaders to empower the community to celebrate Christ's death and resurrection, respond in corporate worship, and reaffirm a common identity in Christ. I have found two paradigms to be helpful for framing the spectrum of Fuller's traditions and current values. These particular lenses help to place *ordos* that are identified into a liturgical genealogy. Furthermore, providing historical contexts for different worship patterns is pedagogically useful in responding to those advocating for certain ordos simply because they are "correct." Rather than engaging in stylistic debates over "right" or "wrong" ways to worship, questions can be posed in such a way as to help students assess whether they are uncritically universalizing their own tradition.

The first framework that has been helpful to understanding chapel at Fuller is James White's description of the "Frontier Tradition," which he describes as being a form of Free Church worship:

> This new tradition has several roots in other traditions but enough distinctive growth of its own to enable us to call it a separate entity. It inherited from the Separatist and Puritan tradition two important characteristics: Biblicism and local autonomy. Biblicism was largely superseded by pragmatism, but autonomy remained prevalent . . . its two staples are a pragmatic bent to do whatever is needed in worship and the freedom to do this uninhibited by

> canons or service books. In a sense, it is a tradition of no tradition,
> but that attitude soon became a tradition in its own right.[11]

I have already discussed how values of autonomy and pragmatism inform chapel worship at Fuller. An additional, particularly helpful historical facet of the Frontier Tradition that White highlights is its self-understanding as a "tradition of no tradition." Many among the worshipping community at Fuller are unaware of the fact that their identification with a local church that is congregational in polity, and their reluctance to label this as a form of denominational expression, is the product of a particular ecclesial heritage. White's definition is pedagogically helpful for shedding light upon this quality, as it is often a slippery point to emphasize. Those who have consciously embraced a tradition that is more self-aware as an actual identity often find such an assertion of traditional neutrality bewildering, if not frustrating. Articulating traditions and anti-traditions within historical paradigms helps to facilitate communication between students and staff coming from the wide diversity of ecclesiologies present at Fuller.

The second paradigm is Lester Ruth's description of "personal-story churches and cosmic story churches." He observes, "there are churches whose worship over time is most focused on the personal stories of the worshipers and how God interacts with their stories. In contrast, there are churches whose worship over time unfolds a more cosmic remembrance of the grand sweep of God's saving activity."[12] In a multi-denominational seminary context, students, faculty, and staff come from churches and traditions along a wide range of this spectrum. Chapel services that challenge each of these perspectives may, therefore, cause discomfort that manifests itself through criticism. Too much emphasis upon "cosmic story" services may lead some to feel that more focus upon personal piety and upon one's relationship with Jesus Christ is needed. Too much emphasis upon "personal story," or what I would call "testimony," can lead others to feel that chapel services are becoming too subjective and "me-focused." Critiques of much worship music fall into these two categories.[13] Understanding the origins and influences that these differences represent can help chapel

---

11. White, *Protestant Worship*, 172.

12. Ruth, "A Rose by Any Other Name," 47.

13. For an exploration of the categories of worship music and how than can be helpful or not helpful, see Witvliet, "Beyond Style," 67–81.

leaders to be intentional about what they want to emphasize during any given season, to be mindful of the potential conflicts that each choice may initiate, and to have well-articulated theological rationales for their choices as a result.

My hope is that the particular way in which I have used White's and Ruth's categories can illustrate a way of ascertaining worship patterns that are otherwise not readily apparent. White has a broad array of histori-cally cogent paradigms that can be used to situate the influences at play in multi-denominational seminary life. In addition, giving consideration to larger movements and trends—such as an evangelical identity, for exam-ple—can clarify an institution's character in a way that is powerful but not seen when strictly considered through the paradigm of denominational-ism.[14] Ruth's categories also provide lenses to understand current trends that may not be neatly captured by historical perspectives. Learning the historical roots and influences which shaped the seminary as an institu-tion and apprising them in light of these different paradigms will frame the seminary's stories and ordos, placing them within the context of spe-cific values and conflicts. In turn, this allows leaders to assess the extent to which chapel worship has either affirmed or reacted to this heritage.

Choosing the Stories

I have used White's and Ruth's paradigms to underscore the value of dis-cerning the "ecclesial DNA" of multi-denominational institutions. This, in turn, can inform one's understanding of why chapel worship may naturally have conformed to certain patterns. The ultimate goal of such an assessment is to make intentional choices about how to lead chapel worship in such a way that nurtures the seminary community, while si-multaneously honoring the diversity of traditions present. Thus, there is a tension between nurturance and challenge that is unavoidable, which further underscores the necessity of articulating the values that inform one's choices.

It is with this in mind that I turn to the issue of chapel leadership. One of the continual challenges to accurate assessment of a seminary's subtexts and stories is that chapel staff will often be excessively attuned to the stories that are most familiar to their own, or with which they other-

14. Ruth, "A Rose by Any Other Name," 45.

COMMON WORSHIP IN THEOLOGICAL EDUCATION

wise resonate due to age, gender, ethnicity, or other factors. Without an awareness of these stories, the subtexts that are discerned will most likely be incomplete or imbalanced. Thus, an equally important task that can help chapel leadership engage communal stories is that of understanding the stories present among the people on their own leadership team.[15] Understanding one's own story, as well as the stories of others with whom one leads, should encompass not only traditions that each person may embrace, but also traditions that one has left, or to which one reacts. On the same team may be some who have remained within a single denomination their entire lives, others who reject the idea of denominationalism, still others who have left mainline denominations for free church traditions, and vice versa. Understanding the traditions that team members have embraced and/or rejected is crucial to understanding a wide range of issues pertaining to liturgical planning. This is true even with respect to the starting points by which one approaches the planning process itself. Some may start with the given scripture around which the sermon will be based, some may start with musical selections, and others may start with the overarching liturgical structure that they think would be ideal. This can either be a point of tension or a point of education. Different starting points reveal values prioritized historically by different traditions and each has their fair share of strengths and weaknesses.

In order to increase our team's level of awareness during the planning process, I have suggested these foci for the consideration of our planning team at the outset of each year:

1) We are all the product of traditions—even if they are "anti-traditions"—that have imbued us with certain values.

15. A staff and student, team-based approach is how chapel planning is approached at Fuller, so it is out of and to this model that I can most naturally speak, although the same need for self-awareness applies all the more acutely if one person plans chapel. John Witvliet makes the important observation that "most students come from a stream of worship practices that have formed them, even though for some the stream may not be long . . . this set of personal experiences is likely to be far more influential than any worship class in shaping their attitudes and habits of leadership. Some interesting recent studies have suggested that how people worshiped when they first became a committed believer is most significant for shaping their views of how worship should go." Witvliet, "Teaching Worship," 127. I maintain that this is the case with all people involved in chapel planning as well as students; in fact, because students are more immersed in theological reflection they may sometimes be more aware of their formative experiences and biases than staff or faculty!

2) We need to consider where we are individually situated within the breadth of church tradition(s), and also, if relevant, understand what factors led us to change from one tradition to another.

3) We need to understand where others on our team are situated in terms of traditions and the tensions that emerge as these interact.

4) We need to consider how we believe worship leadership at Fuller Seminary relates to worship of the broader Christian church.

Using these four reflections can promote intentionality. We can then choose which values and traditions we will reflect in any given week, having a better understanding of which grains they go with and against. With this kind of a hermeneutic being formed, greater light gets shed on many issues that arise, which usually have predictable historical origins.

For example, a common tension that arises on our planning team is the extent to which repetition is "vain repetition" or formation. If the congregation is regularly encouraged to say "Thanks be to God" after hearing "The Word of the Lord" spoken, will this become meaningless or will these words become a formative consistency in what is otherwise a widely varied liturgical life? Or, for some, the sight of clergy in vestments is disconcerting, for others novel, and for yet others welcome. Is a worship leader in an alb and stole viewed as less trustworthy than one in jeans and a t-shirt? More trustworthy? Why? This can either remain on a stylistic or aesthetic level of debate, or discussions can be opened up concerning what messages are conveyed by different types of liturgical attire. Furthermore, such controversies can be framed historically, which can quickly illustrate the extent to which we are all inheritors of traditions. It can be helpful to understand discussions of repetition in light of the tension between ritual and faith[16] that is present between sacramental and free-church or Pentecostal traditions. Or, a discussion surrounding the centrality of the sermon to the worship service can be understood to be

---

16. Ann Taves provides a brief overview of this historic conflict that is particularly helpful. She states, "The Protestant polemic against ritual was premised on a sharp distinction between ritual (understood as liturgy or rite) and faith (understood in terms of belief and/or experience)." Taves, "The Camp Meeting," 120.

reflective of an historic tension between Catholic and Reformed thought concerning the importance of didactic components of the liturgy.

In so doing, it becomes all the more clear to the chapel planning team that the *status quo* is as much historically situated as any changes made to it. This can be helpful for a number of reasons. It can help the team go through a process of recognizing when and why they are making choices to maintain or change things. Greater understanding (and perhaps even a sense of humor!) can develop among team members about the ways that preferences reflect the traditions that each has embraced or rejected. As dialogue happens that becomes more liturgically and historically informed, conflict can become more educational than edgy, and more formative than frustrating.

This process can, in turn, help chapel leaders articulate their choices to the surrounding community. Chapel leadership can become the community's storytellers in the sense that they have become accustomed to attuning to the community's subtexts. They can gain an ability to discern underlying issues behind what may seem like otherwise merely stylistic objections, and use the knowledge gained from the chapel planning process to decipher seemingly petty objections into formative discussions. In other words, the chapel leadership team must engage in the practice of making connections between the past and the present in order to set a course for the future. This approach provides a counterpoint to the pedagogical model that John Witvliet has advocated in discussing the teaching of worship in classroom settings. He observes:

> Teaching worship as a practice requires that students learn certain *knowledge* (e.g., basic literacy), certain *competencies* (e.g., the skill of choosing musical repertoire for liturgical purposes), and certain *virtues* (e.g., pastoral discernment, humility), but it also demands that students see how that knowledge, competency, and virtue are carried out or enacted, how they are 'performed.'[17]

Witvliet is describing the challenge of integrating practical skills of worship planning into classroom discussions that run the risk of being too theoretical. In the context he addresses, knowledge will be the most likely starting point. In the context of chapel planning, the challenge is the opposite—namely, of providing enough theoretical context to make choices that are not simply pragmatically driven. In this setting, competencies are

17. Witvliet, "Teaching Worship", 129–30.

the starting point. Staff and students arrive with skills that they immediately begin to employ. Frequently, these competencies are both a strength and an obstacle, as they may function as a "comfort zone" and are often used unreflectively and without theoretical knowledge (e.g., choosing a "music set" for a chapel service without recognizing this as an intentional starting point or how music functions within the bigger picture).

Thus, it is helpful for those leading chapel to use knowledge and virtues intentionally to form the competencies of students and staff. Theoretical knowledge concerning liturgical and ritual practices must be deliberately articulated in response to concrete situations that arise. To do this requires the ability to translate or "see" the theory behind the pragmatics.[18] For example, to return to the discussion concerning vestments, chapel leadership should have the ability to recognize that this is a conversation about *symbolism*. Different opinions and reactions can provide real-time examples that can readily be framed into a discussion of public versus private meanings of ritual.[19] What were vestments intended to mean? What do they mean to the Fuller community? What do jeans and a t-shirt mean by comparison? Are there historical antecedents behind these values? A number of competencies and virtues can be modeled as a result, among which are the ability to understand current worship practices and conflicts in light of historical developments and the ability to understand and describe the practices of one's own and other traditions in value-neutral terms. Developing these habits as practices among the chapel leadership team can lead to new discoveries about common ground that could otherwise not become apparent when hidden behind assumptions and preconceptions. For example, those from "high" and "low" ecclesial traditions may discover a common concern for creativity that can allow for enough agreement to experiment with different forms of multisensory worship.

Ultimately, the skills that get passed on to students who will be involved in worship leadership in churches will ideally be those of dis-

18. Because students participating in chapel planning are in a variety of degree programs, they will have varying levels of theoretical training. Those in MDiv programs take courses in worship planning, but chapel staff cannot take this as a given.

19. Margaret Mary Kelleher distinguishes the "public world of meaning" from "meanings that are personally appropriated by members of the assembly" and "meanings identified in official texts or commentaries on rite," ("Liturgical Theology," 6). Since there is no "official text" that pertains to chapel worship at Fuller, I have incorporated the idea of "subtexts" and "stories" as an alternative.

cernment, the ability to collaborate and listen, and the ability to assess conflicts in light of historical and generational realities. Working across a diversity of traditions on a practical level often means encountering resistance and tension where one does not at first recognize its source. Developing skills to "read" these underlying tensions will serve students well no matter what denomination or stripe of church they wind up in, as conflict around issues of worship is a true ecumenical reality. This is a gift that multi-denominational seminaries are uniquely positioned to cultivate, but it does require cultivation. The very difficulties and challenges faced by those leading multi-denominational chapels are areas that can give future leaders in the church the abilities and skill sets needed to be conversant across different denominational traditions and able to more effectively gauge the actual *roots*—rather than the symptoms—of congregational conflict around areas of worship.

Conclusion

Planning worship in a multi-denominational chapel context often leads to crisis in the best sense of the word. It is ripe with opportunities for conflict and challenge, but also with opportunities for formation that can teach students how to be translators and interpreters. Because there are no explicitly stated ecclesial norms or expectations around which chapel worship must revolve, leaders must become attuned to the seminary's own history, especially as related to ecclesial traditions and anti-traditions, as well as the stories and hidden expectations present in the seminary's existing community. Chapel leaders must also place these stories within their historical and ecclesial contexts to challenge the notion that "multi-denominational" means "a-traditional." Engaging in these exercises of discernment can empower chapel leadership to name default patterns of worship, so that choices to change or maintain liturgical patterns can be made with intentionality. The ability to "read" the institutional and communal life of the seminary as its own text and translate it into liturgical expression is a skill that is broadly applicable, and that will equip students at multi-denominational seminaries to lead God's people in a wide range of ecclesial settings.

Works Cited:

Anderson, Herbert, and Edward Foley. *Mighty Stories, Dangerous Rituals: Weaving Together the Human and the Divine*. San Francisco: Jossey-Bass, 1998.

Calvin Institute of Christian Worship. "Encouragement." http://www.calvin.edu/worship/wcom/campus/encouragement.php (accessed June 16, 2009).

Foster, Charles, Lisa Dahill, Larry Golemon, and Barbara Wang Tolentino. *Educating Clergy: Teaching Practices and Pastoral Imagination*. San Francisco: Jossey-Bass, 2006.

Fuller Theological Seminary. Office of Enrollment Services. *Final Enrollment Report*. Unpublished chart. October 12, 2008.

Fuller Theological Seminary. Office of Enrollment Services. *Demographic Report*. Unpublished chart. October 12, 2008.

Harper, Lisa Sharon. *Evangelical Does Not Equal Republican . . . or Democrat*. New York: The New Press, 2008.

Kelleher, Margaret Mary. "Liturgical Theology: A Task and a Method." *Worship* 62 (1988) 2–25.

Marsden, George M. *Reforming Fundamentalism: Fuller Seminary and the New Evangelicalism*. Grand Rapids: Eerdmans, 1987.

Ruth, Lester. "A Rose by Any Other Name." In *The Conviction of Things Not Seen: Worship and Ministry in the 21st Century*, edited by Todd E. Johnson, 33–52. Grand Rapids, MI: Brazos, 2002.

Taves, Ann. "The Camp Meeting and the Paradoxes of Evangelical Protestant Ritual." In *Teaching Ritual*, edited by Catherine Bell, 119–32. AAR Teaching Religious Studies Series. Oxford: Oxford University Press, 2007.

White, James F. *Protestant Worship: Traditions in Transition*. Louisville: Westminster John Knox, 1989.

Witvliet, John D. "Teaching Worship as a Christian Practice." In *For Life Abundant: Practical Theology, Theological Education, and Christian Ministry*, edited by Dorothy C. Bass and Craig Dykstra, 117–48. Grand Rapids, MI: Eerdmans, 2008.

———. "Beyond Style." In *The Conviction of Things Not Seen: Worship and Ministry in the 21st Century*, edited by Todd E. Johnson, 67–81. Grand Rapids, MI: Brazos, 2002.

7

"In Spirit and in Truth":
The Liturgical Space as a Territory

CLÁUDIO CARVALHAES

Introduction

Don Saliers writes, we can "interpret human life liturgically."[1] Words uttered and practices done in worship spaces can determine, in unimaginable ways, the stories of our lives and also in many ways, the movements of the world. It would appear that worship spaces are crucial to the hermeneutic quality of worship. What do worship *spaces* then have to do with worship? These places can tell who we are and how we live. Worship spaces are privileged places to understand how Christians see and practice their faith, how worldviews are created and how Christians engage in ethics and mission in and from this loaded space. Yet the world inside our worship spaces shapes the ways we worship, live, and engage with the world, and create a distinction between the liturgical world and the world it interprets. In this way, the world can be interpreted through liturgical lenses.

To accomplish this task, I will position myself within what Don Saliers call the "liberationist moral and political critiques of Christian liturgy," and the "ambiguity of liturgical formation," and continue to press what he affirms when he says that "liturgical theology suffers when it fails to acknowledge 'hidden' power issues and the malformative histories of

1. Saliers, "Afterword," 208.

practice."[2] In order to try to discern Jesus' call to all of us to worship God "in Spirit and in truth," we must visit these ambiguities, these hidden power issues, in our worship spaces.

Each of our stories has a certain beginning, a reference point or social location that shapes the ways we do theology, the ways we look at the world. What we say, the ways we commit ourselves, the ways we use our money, our talents and the ways we see the liturgical space and whatever happens there, are all influenced by our social location. The way I see a liturgical space is related to my story. When I was about eight or nine years old I was a shoe-shine boy. I use to borrow a shoe-shine box from a friend and would go to Largo do Cambuci in São Paulo, Brazil, to work and try to get some money to buy candies or bread. As we learn in liturgical studies, things/objects/images are very important for rituals because they shape peoples lives. That shoe-shining box also had the power to shape me, teaching me about economics, power and the world. The same way that my faith shaped my shoe-shine box. I shined shoes because I learned that I needed to work to help my family. But because we prayed for people in church, I learned that I had to pray for people on the streets. Those whose shoes I had the chance to shine would also hear that God loved them!

My shoe-shine box became not only my professional toolbox but also my mission tools. This confluence came from what I learned in church, that what I practiced in church I was supposed to do in my daily life as well. Looking back, I see that my shoe-shining box also influenced the ways I prayed and moved around the liturgy of the church. It gave me naive eyes to see that there were different people in church according to their shoes. To the surprise of my local Presbyterian church, I started to bring street people with no shoes to worship with everybody else. My shoe-shining box helped me to see that strangers could be welcomed and fed in church. However, there were problems with the church's hospitality and I quickly learned that the liturgical space was a little more than an isolated sacred space where we went to worship God: it was a socially defining space. There was more to that space than I, with my shoe-shine box, could know at that time. What was once a wonderful time of innocence, was now a lost innocence. However, my experience as a Christian shining shoes continues to give me a perspective on our worship today.

2. Saliers, "Afterword," 214.

What would happen today if we brought people without shoes to our liturgical spaces? As it happened in Brazil then, it would happen today. The poor street-people would bring with them some outside problems that could disturb the inner order of things in the worship space. But not only the shoeless people are problems for the liturgical order. What are we supposed to do when the worship space is taken over by strangers or a strange order of things? What are we supposed to do when people/symbols/references/gestures/words not usually there in the liturgical space, happen to occupy that space? I recently learned about a seminary in another country that had a woman dancing in chapel. Because her skirt went up accidentally, she was vehemently rebuked and her dance was called sacrilegious, having offended several people. How do we then negotiate gestures, music, prayers, confessions, bodies, races, ethnicities, colors, class? What or who does this space privilege? Are there items and issues already present in the worship space prior to the worship event that define the values and theology of the community? What is it that marks this space, or rather, this territory? Who are the insiders and who are the outsiders in this space set aside to worship the God of all people?

This cluster of stories and questions guides my scholarship and my practices in the liturgical space. Even though this article is focused upon seminary chapels, it is related to all liturgical spaces, both academic and ecclesial. Needless to say, there are specific issues for worship in seminary chapels, and these will be addressed here.

Those who participate in seminary chapels encompass a wide-ranging diversity. They bring with them their classes, races, sexes, ethnicities, theologies, political commitments, world–views, etc. This diversity is evident to all who choose to see. What do these relationships look like? What do they look like in the worship space? Who is at the center and who is at the margins as defined by the space? What of these relationships are revealed and hidden, accepted and dismissed, illuminated and shadowed while in the worshiping space? The liturgical space is a complex set of lenses that makes us see, as well as not see, the world in which we live in today.

Let's return to who these participants are. Every year someone new appears in the seminary chapel, and with his/her arrival, the anxiety of being new arrives too. Will they fit? Will they understand? Will they adjust? Those who arrive also ask questions: What do they do here? Am I supposed to engage them, like them, confess what they confess, do what they do? Do I improve or betray my worship tradition when I am presented to this "seminary way" of worshiping God?

The new students are always guests of the seminary, which has established safe boundaries for the community. After a process in which the applicants are scrutinized to see if they are a fit for the community, he or she is welcomed inside the gates of higher education. Seminaries can often avoid receiving a complete stranger into their midst which makes worship services somewhat a safe haven. There is a pre-existing tradition, a set of gestures, words, and there is a community who know the rules. The seminary as a whole is often structured around a tradition that is to be passed on. Thus, seminaries, more often than not, never get to know "shoeless students," and do not want to know about the increasing number of students who might have good pairs of shoes but are immersed in terrible financial debts. Conformity appears to be more important than compassion.

Beyond financial debts, the liturgical space is filled with issues that we ignore or avoid in our worship services. Once we establish that the liturgical space provides us a look at both the world and the liturgical realm of prayer, priorities become confused and our starting points become uncertain. Do we start from "God," or from "the world?" If we start from God, does it mean that the liturgical space becomes a value-free space and our faith is an "unreferenced" set of beliefs? However, if we start from the world, i.e., from the location of the seminary and the bodies of students/faculty/staff, does it empty the worship space of its sacredness? It seems that there is no either/or in the liturgical space. On the contrary, our starting points require dual references that sometimes appear contradictory. We look at the world from this space as well as we see the liturgical space from the world already there. The liturgical space is a "territory" where the world is negotiating with competing values and worldviews. It is a concrete territory located in the materiality of the world, with its "contingencies" such as race, class, gender, ethnicity, etc. very much present there.

Paraphrasing Derrida's question, "How do we conceive the outside of a text?"[3] I want to ask for our own purposes here "How do we conceive the outside of a liturgical space"? This complexity of things are seen for instance, in the social class I belong to, the ethnicity I am part of, the gen-

---

3. Derrida, *Writing and Difference*, 247.

der history I carry, the idiom I speak, and my sexual orientation, which are all part of and intrinsically related to the prayers I pray, the language I use, the sermons I preach, the Eucharist I celebrate. All of these are also interconnected with the same variants of those who worship with me. Thus, tangled in a web of relations, we are caught up in the holy practice of worshiping God alone, and trying to figure out how much this "alone" has to do with God. The complexity of the singularity/plurality of God alone cannot be deviated from the plurality/singularity of the worshipers of God. We are undeniably together, and yet, together alone with God.

So, how do our worship services glorify God alone in mined liturgical locations, and perhaps especially in seminary chapels, populated by students, faculty and staff who either could not care less about the service, or have already-defined notions of worship, liturgical theology, proper biblical hermeneutics and preaching expectations? It seems like worshiping God alone in a territory filled with political agendas, mundane business, complex relations, hardcore academic thinking and clear intentions is a very difficult thing to do.

Since a liturgical space is never a truly neutral location, there has never been such a thing as a *disinterested*, or *pure*, worship of God, where one becomes a completely detached being worshiping God alone. For God is never alone, nor are we. Thus, to worship God alone, we must get through our located historical fragile bodies, our failing languages, erratic theologies, and class, racial, sexual, gender, ethnic references. Worship spaces become a territory marked by so many material conditions.

Territories

Why am I calling our worship/liturgical spaces a territory? Merriam-Webster defines "territory" as follows:

> 1 a : a geographic area belonging to or under the jurisdiction of a governmental authority b : an administrative subdivision of a country c : a part of the United States not included within any state but organized with a separate legislature d : a geographic area (as a colonial possession) dependent on an external government but having some degree of autonomy.[4]

---

4. *Merriam-Webster's Collegiate Dictionary*, 11th ed., s.v. "territory."

For a space to become a territory, a process of ownership has to occur. When this process takes place, than the use, access and control start to happen. Territories are loaded with laws, political views, border control, and so on. Territories shape communities. Likewise our liturgical spaces also have laws, political views, border control, and so on. Historically, this shaping of the liturgical space has produced hegemonic discourses and processes that have ended up erasing differences, turning the world into one territory of the same: same definitions of things and concepts, same networking, same politics, same practices, same market control, same companies/worship books controlling most things, same owners/clergy of the capital/sacred, same financial/dogma regulations, same life/worship orders and so on. Moreover, this attempt to turn thoughts/gestures into the same dominant discourse, to make social, political, economic and theological territories even—without edges or anomalies, differences or discrepancies, inner/outer—tries to erase tensions, ambiguities, what makes things "difficult," as well as to prevent people from being critical to those who control the power. Using Kath Holt-Damant's expression, this inner/outer control has also to do with "protecting the indefensible from the Indeterminate."[5]

Thus, the erasure of differences and the expansion of fences, ends up creating more borders, making states, countries, churches and individuals unrelated to gender, political, economic, class, racial and religious references and continue to maintain the boundaries around the liturgical space as private and secure known territories. In this territory, the things available there, such as the baptismal waters and the Eucharistic table/altar are offered only for those allowed to get the proper documents of ecclesiastical citizenship, who vow to do the same gestures of faith, the say the same denominational confessions, to keep the same theological and liturgical borders. In some Protestant seminaries, only faculty can preach when the Eucharist is celebrated, in still others, only faculty can preach.

Power is always an issue. Several seminaries are trying to create diversity by welcoming faculty and students from various minority groups. However, in many places this process does not necessarily mean the participation of minorities or respect for differences in worship services. As seminary chapels acknowledge the diversity of their communities—ethnicity, color, gender, class and sexualities—it raises questions of how

5. Holt-Damant, "The Threat from Within," 163.

this diversity entails different discourses, prayers, theologies, liturgical practices, sacramental understandings, global music, ritual gestures, bodily movements and so on. What seems to be happening with the welcoming of diversity is a certain kind of soft reiteration of the same erasure and nullifying of differences. In other words, one is welcome to become the same as the host. This movement towards diversity in worship services intends mostly to keep the power under the rubrics of a supposed diversity, a diversity that does not diverse/divert what is known and acceptable. Thus, seminaries with diversity continue to worship God without differences, something that would be close to what Derrida calls "a process of autoimmunization,"[6] which has to do with the breaking of its own limits in order to expand its control. Not only mainline worship services do this, but evangelical, contemporary, and postmodern worship services also do the same.

Never outside of the field of clear intentions, liturgical spaces are claimed spaces where politics of identity, theological constructions, ethical limits and social structures are always in the making. Liturgy/*leitourgia* means the work of the people and is meant to be a space where citizens would get together and decide about their lives in community. A political space for sure, where the *polis,* the city—the life together—was to be built together. The liturgical space has always been a political territory, intentionally occupied, controlled by authorities in the name of God. As noted before, these "unmarked" occupations entailed a colonial historical process of domination that served to *de-territorialize* the liturgical space, i.e., make it clean, without references, unintentional, apolitical, as if sacred actions were possibly untainted by human actions.

Liturgical territories are loaded with calculations and representations that through fierce theological, liturgical, gender, racial, sexual, and territorial disputes, try to make God a controlled human object under the rubrics of a transcendent mystery. In this very nervous space, we run the risk of recasting the transcendent into an absolute immanence in order to serve our desires and needs, and to make the worship of God and our sacred actions undifferentiated from our too human material struggles. As a territory, this space is loaded with contradictions, paradoxes, unrelated matters, unresolved issues, and marked by intense disputes of power and access. It is by being exposed, having to be engaged with another, around

6. Derrida and Roudinesco, *For What Tomorrow,* 18–19.

planned and unplanned encounters that we create a relation between people and God. This is what Jean-Luc Nancy called "being with."[7] It is by "being with" God and one another and a whole array of guests, known and unknown, in our worship spaces that we negotiate what to learn and to unlearn, what to worship and not to worship, and how to figure, disfigure and refigure God, our faith and the world.

Understanding liturgical space as a territory reveals it as a loaded space, a mined territory. Here we are caught up between Babel and Pentecost, in the midst of the work of the Holy Spirit. Here we confront ethical demands and complicated relations. We cannot avoid the poor or ignore nameless, senseless deaths. We cling to potential resurrections, possible harmonies and promises of love and hopeful redemptions.

In Spirit and in Truth: John 4:1–30.

How do we live in this territory? How do we honor God and one another in our differences and open spaces for others to come? How do we encounter God and one another at the liturgical space?

In the fourth chapter of John's gospel, we see an encounter between the Samaritan woman and Jesus, an encounter that shook some of the social, political and religious conventions of that time. We all know well that the Jews had issues with the Samaritans, and vice versa. As Gail R. O'Day says:

> The breach between Samaritans and Jews derived from the Assyrian occupation of northern Palestine in 721 B.C.E. (2 Kings 17), but this breach intensified about 200 B.C.E. in a dispute over the location of the cultic center. The Samaritans built a shrine on Mount Gerizin and claimed that this shrine, not Jerusalem temple, was the center of cultic life. Jewish troops destroyed the shrine on Mount Gerizin in 128 B.C.E., and the rift between the two groups continued into Jesus' day. In addition, Jews and Samaritans disagreed over what constituted authoritative scripture, with the Samaritans accepting only the Pentateuch as authoritative.[8]

---

7. Nancy, "Of Being Singular Plural," 26.

8. O'Day, *The Word Disclosed*, 34–35. Jean K. Kim says, "Both Jews and Samaritans were determined to keep alive their father's way of life and customs, and quarreled with each other on the issue of the sanctity of their respective temples." Kim, *Women and Nation*, 95.

Both of them thought that the other group was the schismatic one. We see that for both Samaritans and Jews, the question of the cultic space was central to their faith, so much so that the location of the worship blurred important themes such as nation identity, religious orthodoxy, personal faith, political recognition and ethnic considerations.

I've heard several sermons that talk about the sinfulness of this woman and how Jesus saved her from her impurity. However, when Jesus hears her story, he does not condemn her, but instead, he says: what you say is true. As Jean K. Kim puts it, women at that time were also "objects of transactions in a patriarchal society . . . "[9] This unnamed woman engages Jesus in a theological discussion and asks him about the right place for worship. Jesus answers that it does not really matter where you worship, and that there will be a time when it will be neither here nor there for worshipers to worship God. Jean Kim says that, "by addressing the question of territorialism, John offers Jesus as a replacement for the land or for a holy place."[10]

Jesus keeps the wall of separation between the Jews and the Samaritans when he says: "You worship what you do not know and we worship what we know, for salvation is from the Jews." As Kim says, Jesus addresses the right place of worship using the repetitive expression "we-you" relationship. Jesus is associating true worship with a proper knowledge of God that can only be found within the Jews. However, as the conversation goes on, he breaks down these walls and offers a new space of worship, a space for anyone, saying that "the hour is coming, and it is now here, when the true worshipers will worship God in spirit and truth, for God seeks such as these to worship him" (4:23).

Here is Jesus saying neither here nor there. How shall we understand that? Our job as Christians has to do with an endless theological and liturgical work of figuring out what it means to worship God in spirit and truth and how we become such true worshipers of God, here and elsewhere. One could say that to be true worshipers of God one has to adore Christ in the inner space of our hearts, that it is there, in the most intimate of our beings that God lives and should be worshipped. To which I say a resounding yes!

9. Kim, *Women and Nation*, 93.

10. Ibid.

However, any worshipful gesture that moves our hearts also depends on the ways of our bodies, depends if we are able to eat, if we are coping with pain or not, if our beloved ones are going through difficult times, etc. Any worshipful gesture of our heart is thus marked by the ways that our territories are marked, depending if we have a house to live in or we live on the streets; if we are employed, if we live in the midst of a civil war or not, if I am Black, an immigrant, gay, a child, have an illness or am a woman. One might say that the grace of God comes to us in any situation, circumstance or territorial bonds, and we do not depend on the material aspects of our lives to receive God's grace. To this, I would say "yes. " But also a resounding "no." It might be true that the grace of God works on God's logic, which is a logic unknown to us. However, the grace of God also moves through human and material channels that we, as Christians, are supposed to create in order to see the grace of God flow. Without compassion for those in need, it will be harder to see the undeniable grace of God flowing in our lives. It is true though, that sometimes the grace of God will go beyond any material contour, and at other times we become the means of grace.

In one way or another, our lives will always have an indelible mark of the world, referenced by some social something that will define how the grace of God will be expressed in our lives. Liturgical spaces are edged, fenced territories that define and are defined by the ways we relate to God and to the world. For this reason, liturgical spaces are territories that define our faith as it gives us world–views in every movement we do or not do here, every word we say or not say here. However, if one is not convinced about the ways that the liturgical territory forms our liturgical world–view, we could say the following:

- If we ask who has the power to preside at the Eucharist, or to preach in our churches/seminaries today we will discover that liturgical space has gendered/sexualized boundaries.

- If we consider that our Black ancestors in this country were required to sit the balcony of those White churches, dislocated and disenfranchised. Then, when we look at our worship patterns today, we realize that the most worship in North America remains *racially segregated,*

- If we consider how our world is economically divided with a minority of the world's population controlling the majority of the world's wealth, and we reflect on how our worship spaces reinforce values of wealth and privilege. Then, we see that economic inequity and class structure deeply marks worship spaces.

- If we consider that queer people who are marginalized from Eucharistic fellowship and worship in general, then we realize that the borders of our sacraments and worship are loaded with sexual references and sexual markers.

- If we consider the borders between nations, and how our sisters and brothers in Christ are treated in dehumanizing ways, then we realize that our worship is ethnocentric and devalues the worth of the intrinsic value of the "other"—their personhood and their labor.

- All these are issues that should concern those who seek to worship in Spirit and in truth; and worship in the name of the One who reached out across territorial boarders to a Samaritan woman.

Jesus said that God desires true worshipers. Who are they? Where are they found? These are key questions for all of us to think about worship in our seminaries. How do we form each other as true worshipers of God? As we worship God together in our seminaries, we learn as we go, with one another, "being with" one another, learning with one another how to worship God in spirit and in truth. We learn as we engage in an unending flux of knowledge, experiences, traditions, prayers and practices. The very place of our liturgies—a loaded territory—must become a safe place for us to discern our faith together, to create a space for differences and dialogue, and linger a little longer with the other who does not worship like I do. Like Jesus and that woman, we are to gather at the well and negotiate our lives and our faith together. Our spaces must be hospitable, negotiable and under constant reflection.

In Spirit and in Truth. . . in the Pews

Let me briefly engage one element of a worship space that is pivotal to the theological/liturgical controlling of people's bodies, namely, the pews and seats of our worship spaces. If there is one thing on which we almost universally expect in worship, it is a place to sit on during our worship services. Frequently these seats come in the form of fixed pews. It is hard to imagine a worship space with no seating.

When I think about diversity of approaches in my teaching I feel behind my other colleagues because of the presence of fixed pews, which offers me only one way of being present in the worship space. On the one hand, theology professors can deal with theologies from all over the world in their classrooms, pastoral care professors can talk about various pastoral care approaches, and Bible professors can try different herme-neutic readings on the Bible, professors of education can play with various pedagogies, and so on. However, I find pews prevent variety and diversity in worship in the chapel because the pews do not allow us to create new movements. This is all to say that pews are theological statements and they intend to create homogeneity and give a sense of fixed structures. They teach how our bodies must behave and by creating a rigidity of movements, they impede theological movements as well. Nancy Pereira Cardoso, a Biblical scholar and theologian from Brazil talks about faith, morality and Christian faith:

> The interior part of our knees is also the bending of our morality, and of our shame. The construction of bodies and the metabolisms of knowledge production, the domestication of objective and sub-jective bending of men and women. Knees are educated and evan-gelized in distinctive ways, with different dislocations, vertices and openings. Knees learn to control and are controlled.[11]

To worship God in our liturgical spaces is to sing with our African slaves ancestors who shout "Gimme de kneebone bent." Without pews, we might be able to bend our knees to each other, find forms of resilience and habits of resistance. Without pews we might engage with differences of bodies in pause and in movement, and try other spatial and territorial approaches to each other and God. Then, we might even discover other possibilities of God in relation to our bodies, our traditions, and our world.

11. Cardoso Pereira, quoted in Cláudio Carvalhaes, "Gimme de kneebone bent," p.12.

Conclusion: At the well . . .

Here is where we try to find what we have abandoned at some point in our thinking and in our practices, that which could have not been abandoned . . .

It is there, at this unknown and dangerous crossroad, with familiar and strange faces, with concrete liturgical objects such as the well, the water and the abandoned jar, that the theological discourse should be constructed.

Beyond the "colonization of subjectivities," here we are to rub our shoulders together, here is where we paint each other's faces with the colors of hope.

Here, in this chartered and unchartered territory, we are to look and perhaps to find theological maps for the road, to create signs for the lost to be found, and signs to those who are found to be lost.

This territory is not here *in spite* of our differences but *because* of our differences. Here, in this mined territory, we construct a liturgy of the neighbor and we confess that a new world is possible. As the Brazilian pastor and theologian Pedro Casaldáliga said: "Here we reveal what our faith is: We either serve the God of Life or we use God's name to serve those who promote death."[12]

It is our aspiration to be a true worshiper of God, in spirit and in truth, and our task is to deconstruct and reconstruct our worship together in our liturgical territories, in seminary chapels or elsewhere. The Bible text tells us a story of an encounter and the liturgical territory must be a place for encounters. Nancy Pereira Cardoso describes this encounter.

> Two strangers: he and she. They were not supposed to meet each other. There was no common space, a reason or a why. The point of encounter: a well. And they have different thirsts. She was a woman. He was a man. He a Jew, even if from Galilee. She a Samaritan. He, a passer by, she a resident. But at that moment, they were both vulnerable in the presence of each other. And it is this identity that facilitates the encounter: to be vulnerable. She and he. He is passing through a non-place, alone, in a strange land. She is familiar with her territory. A territory is also made of relations. They are both so alone that the social and relational markers of that terri-

12. Pedro Casaldáliga in one of his texts to the 2008 Campanha da Fraternidade in Brazil: *Fraternidade e Defesa da Vida. Escolhe, pois, a vida.* No longer available on the internet.

tory are suspended. A man and a woman meet each other at the well. At that moment, water was also relation.

And the theology of this encounter around the well has its own liturgy:

At first, they introduce themselves to each other and let each other know their differences as they move around the heavy furniture of the past . . . the concrete ground that now they share. They make themselves present to each other, they see . . . and let each other be seen.

At a second moment, there was an affirmation of faith: we are humans and we share the world. They recognize each other by the concrete presence of what sustain their lives: the water;

On a third moment comes the word. It comes as a necessary conversation, a dialogue with the precision of their words. The word circulates between the materiality and the representations of the place. Words that do not negate the conflict. The word that do not fear problems and questions. Here's the itinerary: from life to theology.

Then, they agree that what he and she have in common is the desire for the well, for the water, beyond the name of the well, its history and its control. They want to be in the same territory, re-signifying identities, offering again new subjectivities and relations, and making history. God with us. Neither here nor there but somewhere in between where we are, which is the best place for adoration.

And then there is the fourth and last moment, the moment for commitment: I give you my cup and I call my people; I introduce my friends to you and I kiss your cup; I recognize you and I call you mine. We offer ourselves to one another, an offering that creates the territory where we worship God. Community.[13]

Our seminary chapels are like the well in this gospel text, a place for unexpected encounters, for gathering of strangers, and the sharing of water, food and wisdom. At that place, you tell me about you, I drink from your cup, we call upon God's name together and in Jesus, we worship God and learn to share this blessed, taught, graceful, difficult and changing world, shifting from political territory to liturgical meeting place. And here at this well, we might interpret the world liturgically, through the lens of God's inclusive realm, daring to challenge the territories established in that God's name.

13. Nancy Pereira Cardoso, personal correspondence on John 4:1–30 (unpublished, used with permission).

Works Cited:

Carvalhaes, Cláudio. "'Gimme de kneebone bent': Liturgics, Dance, Resistance and a Hermeneutics of the Knees." *Studies in World Christianity 14* (2008) 1–18.

Derrida, Jacques. *Of Grammatology.* Corrected ed. Translated by Gayatri Spivak. Baltimore: Johns Hopkins University Press, 1998.

———. *Writing and Difference.* Translated by Alan Bass. Chicago: University of Chicago Press, 1978.

Derrida, Jacques, and Elisabeth Roudinesco. *For What Tomorrow . . . A Dialogue.* Translated by Jeff Fort. Cultural Memory in the Present. Stanford, CA: Stanford University Press, 2004.

Holt-Damant, Kath. "The Threat from Within. Protecting the Indefensible from the Indeterminate." In *Indefensible Space: The Architecture of the National Insecurity State,* edited by Michael Sorkin, 163–76. Routledge: New York, 2008.

Kim, Jean Kyoung. *Woman and Nation: An Intercontextual Reading of the Gospel of John from a Postcolonial Feminist Perspective. Biblical Interpretation Series 69.* Boston: Brill, 2004.

Nancy, Jean-Luc. "Of Being Singular Plural." In *Being Singular Plural,* translated by Robert D. Richardson and Anne E. O'Byrne, 1–100. Meridian, Crossing Aesthetics. Stanford, CA: Stanford University Press, 2000.

O'Day, Gail R. *The Word Disclosed: Preaching the Gospel of John. Revised and expanded ed.* St. Louis: Chalice Press, 2002.

Saliers, Don. "Afterword: Liturgy and Ethics Revised." In *Liturgy and the Moral Self: Humanity at Full Stretch before God,* edited by E. Byron Anderson and Bruce T. Morrill, 209–24. Collegeville, MN: Liturgical, 1998.

8

Table Teaching:
Practicing the Lord's Supper at Seminary

RON RIENSTRA

Introduction

The modern seminary has a liminal character and history. It stands uneasily between two strong cultural institutions—the church and the academy—like the child of separated parents. It struggles to please both, to balance the expectations and criteria for excellence each demands.[1] And mealtime is particularly awkward. When an educational community gathers to practice the Eucharist[2] there is tension and ambiguity in

1. D. H. Kelsey writes of the tension within theological education between two "controlling traditions," *paideia* and *wissenschaft,* the first focused on transformation and the second on information. Though not mutually exclusive, they sit uneasily alongside one another because of their "incommensurate sets of criteria of excellence." See Kelsey, 92. These two may be said roughly to correspond to the two institutions in view here, church and academy. Approaches that embrace *paideia* value spiritual growth, devotional practices, shaping ministerial identity and pastoral imagination; approaches that embrace *wissenschaft* focus on the transmission and preservation of specialized knowledge, and critical inquiry. Judging by the frequency with this is referred to in the professional literature, it could be argued that there has been a turning—or a returning—to the *paideia* model in recent years. See, for example, the discussions in Dykstra, 141–48; Jones and Paulsell, *The Scope of Our Art,* 2002, especially the first three chapters.

2. I will use the terms "Lord's Supper," "Eucharist," and "Communion" interchangeably to refer to the meal Jesus instituted. Each of these terms highlights particular theological emphases and thus certain terms are preferred by certain denominations or theological traditions. But in keeping with the ecumenical aims of this paper (if not the ecumenical character of the meal itself), I will use all of them—both for the sake of even-handedness

the room. There is tension between formation and expression, and between unity and diversity. And there is ambiguity, born of the seminary's parentage—ambiguity of persons and purpose. Who is it that gathers for this event: a small congregation of Christians or a class of students and teachers? Why do they gather: for devotion or education?[3] Of course, this is an over-simplified picture, but all the complexity, awkwardness, and tensions of clerical training are compressed in the moment when a presider in a classroom or chapel offers a prayer, lifts a loaf and a cup, and says, "The gifts of God for the people of God," and the liturgy professor thinks (or says) "Lift them up a bit higher. And stop mumbling."

Despite these tensions and the inherent pedagogical and polity problems they pose, more and more seminaries are coming to value Eucharist as central to worship, worship as central to ministerial formation, and formation central to the task of the seminary.[4] Hence, the Table is increasingly seen as an important expression of the seminary's ecclesial identity and as a place to fulfill the seminary's obligation to train the next generation of liturgical leaders.

This is borne out in Lutheran and Presbyterian schools where Holy Communion, once celebrated a handful of times per year on campus, is now celebrated weekly. Methodist seminaries that celebrated weekly now celebrate three times a week. In other quarters there is intermittent sacramental celebration and vigorous conversation where a generation ago the subject was a non-starter. Pedagogically the same trend is evident: a school that previously offered worship only as an elective now requires two substantive courses, one folded into the introductory theology course, and the other as a senior capstone. Another offers one required course and a dozen elective practica in various aspects of worship leadership. Another school requires a four-course sequence of all MDiv students in addition to regular responsibilities leading worship on campus and in a parish field setting.

and for the sake of rhetorical variety.

3. See Anderson, "Worship and Theological Education," 117–30.

4. See for example Murphy, *Teaching that Transforms*. Other examples abound: two years ago at the Episcopalian pre-meeting at the North American Academy of Liturgy (the professional organization of liturgy academics), the conversation topic was "Teaching Worship." A similar theme was explored in the 2008 meeting among the Lutherans, and the Association for Reformed and Liturgical Worship is in the middle of a three-year initiative to "strengthen the church in forming leaders for worship." See http://arlw.worshiprenewal.googlepages.com/revisedproposal.doc.

The move in this direction, while widespread, is not uniform. Different denominations have different understandings of the liturgical traditions they want to pass on and in which they wish to shape their students. Schools in the same families may differ in the *manner* in which they wish to model and pass on their traditions. And many schools embrace an explicitly ecumenical identity, and so celebration and teaching around the Table is fraught with all the danger—and all the potential—of a richly diverse community. Just as importantly, across the ecclesial spectrum there are different theological views of what constitutes a *church*. Consequently, there is disagreement concerning the fittingness of sacramental celebration in the seminary community.[5]

It is not my aim in this essay to adjudicate these disputes, or to evaluate one group by the theological lights of another. It is, rather, to describe, in the abstract and in anecdote, what sort of table teaching is happening at Protestant seminaries in North America. My intent is to map out the territory, identifying some landmarks that a school can use to assess its own thinking and practice, and to begin to find a common way to talk about common challenges in light of the wise ways many are meeting them.[6] Along the way—to return to the opening metaphor—I hope this will help seminaries think about ways to negotiate a relationship with both their institutional parents without having to choose one over the other.

I will use the simple lens with which I began this essay: the seminary as an institution that stands somewhere between church and academy.[7] I will thus begin with church polity, looking at some ecclesial implications for practicing Eucharist at seminary. I will then turn briefly to an exploration of pedagogical concerns.[8]

5. This will be more of an issue in some traditions than others, as we will see.

6. Though I am sure there would be much gained, including Roman Catholic and Orthodox as well as international voices, for the purposes of this short essay, I have limited the field of vision and research to manageable parameters, focusing only on Protestant seminaries in North America. Within this field of vision, I hope to be broadly ecumenical, but I suspect that my own Reformed sensibilities and interests will be evident on occasion.

7. I don't want to probe the specifics of the relationship between the two, but to look at each as something like the other. For a more subtle and historically grounded examination, see Richard Mouw, President of Fuller Seminary, who argues that "the ontology of the theological school seems to me to be captured in a formula of this sort: it is *of* the academy and *for* the church" ("The Seminary," 462).

8. A research note: the published data on this topic is fine, but rather meager. Thus, much of the material for this essay comes from unpublished papers, local customaries,

The School as Church

What is the church? A fully orbed study of comparative ecclesiology is beyond the scope of this essay. But we can start with a few premises, ask a few questions, and make a few observations. I presume first of all that the seminary is considered to be a *school* in some meaningful sense. Secondly, it is not self-evident to all that as a school it can legitimately and fittingly celebrate the Eucharist any more than a family of believers around the dinner table could, or the bible-study fellowship at the GM plant, or the congressional men's prayer breakfast.[9] The sacraments belong not to the state or the guild or the family—or the academy—but to Christ and to the Church that God calls into being by the power of the Holy Spirit. The question, then, is whether or not the academically congregated *seminary* community can be considered a *church*. If it is, in what sense and of what sort? Or to put it in the terminology of church polity, by what ecclesial sanction does the seminary celebrate this meal?[10]

These questions may be answered differently depending in part on whether one's first impulse is to conceive of the church as *organism* or as *institution*. Understood as an *organism*, the Church is the living body of Christ, an existentially known assembly of believers who simply do the things Christians do when two or three of them gather. Understood as an *institution*, an identifiable community of the faithful, the Church is called out to be led and served and ordered by particular offices and rites and governmental structures for the up-building of the whole people of God. Of course, these are not incompatible views, but they do pull in different directions.

---

and a substantial series of email and telephone interviews with faculty and clergy at dozens of seminaries, conducted during 2007–2008. Where appropriate, citations will point to my own (unpublished) records. Furthermore, because this topic at institutions of higher education is politically sensitive, and the people responsible for Table celebration are often in vulnerable positions, I am anonymizing quotations from my research participants in order to protect their identities, except where specific permission for naming has been granted.

9. The Westminster Assembly, for example, is one of the documents that explicitly rejects these sorts of private celebrations.

10. I am thinking now primarily of the celebrations which happen in chapels and sanctuaries, when the communities gather explicitly for the purpose of prayer and worship. We will look at what happens in the liturgics *practica* at a few points later on.

Consider, for example, the following responses to the questions above (about the ecclesial status of the seminary, and the fittingness of Table celebration), culled from surveys and interviews with professors and administrators at seminaries from a broad range of denominational backgrounds:[11]

- "We celebrate the Lord's Supper because we're *Christians*."
- "We're part of the body of Christ; we would be bereft without the Lord's Supper. We need it to sustain us."
- "We *are* a church. We celebrate the Eucharist as a peculiar church of the local diocese, under the authority of the bishop."
- "We do not operate as a church, so we do not celebrate the Lord's Supper."
- "We're a community of faith, but we're not a church. We're a learning community—and a religious community. So Chapel is one of the main places we learn tolerance and diversity."

In these representative quotes, the language sometimes leans in an organic or in an institutional direction. Where the organic impulse is strong, so is the need to celebrate ("we would be bereft"). When institutional considerations are also taken into account, there seem to be a handful of options. Among them are these: a seminary may: a) celebrate in conformity to relevant ecclesial conventions; or b) refrain from celebrating because those institutional considerations define church in such a way as to exclude the seminary community. Especially in ecumenical contexts, a number of additional options are pursued. For example, some seminaries: c) refrain from celebrating because the seminary finds the negotiation of competing polity considerations hopelessly vexed; d) pick a tradition in which to celebrate, and through an authorized representative, borrow the sanction of that tradition; or e) fall back on the organic sense of the Church, and celebrate ecumenically.[12] These options provide a helpful starting point for the seminary considering the fittingness of its own Table celebration.

11. The data in this essay was gained through three distinct means. First, a survey of 120 North American seminaries was made using public information posted on the schools' web sights. Second, approximately forty seminaries filled out a survey and a returned it for this study. Finally, about 25 phone interviews were held with leaders of seminary chapels.

12. Consider a prominent divinity school that understands itself primarily as a learn-

On the Nature of the Church

Perhaps the organic/institutional distinction is too simple as an interpretive tool. The ecumenical theologian Lesslie Newbigin offers a helpful alternative framework in his landmark study of the Church, *The Household of God*. First, Newbigin offers a gentle critique of the distinction between the visible and the invisible church (a critique that may have some traction in this discussion).[13] He then outlines three ways that Christians have understood the manner in which those who are called out by God are ingrafted into Christ and made his Church.[14]

The first group that draws Newbigin's attention is the one centered in *evangelical proclamation*. On this view, the Church is the "congregation of the faithful"—with the faithful being identified as those who have heard and believed the Gospel. This view holds tightly to the Protestant

---

ing community made up of people, many of whom are individually part of a church community, but who would be hesitant to consider themselves "church" when they come together. Celebration in these contexts is particularly vexed, because of the primacy of educational concerns—especially learning tolerance and diversity—overshadows devotional ones. To demonstrate the pull in the other direction, consider one seminary which claims no ecclesial status for itself, and furthermore, affirms the primacy of its *educational* purpose, but with a different agenda. According to the person in charge of worship at this place: "We are an academic institution run on behalf of the church body. We want our students to know, defend, promote, and practice official church doctrine. We aren't burdened by the need to receive every ecumenical part of the church" (personal interview with liturgy professor, October 21, 2008).

13. The distinction between the "organic" and "institutional" church is not the same as that between the "visible" and "invisible church." (For those who accept this latter distinction, see the discussion in Berkhof, *Systematic Theology*, 565–67.) Yet Newbigin's critique is trenchant. He says: "The idea of the invisible Church . . . derives its main attraction—unless I am much mistaken—from the fact that each of us can determine its membership as he [sic] will. It is our ideal Church, containing the people whom we—in our present stage of spiritual development—would regard as fit members" (*Household*, 28). Those whose first or stronger impulse is to think of the church as organism would be wise to ground their notion of church in flesh and blood, and avoid allowing the spiritual character of its organic unity to drift away into the platonic stratosphere, a celebration of an abstract, if heavily modified noun (e.g., the True Assembly of the Redeemed from every tribe, tongue, people and nation, etc.)

14. For the purposes of this paper, I prefer this Christocentric approach, rather than other interesting, but perhaps overly controversial or expansive frameworks one might consider, e.g. the marks of the Church, either creedal (One, Holy, Catholic, Apostolic) or confessional (sincere proclamation and hearing of the Word, right administration of the sacraments, exercise of discipline, prayer/reconciliation, etc.), or contemporary (practices of Sabbath, Singing, Non-violence, etc.)

affirmations of *sola fides,* and *sola gratia,* and recognizes Christ's presence made known in both preaching and sacramental celebration.[15] Newbigin charges that this view, in its focus on the 'event character,' of the Church, can give insufficient attention to the ongoing life of Christian fellowship.

The second group Newbigin explores is the one centered in *sacramental unity and continuity.* On this view, Christians are ingrafted into Christ "primarily and essentially by sacramental incorporation into the life of His Church."[16] Here, the notion of the Body of Christ is central, expressed institutionally in both a physical and spiritual sense, in visible people, tangible things, stable structures. The key flaw of this view, according to Newbigin, is that the church often assumes the grace of God comes automatically with these physical, visible, tangible, stable things, so that the Church holds in itself the plenitude of God's grace.[17]

The third group Newbigin introduces is centered in *pentecostal power.* On this view, the Christian life is a matter of the experienced presence of the Holy Spirit. Whereas the other views hold to what has been passed on, either in message or structure, this view identifies the Church with those people who in the present know the power of the abiding life of the Holy Spirit. This view of the Church is flawed when it locates the church in the power of the Spirit entirely *independent* of Christ's work and presence in historical message and structure.

Theological Implications: Congregation of the Faithful

Though these three notions of Church are sometimes associated with specific denominations and Christian traditions, one may find (and perhaps *should* find) all of them impulses present in any particular seminary community. I outline them here not to line up seminaries and traditions, or sort them into the right boxes, but to explore in a suggestive or illustrative way how these impulses—along with their theological strengths and weaknesses—inform the consideration of seminary as Church.

15. Here Newbigin favorably quotes both Calvin and Luther in their maintenance that wherever the Gospel is truly preached and the sacraments duly administered, there the church is. Newbigin, *Household,* 49.

16. Newbigin, *Household,* 60.

17. Newbigin, *Household,* 83.

So, for example, the first impulse—to see Church as a "congregation of the faithful"—is plainly evident in the liturgical language of the invitation to the Table. These often set forth the preconditions for participation primarily in terms of faith or belief. Consider this one commonly used at Presbyterian seminaries—Princeton, Austin, Union, and others: "This is the Lord's Table. Our Savior invites those who trust him to share the feast which he has prepared."[18]

Or consider this excerpt from a "communion card" used at Concordia, the Lutheran Church—Missouri Synod seminary, which gives denominational and confessional specificity to what it means to trust in Jesus and thus constitute a congregation of the faithful:

> Our Lord invites to his table those who trust his words, repent of all sin, and set aside any refusal to forgive and love as he forgives and loves us, that they may show forth his death until he comes. Because . . . Holy Communion is a confession of the faith which is confessed at this altar, any who are not yet instructed, in doubt, or who hold a confession differing from that of this congregation . . . are asked first to speak with the pastor or an usher.[19]

Of course, if the Meal is a communion of the faithful, what might such a notion of church say to its public celebration in ecumenical or even interfaith contexts? Can the Church celebrate hospitably, while simultaneously protecting the integrity of the community and the meal, ensuring

---

18. *Book of Common Worship*, 68. It is worth noting that though the emphasis here is on *belief*, the expected *response* of faith—baptism, and membership in the body of Christ—is not altogether out of view. For example, in the *Directory for Worship* of the PCUSA and in Principle 39 of the ELCA's *Principles for Worship*, both of which deal with the celebration of the Meal, a primary emphasis on belief and faith is augmented by a requirement for that belief to have found expression in baptism, though this is not always expressed liturgically. Principle 39 reads: "The gathered people of God celebrate the sacrament. Holy Communion, usually celebrated within a congregation, also may be celebrated in synodical, churchwide, and other settings *where the baptized gather*" (italics mine). See also the PC(USA) Book of Order, the Directory for Worship section on Baptism, W-2.4011: "Who may receive: The invitation to the Lord's Supper is extended *to all who have been baptized*, remembering that access to the Table is not a right conferred upon the worthy, but a privilege given to the undeserving *who come in faith, repentance, and love*." An online copy can be found at: http://www.elca.org/Growing-In -Faith/Worship/Learning-Center/Principles-of-Worship.aspx.

19. *Model Communion Card Statement*. Can be found online at: http://www.iclnet.org/pub/resources/text/wittenberg/mosynod/clcommunion.txt.

that it is the "faithful" who come?[20] This is more difficult—though not impossible—if there are not structural or disciplinary mechanisms in the community as there are in a local congregation. My research suggests that some seminary communities function more effectively than many congregations as a loving community of discipleship and accountability and prayer—even for extended families of seminarians.

Of course, protecting the table as a place for the faithful alone is not a concern for all. The Methodist tradition has long seen the Meal as a "converting ordinance," and scholars such as Gordon Lathrop and N. T. Wright have argued in this direction as well. Consider the recent reflections on open, converting table practice at St. Gregory of Nyssa in San Francisco as related in *Take This Bread* by Sara Miles. The president of an ecumenical school in the Reformed tradition said to me: "In a post-Christian culture, our students are engaged with populations who do not see the difference between the Baptist altar-call and our Invitation to the Table. Our ecclesial bodies are far from this, but it's where our people are."[21]

Theological Implications: Sacramental Unity

On consideration of the second view of Church as a sacramentally united people under a continuous ecclesial structure, the question of baptism, as we have seen, takes on great significance. We will look more carefully at some institutional questions in the next section, but for now, it is worth puzzling briefly over the relationship between Bath and Meal in the seminary context.

Across the denominational spectrum, no seminary community with whom I had contact would happily allow a baptism. Some Lutheran and Episcopalian schools might allow it for the child of a community member, but only if it were a ceremony held in the campus worship space on behalf of a local parish and the baptism registered to that local congregation.[22]

---

20. There are a few seminaries where the community is not necessarily understood as the "congregation of the faithful." In such places, worship is "but one piece of an interfaith dialogue" (personal interview with liturgy professor, October 21, 2008). In such contexts, it may be worthwhile considering how the classical biblical meanings of the sacrament (see Appendix) are to be interpreted.

21. Personal interview, October 21, 2008.

22. Telephone interviews, September 26, 2008 and August 22, 2008.

Most other schools would categorically refrain from baptisms in recognition of its initiatory significance into the local as well as the universal Body of Christ.[23] Some also cited the absence of appropriate mechanisms of oversight and nurture for new Christians.[24]

Where there is refusal to celebrate baptism, but regular celebration of the meal, the sacraments are decoupled, and this can cause considerable theological tension.[25] At one seminary, for example, the recent renovation of the worship space occasioned reflection on how to embody their theological convictions in the presence or absence of liturgical furniture. Consequently, because the community celebrates the Lord's Supper each week, there is a table; but because they do not celebrate baptism, there is no font in the sanctuary. According to one administrator, "if we follow through with our 'baptismal *no*,' we should probably also say 'no' to the Lord's Supper." In another school there is a bowl of holy water at the entrance to the sanctuary. A faculty member told me: "Just because we don't do regular baptisms doesn't mean we don't *remember* our baptisms. We embrace a richly baptismal ecclesiology."[26] Indeed, it seems especially appropriate that at seminary, where students try work out the particular configurations of their baptismal callings to serve God in the Church, students might regularly remember those baptisms and the gifts of the Spirit given at baptism.

Theological Implications: Pentecostal Power

Among those spiritual gifts given at baptism is union with Christ—a union that on Newbigin's third view is also experienced through the power of the Spirit. The experience—as it happens in the meal or in other places—is not commonly associated with the Evangelical and Sacramental traditions

23. So, for example, a faculty member at one seminary said that he would not do a baptism because of its initiatory significance into a local church. But as we chatted through the complexities, he suggested somewhat wistfully, "we would be well-served to articulate a policy on this more clearly" (telephone interview, September 22, 2008).

24. Personal interview, October 31, 2008.

25. It is, in fact, determinative in some cases, as at Calvin Theological Seminary, where the potential decoupling of the sacraments from their proper home in the local congregation was cited as the primary reason there is no Lord's Supper celebration there (personal correspondence with President Neal Plantinga, August 19, 2008).

26. Telephone interview, August 22, 2008.

under discussion here.[27] Yet even in these schools there is recognition that the Holy Spirit can intervene in surprising ways. So, for example, many liturgy professors testify to the movement of the Holy Spirit not only at seminary chapel, but in classroom practica where the Meal is practiced, where a community of baptized believers, soaked in the Gospel message, gathers around bread and cup, and speak words of prayer and thanksgiving and remembrance and sacrifice and unity. "We find this isn't a *live* context, but it is *living,*" says a faculty member at one seminary. "The Holy Spirit comes. There are norms for the Lord's Supper, but norms are not the *sine qua non* of Christian experience. There are boundaries we want to hold on to, but God breaks out of those boundaries with startling frequency."[28]

We have been considering Newbigin's three views of the nature of the Church as a helpful framework for thinking about seminary communities as church. As we have seen, these three are not mutually exclusive. Indeed, Newbigin will insist that no one of them has full grasp of the full truth; they are complimentary, and each needs the others. More than this, Newbigin concludes his book on ecclesiology arguing that the fundamental character of the Church's identity is to be found beyond these: in union with Christ understood both eschatologically and missionally. That is to say, the Church is never defined in terms of what it has been, or is right now, but it must be understood "in terms of the eschatological tension of faith and hope," drawn both into the future, and unto the nations.[29]

On the Order of the Church

Seminary communities assembling around the Table appear to be very church-like. They are united to Christ in crucial organic ways: they gather as believers in Jesus, they participate in the communal life of the body, and they are moved by the power of the Spirit. But institutionally-speaking, the picture is a bit more complicated. The Church has always found it important to express and safeguard the unity of the body through a

27. To be fair, the majority of congregations in North America that would self-label with Newbigin's term, "Pentecostal," come from traditions that do not celebrate the Meal as regularly as others; furthermore, they often do not send their clergy to academic institutions for preparatory training, and are thus underrepresented in this study.

28. Personal interview, September 22, 2008.

29. Newbigin, *Household,* 111–52.

ministry of *institutional* oversight, of structure and order, accountability and affirmation.[30] This oversight—*episkopē* in the Greek—and the shape it takes is a matter of substantial disagreement. Even so, there is unity. First, even though they are places of liturgical training, seminaries almost uniformly insist on the presence of an *ordained* person—usually *not* a student—to preside at the Table. As BEM notes, "It is especially in the Eucharistic celebration that the ordained ministry is the visible focus of the deep and all-embracing communion between Christ and the members of his body."[31] Second, seminaries look for authorization or sanction for their celebrations from the broader institutional structures that grant ordination. How they do so depends upon the operative ecclesiological polities at work in each community. The more pointed questions to consider then, are these: where does a seminary's particular church tradition locate the *episkopē*, the foundation of ordained ministry, and does it seek and find sanction from those quarters?

There are three broad traditions concerning the location of the episcopal function of the Church. According to Congregational polity, oversight and authority rests with the congregation itself. In Presbyterian polity, it rests with a congregationally-located board of elders. In Episcopal polity, it rests with the bishop. We will consider each of these briefly.

Congregational Polity

A seminary that claims congregational polity may feel quite free to celebrate the Meal whenever it deems appropriate. The same may be true of an ecumenical seminary that has no denominationally-directed polity connections. Decisions about that appropriateness might lie with the presumed representative of the seminary "congregation": the President, the Faculty or a committee thereof, or with the person designated to be in charge of community worship. In such situations, the authorization to celebrate in these contexts often comes not so much through the institutional channels of the seminary conceived as church, but through more traditional ecclesial channels. So, for example, the "Worship Guidelines" at one ecumenical seminary state that the director of worship "selects peo-

---

30. See Newbigin, *Household*, 73; and *Baptism, Eucharist and Ministry* (BEM), III.A.23.

31. BEM, II.A.14.

ple to preside at the Table who are authorized by their denominations."[32] Indeed, at many schools, the authority to celebrate the supper—the oversight—is borrowed from the tradition of the chosen presider.[33]

Of course, other ecumenical or congregational schools, having determined by their lights that the seminary is not a church, choose to celebrate rarely, if at all. At Fuller Seminary, for example, the Lord's Supper typically happens only once or twice a year, and while students seem to embrace it, faculty often raise strong objections. The same is true at a Baptist seminary, where, according to one faculty member, "For the most part students do not even consider the concept that the Supper is to be offered under the authority of the church. . . . On the other hand, when the Supper is offered in a chapel service, some seminary faculty respond negatively, saying that the seminary is not a church and that the Supper has no place within the seminary context."[34]

Episcopal Polity

The question of ecclesial sanction for seminary supper celebrations for those in the Episcopal political tradition is a bit more straightforward. Under the authority of a presiding bishop, the seminary community is understood in its own right as a legitimate ecclesial body. The customary of the Church Divinity School of the Pacific says: "At a seminary and graduate theological center such as this, our prayer in common is both the *real worship of a real community* and an opportunity for reflection and practice for preachers and future liturgical leaders."[35] Adds an Episcopal administrator: "In the Anglican tradition, Collegiate and other chapels

---

32. Philips Theological Seminary, "PTS Worship Guidelines."

33. See, for example, this statement from a divinity school: "Presiders are responsible to their own polity. If they come from a denomination which requires special permission to celebrate the Eucharist in another location, then they are responsible for either securing such permission or taking the decision to ignore it. The chapel staff can neither administer the former nor request the latter. The presider must be ordained or otherwise authorized within their own denomination/congregation" (private correspondence, August 8, 2008).

34. Personal correspondence, August 1, 2008. This judgment might be logically extended to the preaching of the Word. So, for example, one seminary president wrote about a faculty member who refused to preach in chapel, "since a seminary chapel is not a properly constituted ecclesial gathering" (personal correspondence, July 19, 2008).

35. Divinity School of the Pacific, *Customary*, 3.

have always been considered part of the Church. There is simply no issue for us here."[36] Likewise, Lutheran seminaries locate the episcopate at the diocesan level and secure permission to celebrate from the presiding bishop.[37] (However, anecdotally, it seems the official solicitation of said permission is assumed as much as it is actually requested).[38]

Presbyterian/Reformed Polity

In the Presbyterian tradition, the sacramental ministries must always be conducted by an ordained pastor under the supervision of the ruling elders, where the "episcopate" is seen to be located. They, or a broader assembly (such as a regional or general synod) may authorize Eucharistic celebrations in other contexts where congregational elders are not present—like a seminary. Some seminaries from this tradition seek and receive this sanction to celebrate, some do not seek it and do not celebrate. Others fall somewhere in between.

So, for example, at least two schools of the PC(USA) petition for and receive permission every other year from the General Assembly Council to celebrate Eucharist. This permission is granted to the seminary president, who then delegates supervisory authority to a chapel committee made up of faculty members.[39] At another Presbyterian-family seminary, there is no board of elders, and no link to a broader presbytery. This school has not communed in years. However, if they were to celebrate, it would require sponsorship by a local congregation, with their pastor presiding and their session (board of elders) present as a focus of the church's uni-

36. Personal correspondence, Aug. 1, 2008.

37. See, for example, *Lutheran Principles*, 39b, 39d: "In established centers of the church—e.g., seminaries, colleges, retreat centers, . . . authorization for the celebration of Holy Communion shall be given, either for a limited or unlimited time, by the presiding bishop of this church, or where only one synod is concerned, by the bishop of that synod. 39d: The authorizing role of bishops is a sign of our interconnectedness. This church provides for ministry in many settings. Chaplains, for example, bring the means of grace to people in institutions on behalf of the whole Church."

38. Telephone interview, September 26, 2008.

39. Personal interview, October 10, 2008. See also Columbia Theological Seminary, "Planning Chapel Worship," 12: "Upon recommendation of the Worship and Convocations Committee, every occasion of the Lord's Supper at Columbia Theological Seminary is authorized by the faculty, under the authority granted by the GA of the PCUSA."

ty.[40] At Western Theological Seminary, where I teach, there are tales told of a process similar to this one: permission for weekly celebration granted years ago by a General Synod, the broadest ecclesial assembly, and the one to which seminary professors are amenable. A past president swears he has seen this permission written somewhere. But a thorough scouring of the General Synod *Minutes* for the past forty years yields no evidence of it. Nevertheless, its existence is assumed in practice.

Ecclesial Model

Though attending to these polity considerations may seem unimportant, even fussy, the alternative is worse—especially for those who believe a seminary should model good ecclesial practice for its students. There is a certain sloppiness that can reinforce an "anything goes" mentality.[41] As one administrator told me: "What the parents do in moderation, the children do in excess. Where we choose to color outside the lines in our practice, we give license to students to color off the page."[42] So, the seminaries that attend carefully to matters of ecclesial polity function not only more legitimately and fittingly *as church*, but in their conscientious modeling, they demonstrate excellence *as school*.[43]

40. *Personal Interview*, October 17, 2008.

41. This sloppiness is not just a Protestant problem. Rich Mouw notes that in a recent Reformed/Roman Catholic dialogue, there was commiseration on all sides about the way the Meal is often handled outside "normal" congregational contexts (personal correspondence, July 19, 2008).

42. Personal interview, September 22, 2008.

43. Examples of the type of compromises that diminish a seminary's effectiveness at modeling good worship could be multiplied a hundredfold. For example, in my research I often heard how *time* pressures drove liturgical decisions—hence, *theological* decisions. So, for example, at one school the Great Prayer of Thanksgiving is trimmed each time it is celebrated, eliminating the *sursum corda* or the *sanctus*. Or another seminary where time pressures inhibit the celebration of the Meal all but twice a semester—here, at a school where students are being trained to lead in parishes where they will preside at the table every week. Of course, there are time pressures in the parish, too. To put the matter more pointedly: the question for seminaries informed by the program of liturgical renewal and convinced of the importance of weekly congregational celebration of the Lord's Supper is this: how best to model a way for their pastors to deal with congregants who complain about the time crunch? How can the seminary model healthy ways to *adapt* the liturgy? How to model a congruent approach to what is said and done with regard to the importance of the supper? It's difficult for pastors to make the argument to their congregations that the Meal is important when the seminary doesn't seem to treat it as such.

The Church as School

At a recent meeting of the North American Academy of Liturgy, Bishop Neil Alexander delivered some remarks to the gathered Episcopalians about teaching worship on seminary campuses. Among his observations was this: "Seminarians of today come to us, by and large, with significantly less catechesis, liturgical and otherwise, than seminarians in times past. The number who have had fairly significant experiences of ecclesial formation is generally quite small."[44] I think that pressed on this point, Bishop Alexander would acknowledge that students today have indeed had significant experiences in ecclesial and liturgical formation—but not always, perhaps, of the best sort. Another way of saying this is to acknowledge that when students come to seminary to be shaped as liturgical leaders, they come *having already been formed* in important ways. In the sanctuaries of their youth, in college chapel, in their present congregations—the church itself is a significant and powerful locus of teaching about worship in general and about the meaning, purpose, and implications of the Eucharist in particular.[45]

And of course, students at seminary continue to learn from local congregations where they attend worship on Sundays, where they work part time in ministry, and where they have field placements. Yet the church gives to the seminary a significant responsibility to shape pastors-in-training—to teach students about their own traditions, to expose them to the traditions of others, and to help them grow into confident liturgical leaders. The seminary has pedagogical tools at its disposal—lecture and essay, observation and analysis, modeling, exercise, and practice. And it has two primary loci to employ its tools: the *classroom*, where sacramental theology and liturgical history can be passed on, explored and applied, and where ritual embodiment can be analyzed, rehearsed, and refined; and the *chapel*, where students can fashion new liturgies, inhabit and vivify old, observe traditions other than their own, and see modeled that which they will inevitably imitate—whether that is excellence or me-

44. Alexander, "Chapel Worship," 9.

45. This is to say nothing of those in seminary who have been primarily shaped not by the church, but by the cultural liturgies of the mall and the sports complex, the movie theater and the all-you-can-eat buffet. "When and where" Ron Anderson asks, "will *these* students receive what can only be called 'remedial' catechesis and formation in the Christian faith?" ("Worship and Theological Education," 121).

diocrity, familiarity or experimentation, indifference or careful, prayerful, authentic celebration.

Classroom

The primary place for learning and practicing the practice of Holy Communion is the classroom. Much valuable and inevitable learning happens in chapel, but there the primary purpose is the glorification of God. In the classroom, however, students receive the wisdom of the church's traditions, they are given the time and resources to research and renew their understandings of the theological meaning and pastoral significance of the Meal, and they rehearse its contours. How this happens varies from school to school, and the centrality of the Eucharist to the worship of a particular tradition may determine how much attention it receives in class, and of what sort.

So for example, at one Reformed school, where pastoral students are required to take one basic course in worship, only a few class periods can be devoted to the theology and practice of the Lord's Supper. So the liturgy Professor's approach is to focus on Reformed sacramental theology and on the pieces of the liturgical puzzle in order to help his students become *thinking* liturgical people.[46] On this model, the classroom functions as it has for centuries, as a place for the transmission of primarily cognitively-apprehended information.

But there is more to the picture. In the Anglican tradition, for example, it is also important to address issues of the fully embodied presence of the *presider* at the Meal as to explore the mysterious presence of Christ. So, for instance, at one Episcopal seminary there is a four course sequence all pastoral students must take. The first course is on the Fundamentals of Worship, walking through the Eucharistic liturgy of the Book of Common Prayer, examining each element—where it comes from, what it is, how it is done. A second class is devoted to Liturgical History, a third to Sacramental Theology, and the Senior capstone course is on "Liturgical Leadership," where students design services, preside at practice rites, are videotaped in their presidency, and reflect together as a group on their performance.

46. Personal interview, October 17, 2008.

At these Eucharistic "practice sessions," real elements are used, the community is a gathering of believers, ecclesially-sanctioned words are spoken, yet, says the liturgy professor, "We're very clear that it is not the will of the church that this is an actual liturgy. While it may not be a sacramental event of the church, the experience of students year after year is that it is very prayerful."[47]

Concern to make this "rehearsal" character of the classroom plain means that sometimes parts of a liturgy are omitted (the words of institution, perhaps), or water is used instead of wine, or some way of breaking up the liturgical sequence so that it does not "feel" so much like a live celebration. Even so, there is sometimes, a sense that something more than prayer happens even during academically-purposed practice sessions for the Eucharist. One professor of liturgy speaks of sacramental potentiality in *every* moment and the sovereignty of God to use any event to be present to the church, even the part of the church gathered in a class. In speaking this way, he acknowledges the mystery of human cooperation with God's will.[48]

In my review of syllabi, and in conversation with those who teach liturgy, there are at least three distinct areas of practice—beyond issues of sacramental theology and broad liturgical contours—that are important for students:

1. The skills of presidency, i.e., embodying the meaning of the meal in both word and action, in vesture, posture, gesture, and so on.

2. The selection or adaptation or composition of the words that surround the meal itself.[49]

3. The logistical details and ritual significance of the manner of celebrating the ritual itself, the distribution of the elements (i.e., in circles around a table, in rows coming forward, in pews passing plates, etc.)

47. Personal interview, August 22, 2008.

48. Personal interview, October 22, 2008.

49. So, for example, at one Reformed seminary, students will study commonly used prayers for their structure and theological emphases. As part of an assignment in the basic worship class, they will compile a prayerbook of their own including a Great Prayer of their own composition modeled on those they have studied.

Chapel

One of the central difficulties in studying these sorts of "practice" details in a course is the tension students may experience between what is taught in the classroom and what is modeled in the sanctuary. In some places these are very congruent—we pray what we teach, and we teach what we pray. In others, it is less so. Says one professor, "The basic pedagogical challenge is that worship in the chapel speaks much louder than anything I can say in class."[50]

Bishop Alexander outlines four theoretical models for seminary worship that define a range for balancing the pedagogical and devotional purposes of community worship. They are not comprehensive, nor mutually exclusive—no seminary's worship practices are to be circumscribed by one of these models. They do, however, offer a helpful starting point for thinking about the purposes of community worship, especially with regard to the Meal.

The first model is a *Pedagogical* one. It emphasizes the seminary chapel as a "liturgics laboratory," an extension of the academic program. Writes Alexander, "Liturgical planning, variously organized, becomes the focus of the chapel's life."[51] We see this impulse at work in schools where students take a substantial role in the preparation of the community's worship. At some Episcopalian and Lutheran schools, for example, worship for an entire week is planned by a committee made of a faculty member, a senior student (who chairs the committee), a middler student, and a junior observer. At Yale Divinity School, the educational impulse is extended beyond those who participate in preparation—*all* who come to worship are invited to learn something about what they are doing and why. To that end, the worship director prepares a short but rich "Reader" each week. It is available for all students, and includes in it "articles about the background of practices to be used in the upcoming week and the reasons for adaptations for ecumenical purposes, where relevant."[52]

The second model Alexander calls *Institutional.* It is characterized by stability and predictability. The approach here is not so much to work on the liturgy as to allow the liturgy to work on the institution and its

---

50. Personal interview, October 22, 2008.

51. Alexander, "Chapel Worship," 17.

52. Personal correspondence, August 8, 2008.

people.[53] Alexander writes: "This model is almost always strong in those institutions that consider common worship and liturgical formation as essential elements of their institutional identity . . . "[54] One can see this approach in one professor's comments about worship at her institution: "We have struggled as a school to articulate to ATS (and to others) why we spend so much time in chapel. This is both the real worship of a real community, and it is the heart of what we do as a seminary . . . It is the primary means of spiritual and ministerial formation."[55] This model is at work at schools where lengthy customaries set forth not only "standard" practice, but also the local practices surrounding the table.

This approach is also part of the institutional DNA at one Reformed school where Eucharist is celebrated every Friday. While supervised students plan and lead daily prayer Monday through Thursday, faculty members are responsible for preparing Friday's Eucharistic service. They employ a fixed liturgy that has enough flexibility for seasonal and thematic variation, and enough stability and predictability that it can work its way into minds and hearts of those in the community, fostering a familiarity and affection for it. Since most students at this school come from backgrounds where weekly celebration is not the norm, the Friday Eucharist has a profound effect, shaping them to value the Lord's Supper deeply. This is a conscious institutional effort to reverse a denominational trend and to produce congregations that produce students in another generation who love the presence of Christ in the Lord's Supper as deeply as the faculty and administration do.

A third model Alexander discusses is the *Parish* model. This paradigm is found in desire for seminary chapel to replicate what is happening in the worship of the congregations sending and calling a seminary's students. The interest in *liturgical* formation is not as strong here as the interest in *spiritual* formation through a comforting exercise of corporate devotion. So, for example, when the All-Seminary chapel at Fuller Theological Seminary employs a songset-sermon-songset ordo, interspersed with prayer and scripture reading, it is using a liturgical formula very familiar to most of its students, and to the congregations from which they came and to which they will be sent.

53. Or, perhaps more accurately, to allow God to work *through* the liturgy on the people.

54. Alexander, "Chapel Worship," 11.

55. Personal interview, August 22, 2008

Alexander does not give this model much detail in description, and while it seems to me that some seminaries might recognize this model in what they do, at least on some days, it would be a difficult thing to do with any intentionality. Even seminaries dominated by a denominational tradition find remarkable variety in the particular parish experiences their incoming students bring to the table. It is hard to see what sort of replication would be sought. Furthermore, a key question to address in the use of this model is whether seminaries seek to replicate on campus the *actual* worship of the congregations in their constituencies, or whether they replicate a *past paradigm* of worship. Though we cannot know with certainty, it seems wise to anticipate changes coming down the cultural pike, and prepare students not for the church they know, but for the church they will likely have.

Alexander calls his final model the *Worship Leader* model. This approach values variety, creativity, and student planning and leading—and perhaps from time to time, failing, which also has important pedagogical purposes. This approach is much more a part of the mix at ecumenical and inter- and non-denominational seminaries. In these places, diversity is especially valued and it is important that no particular voice be dominant. This impulse is evident, for instance, at one ecumenical school where individual students or student groups, faculty, or administrative departments can all sign up to plan and lead chapel. The parameters are wide open, except that there is a time limit, and a request to use the lectionary.[56] Though the participation of the congregation at such services can be high, it can also be quite low, if a particular approach is put forth in a presentational rather than an invitational way. So, for instance, at one Presbyterian school, during the celebration of the Lord's Supper, there are some faculty who prefer the elements be distributed via coming forward for intinction. Others prefer individual cups and bread squares to be passed in the pews. Demonstrating this variety is pedagogically helpful, especially when faculty explain plainly *why* the liturgy is taking a particular form. On the other hand, it is hard for students exposed to a mild polemic in the midst of a Eucharistic prayer not to pick up on a bit of underlying antagonism that may undercut the union of the Table everything else is meant to express.[57]

56. Personal interview, October 22, 2008.
57. Personal interview, October 10, 2008.

Conclusion

Seminary students will learn about the Lord's Supper from multiple sources: from a professor and peers in classroom discussion, from the regular repetition or thoughtful exploration modeled in community worship—and also from the churches in which they grew up, in which they serve, and to which they will be sent. Not all of these sources need speak univocally, and each has particular pedagogical strengths. The inherent inclination of the church is to define and reinforce boundaries, to pass on traditions and practices, to safeguard the unity of the body by institutional oversight. The academy, on the other hand, while it also passes on knowledge, is often in the business of challenging boundaries.

While it is confusing for students when one pedagogical source undermines another, the seminary can be a remarkable place where these two impulses at the heart of the seminary enterprise—educational and ecclesial—exist in a creative and stimulating tension. It may be that the next generation of seminary students will know a rich and intentional education in the practice of the Lord's Supper, informed by careful study in the classroom, thoughtful practice in the parish, and the unifying presence of Christ in the seminary chapel.

Appendix

Questions to Prompt Conversation

The following questions are offered merely as a conversational starting place. They may help seminary instructors, students, and administrators to have a conversation about the Meal Christ instituted—how it is both taught and how it is celebrated within the community.

Narratives

It may be helpful to begin a conversation by having participants share *narratives* about the community's celebration of the sacrament/ordinance. This helps people to be engaged on a more personal rather than abstract level. Such stories, when told honestly and heard with empathy, may disclose important but previously unarticulated theological assumptions, or help to identify a community's particular gifts and challenges. Here are some possible ways to begin:

1. What was the most meaningful experience around the Table in your memory? and why was it so?

2. What was the most disastrous experience around the Table in your memory? and why was it so?

Theological Meanings of the Meal

Combining ecumenical scholar Jim White's treatment of the Sacrament,[58] and the relevant material from the ecumenical document *Baptism, Eucharist, and Ministry*[59] yields the following list of common biblical metaphors or meaning systems for understanding the Meal Christ instituted. The list is not comprehensive, but suggestive, as the meanings overlap and intertwine. Each will be important for nearly any Christian community, though some may be more important than others—either by design or

58. See especially White, *Introduction*, 248–59.

59. *Baptism, Eucharist, and Ministry*.

by accident. How should these commonly held meanings for the Meal inform our pedagogy and practice as an institution of ministerial formation and theological education?

Thanksgiving to the Father (*eucharista*—a proclamation and celebration of God's work, an offering of gifts and lives)

Memorial of Christ (*anamnesis*, a present-making commemoration of Christ's work on behalf of those he came to save)

Invocation of the Spirit (*epiklesis*—a recognition of the Spirit's role in the meal being what God promises it to be)

Communion of the Faithful (*koinonia*—union with the Body of Christ, the Church)

The Mystery of the **Presence** of Christ at the feast (understood in many different ways by different Christian traditions)

Meal of the Kingdom (eschatological anticipation, nourishment for discipleship and mission)

Sacrifice of Christ (memorialized in the meal) and of our own praise and gifts (offered in gratitude and obedience).

1. If this list helps us to see what the supper means for Christians generally and ecumenically, what do these pieces tell us about what it means for us to celebrate it here in *this* community?

2. What do these meanings tell us about how we ought to *practice* the meal as a community?

3. What do they tell us about how we ought to *teach* it as a community to those who will become liturgical leaders?

Polity

Each seminary will approach these questions differently, taking into account the nature of the community, its denominational affiliation, etc. But here are some basic questions to identify places of congruence and incongruence:

1. With which of Newbegin's three "Great Christian Communities"—Evangelical, Sacramental, Pentecostal—does your own seminary community primarily identify? What are the ecclesial implications of that identification? Does your community also have eschatological and missional dimensions? How are they expressed in your celebrations of the Meal?

2. Are there particular principals that guide your celebration of the Meal? Are these principals articulated anywhere? Are they commonly used/do they actually guide practice?

3. Who may fittingly preside at the Table? Who may assist? Who may come to the Table? Are these understandings apparent to those who are asked to lead? To students? To visitors?

Pedagogy

1. What pedagogical challenges do you face in shaping the next generation's liturgical leaders?

2. Are there opportunities for students to be shaped by both experimentation (success/failure and reflection on practice) as well as the modeling of best practices? Think in terms of:

   a. The manner of celebrating the ritual itself (in circles around a table, in rows coming forward, in pews passing plates, etc.)

   b. The skills of presidency—embodying the meaning of the meal in both word and action

   c. The selection or adaptation or composition of the words that surround the meal itself

3. What is the relationship between the classroom, the chapel, and the local church? Do they work in concert or at cross-purposes? How can these relationships be improved?

Works Cited

Aleshire, Daniel. *Earthen Vessels: Hopeful Reflections on the Work and Future of Theological Schools*. Grand Rapids: Eerdmans, 2008.

Alexander, Neil. "Chapel Worship and Liturgical Formation in Episcopal Seminaries." Unpublished paper delivered at the North American Academy of Liturgy, 2006.

Anderson, Ron. "Worship and Theological Education." *Theological Education* 39.1 (2003) 117–30.

Baptism, Eucharist, and Ministry. Faith & Order Paper No. 111. Geneva: World Council of Churches, 1982.

Berkhof, Louis. *Systematic Theology.* Grand Rapids: Eerdmans, 1939.

Columbia Theological Seminary. Faculty. "Planning Chapel Worship at Columbia Theological Seminary: Guidelines, Requirements, and Recommendations." Decatur, GA: revised faculty document, April 2008.

Divinity School of the Pacific. *Customary* Privately published. n.d.

Eisner, Elliot W. *The Educational Imagination: On the Design and Evaluation of School Programs.* Third ed. Upper Saddle River, NJ: Prentice Hall, 2002.

Evangelical Church in America, *Renewing Worship, Vol. 2: Principles for Worship,* Augsburg, 2002.

Foster, Charles R., Lisa E. Dahill, Lawrence A. Goleman, and Barbara Wang Tolentino. *Educating Clergy: Teaching Practices and Pastoral Imagination.* The Carnegie Foundation for the Achievement of Teachers: Preparation for Professions. San Francisco: Jossey-Bass, 2006.

Jones, L. Gregory, and Stephanie Paulsell, editors. *The Scope of Our Art: The Vocation of the Theological Teacher.* Grand Rapids: Eerdmans, 2002.

Miles, Sara. *Take This Bread: A Radical Conversion.* New York: Ballantine, 2007.

Mouw, Richard. "The Seminary, the Church, and the Academy." *Calvin Theological Journal* 33 (1988) 457–68.

Murphy, Debra Dean. *Teaching that Transforms: Worship as the Heart of Christian Education* Grand Rapids: Brazos, 2004.

Newbigin, Lesslie. *The Household of God: Lectures on the Nature of the Church.* London: SCM, 1953.

Philips Theological Seminary. Faculty. "PTS Worship Guidelines." Tulsa, OK: unpublished, 2003.

Presbyterian Church (U.S.A.). Theology and Worship Ministry Unit. *Book of Common Worship.* Louisville: Westminster John Knox, 1993.

White, James F. *Introduction to Christian Worship.* Nashville: Abingdon, 1980.

9

Worship and Formation for Ministry

E. BYRON ANDERSON

In general, the conflicts that so often find their expression in seminary chapels tend to focus on two interrelated issues—the content of worship and the place of worship in a theological curriculum.[1] In contrast to the seminary classroom where course content is directly related to the course's place in the curriculum, the content of what happens in the seminary chapel has a more ambiguous relationship to the curriculum. In schools with strong denominational identities and similarly strong liturgical traditions, the seminary chapel plays a central role in theological and pastoral formation. Here, generally, worship has both a central place in the life of the seminary community, and a well-articulated place in the theological curriculum. Conflicts about content are muted (though never absent or silenced) by normative traditions into which the students are to be formed. In schools whose denominational identity (or lack thereof) does not provide a determinative role in the shape and practice of worship or whose liturgical traditions are marked by greater freedom from particular patterns and practices, and in schools with more diverse theological and denominational student bodies, the chapel is as likely to have a strong and visible place in the community's life as it is to be relegated to the margins as "extra-curricular," available for those "who like that kind of thing."[2] Especially when seen as an extra-curricular activity,

1. Portions of this first section are adapted from my article "Worship and Theological Education."

2. Examples of these models are discussed in Foster, Dahill, Goleman, and Tolentino, *Educating Clergy*, 276–80.

the chapel—communal worship—has little place in the curriculum. As will be clear in what follows, it should have a central and well-articulated place in the curriculum.

The changing character of student bodies over the past generation has also had an effect on the content and place of worship. While it is, or was, far easier to think about the formative character of communal liturgical life when the student body is largely full-time and in residence, the growing number of part-time commuter students has made planning, scheduling and participation in communal worship difficult. Communal worship from which students are absent can hardly be a formative part of the theological curriculum. Yet students absent themselves from the worship life of the seminary, either because it is optional or because it does not fit their schedule. They do not sense that the seminary chapel—or even the worship life of the local church—has any role to play in their pastoral formation and do not see their absence from worship in the seminary as an obstacle to their enrollment in course work.

This lack of concern about participation in the seminary chapel probably should not surprise us. Many of the conflicts about the content and place of worship in the theological curriculum, as well as student decisions to absent themselves from worship, arise from a shared cultural expectation that emphasizes an *expressive* rather than *formative* character of worship, an expectation that finds expression across many denominational and liturgical traditions. For students this often means that worship should express "my" faith and belief. Those seven dreadful words that pastors hate to hear—*"We've never done it that way before"*—are enacted by seminarians not only as "That's not the way my tradition does it" but, with increasing frequency, as "That's not the way I want to do it."[3] The response to these expressive expectations in some schools often takes the form of

---

3. Nathan Mitchell notes that the various relationships students negotiate in seminary occur "in a 'tribal village' atmosphere where competition and scrutiny are intensified. The tribal village quickly becomes guerilla theatre, with everyone participating as both actor and critic." In such a context, Mitchell writes, "Worship is judged successful when it 'contributes to my personal growth' or when it 'offers me insight into myself'" (Mitchell, "Teaching Worship," 323). Although Mitchell wrote these words in 1981, they continue to reflect the reality of many protestant seminaries today. Thomas Troeger and Carol Doran, in their discussion about the conflicts around music in worship, encourage the church to find ways to worship that draw "on the best of what each tribe has to offer without reinforcing the fragmentation and the struggle for domination that characterizes our culture" (Troeger and Doran, *Trouble at the Table*, 16).

a worship program that emphasizes a variety of experiences and expressions to which students may be exposed, from which they may sample, and in which they may experiment. Students and faculty members are thus presented with a "smorgasbord" of liturgical experiences—a little of something for everyone according to taste, temperament, or desire. Such variation permits the seminary chapel to be a place of instruction, comparable perhaps to an introductory survey course in Christian theology, or a place of artistic experimentation, comparable perhaps to an artist's workshop or an open performance venue. The chapel thus provides a place in which to survey the varieties of piety and worship traditions represented in the student body, offer opportunities to explore liturgical possibilities outside of such traditions, and invite considerable attention to the place of the arts in Christian worship. Rarely, however, does such a program suggest that the seminary chapel has a central or carefully articulated place in a curriculum intent on preparing persons for pastoral leadership. To the contrary, it enacts a three-fold "curriculum", generally implicit, of individualism, theological and ethnic segregation, and consumerism.

First, free to pick and choose among the options, students often prefer a worship tradition most like themselves and from which they believe they will most likely "get" something. Such liturgical self-selection may function as a form of self-care for those who, even in the first years of seminary, are already providing regular worship leadership in the local church, but nothing in this approach challenges the rupture of community and the individualism it represents.

Second, while the seminary community benefits by engaging the varied liturgical practices reflected in many ethnic traditions and in the prayer book, sacramental, preaching, charismatic, formal, traditional, or contemporary traditions that find a place in the schedule, the optional nature of worship perpetuates a kind of ethnic, liturgical, theological segregation.[4] There is little understanding that choosing to worship together, even when it is not from one's own tradition, invites an encounter with the otherness of one's neighbors as well as the Transcendent Other. Nor is there an understanding that choosing not to worship together is itself a reflection of the lack of community about which students and faculty so

4. Foster, Dahill, Goleman, and Tolentino encourage us to ask how much diversity in conducive to pastoral formation, how much is needed to stretch students' imaginations, how much starts to limit formation, and what kinds of diversities are not beneficial for pastoral formation (*Educating Clergy,* 278).

often complain.[5] Susan Wood writes, "What distinguishes liturgical prayer from other prayer of the church is that it is a corporate gesture of praise of God neither originating from nor directed toward any one individual or group in the church. It is the church as church glorifying God."[6] When we demythologize all ethnocentric expressions of the Christian faith, as Albert Pero argues we must do, we "may discover that the essence of the Christian faith not only ultimately transcends the ethnocentric culture of white people, but that of blacks as well."[7] We do not gather to worship for our own sake. "The seminary community gathers together in God's name for the sake of the world to which it ministers."[8] When we gather to worship in black or in white, we perpetuate the segregation that is present in our churches as well as in our civic communities. When we find ways to gather in corporate worship that move beyond such divisions, we provide a witness to the Church and form leaders for a more inclusive and diverse church.

Third, communal worship offered as an extra-curricular and optional activity takes on the character of a service to the student as consumer. The chapel comes to be seen as part of "student services" rather than as part of the theological curriculum. Unfortunately, seminarian consumers act no differently than those they are called to serve. Catechized by consumerism, students are defined by what they produce, purchase, and consume rather than by the practices through which they seek, love, and glorify God.[9] The seminarian/pastor, like many people in the local church, seeks liturgical forms that best fit his or her personal spirituality, psychological history, and experience and avoids those that do not so fit.

Given the difficulties many seminaries face when addressing the worship life of the community, why should we worry about it? Worship in the seminary is an antiquated remnant of a monastic mode of formation,

---

5. J. Robert Nelson suggested that the "daily rhythm of chapel worship, godly learning, and communal living" is a "beatific public vision" that is "not only inaccurate but pathetic and ludicrous." He continued, "Who of us has not heard *ad nauseum* the continual complaint about the lack of Christian community among students and faculty alike." What may surprise some is that this was not written recently; Nelson provided these comments in the first issue of *Theological Education* in 1964 (see Nelson, "Seminary.")

6. Wood, "Participatory Knowledge," 32

7. Pero, "Worship and Theology," 230

8. Duke, "Seminary Worship," 44.

9. Waddell, "Teaching," 121.

so why not leave worship to local congregations and let the seminary get on with the "real" work of theological education? Because, to give a brief answer here, we have discovered that preparation for pastoral leadership is not only about *information* as gained in the classroom and study, but also about *formation* through liturgy, prayer, and other spiritual disciplines.

A historical review of the relationship between worship and formation would demonstrate a long integral relationship between them. In some cases, we would be hard pressed to see where they were separate activities. Worship as prayer, scripture, and interpretation through preaching and teaching, was the church's primary mode of formation and instruction. The sanctuary was the classroom. Worship and formation in the context of and through worship served as a primary strategy for the socialization of persons into a moral and sacramental way of life, a way that was counter-cultural and life-endangering. When this socialization turned more toward the mainstream of culture it gave rise, in part, to the flight to desert and monastery where the school of the church could be enacted in life together and in worship and prayer. And, when it later encountered the culture of rationalism, sanctuary and classroom seemed to be permanently separated from one another.

In the late Twentieth century, seminaries and churches found a renewed awareness and expectation that corporate worship could and should be part of the formational theological curriculum, that it had a distinctive role to play in the formation of persons for pastoral leadership. In 1964 J. Robert Nelson asked if we had "simply cherished an inappropriate ideal of worship," to which he responded by arguing "the chapel should surely inform the academy with the viewpoint, attitude, and appreciation of what is valid and valuable in the curriculum." "The foremost element of seminary education," he argues, "is the discovery of the full dimensions of Christian worship…both Word and Sacrament, both liturgy and life, both confession of sin and confession of faith, both doxology and self-sacrifice, both the heart and the head."[10] Robert Duke, addressing the same question a year after Nelson, argued "It is possible to think theologically with attention paid to theology's central affirmation expressed in worship. It is not possible, however, to live theologically unless that reflecting, unfolding, and developing faith is rooted in thanksgiving, confession, and

---

10. Nelson, "Seminary," 57, 59.

forgiveness."[11] Sallie McFague Teselle, a decade later, argued that the formational task of theological education sets it "within the context of church and the faith. The *sine qua non* of such formation is a worshipping community.... The context for our intellectual work must be that of worship, or we deny our basic loyalty."[12] John Westerhoff, writing primarily about the work of religious education in the local congregation, similarly argues, "because we have failed to understand the importance of unity between our ritual and educational endeavors we have both improperly prepared persons for meaningful participation in the faith community's ceremonial life and continued to encourage people to mindlessly participate in rituals which are often antithetical to Christian faith."[13] Marjorie Procter-Smith, writing another decade after McFague and Westerhoff, asked "If ministers-in-training do not learn the disciplines of prayer and worship as they learn their Bible and systematic theology, when will they learn it?"[14] Most recently, L. Gregory Jones has argued that the process of forming students for ministerial leadership requires more attention "to the character and quality of seminary-sponsored worship."[15] Each writer, all from within mainline protestant traditions, agrees that worship in the seminary is part of the formational and curricular program of theological education.

Yet, because we have emphasized the expressive over the formative role of corporate worship, the chapel continues to have an ambivalent place in the theological curriculum. We may be explicitly aware of how we express our faith in worship, but we are not generally aware of worship's formative power. We have not recognized that worship is itself a primary formative practice. Rebecca Chopp describes such practices as "socially shared forms of behavior that mediate between what are often

11. Ibid.

12. McFague, 89. James White concludes his 1980 review of the teaching of worship in North American seminaries with similar words: "Worship is a basic art of the whole personal being of all in Christian ministry, both ordained and lay. The classroom has to be balanced by the chapel. A strong worship life in the seminary is as basic as a good library in equipping men and women for ministry" ("The Teaching of Worship," 318). Unfortunately, White's research did not include attention to the specific liturgical structures and practices of these seminaries.

13. Westerhoff, "Liturgical Imperative," 97.

14. Procter-Smith, "Daily Worship," 125.

15. Jones, "Beliefs," 203.

called subjective and objective dimensions,"[16] through which we develop common languages and processes of interpretation. This is to say that in worship persons and communities are formed intentionally and unintentionally in particular understandings of self, church and God. In worship we learn a Christian "grammar" through which we interpret our relationships to God and neighbor. What we do in and as we worship—what and how we sing, the language of our prayer, how we participate in prayer, who and what we pray for, the roles played by the community and by leaders in worship, the ways in which scripture is read and interpreted— is teaching us a way of being together as community and preparing us for a way of being in the church and world. When our language is exclusive, when the congregation is made to be passive observers and listeners, when children are neither seen nor heard, when prayer never extends beyond the immediate concerns of the congregation, worship is forming an exclusive, passive, isolated adult community. When our language is inclusive of human difference, when the congregation's voice is heard in prayer and song, when persons of all ages and abilities are welcomed in worship leadership, when prayer extends to the suffering of the world, worship is becoming a polyphonic expression of life in God and a means for our participation in the mission of Jesus Christ in the world.

As we can say of the Christian life as a whole, self-expression in praise of God is a sign of the grace-filled life. But Christian self-expression requires formation in the way of discipleship. Corporate worship, like personal devotion, intellectual inquiry, and ethical action, is part of the Christian *askesis*, the disciplined training—the traditioning—of persons for the Christian life and a means of inhabiting and imagining that life.[17] Clearly, worship in the seminary must enable both expression and formation. But the work of theological education—and therefore of communal worship in the context of theological education—is first and foremost about formation for leadership in the church. Such formation does not occur primarily by talking about worship but by engaging in common liturgical action embodied and enacted in liturgical prayer, song, preach-

16. Chopp, *Saving Work*, 15.

17. Albert Pero challenges notions that free church worship traditions, especially those within the Black community are unritualized. He argues that in many contexts, spontaneity is ritualized, making it possible to predict "who will be spontaneous, when, and how . . . as with all gifts of the Spirit, there is an implicit order" ("Worship and Theology," 243).

ing, and sacrament.[18] The seminary chapel and the corporate worship enacted there provide a place and occasion for formation in the practiced liturgical life of a community. A pastoral leader is not equipped to lead Christian worship unless he or she has been formed in the patterns and practices of Christian worship. And, it is only in and through worship we learn to inhabit the practice of worship. The disciplines of corporate worship and theological study are therefore companion formative practices of the seminary through which new pastoral leaders learn to inhabit, imagine and embody the Christian tradition.

Traditioning

One of the things accomplished in the chapel is the traditioning of pastoral leaders in the forms and actions of prayer and sacrament, in the language of praise and lament, and in the church's way of being community. The ongoing conflicts between "contemporary" and "traditional" worship have made more difficult any discussion of tradition in regard to liturgical formation. Not only do we fail to see that everything that is "contemporary" is transient, passing by, potentially left behind, but we also confuse tradition with what is "traditional." Tradition is not, much as we have come to think of it, primarily about the past. It is the past reaching through the present to shape a future in which all may have life (John 3:16–17). It is handing on and receiving a way of life. Edward Shils describes tradition as the ways in which institutions, beliefs, and practices of earlier times "live forward into the present," creating "a consensus between the living and the dead" that, from the beginning, has exercised processes of selection, adaptation, and interpretation.[19] Even the tradition we call Scripture emerged from such a process in the church. And, as appears in various ways throughout the New Testament, but more clearly in the history of the church in its first centuries, the content of the apostolic tradition was not first a tradition of dogmatic theology but of liturgical

18. See, for example, the Roman Catholic Instruction on Liturgical Formation in Seminaries: Introduction, paragraph a.2: "All genuine liturgical formation involves not only doctrine but also practice. This practice, as a 'mystagogical' formation, is obtained first and mainly through the very liturgical life of the students into which they are daily most deeply initiated through liturgical actions celebrated in common" (www.ewtn.com/library/CURIA/CCESEMS.HTM) accessed September 15, 2009.

19. Shils, *Tradition*, 168.

theology, not first a tradition of creed but of the rule of prayer through which we bless and thank God for salvation and redemption, petition God on behalf of the world, and lament with God over the condition of our world.[20] Prayer and liturgical practice lead us to questions of belief and theological explanation. Tradition is about knowing how to live today, not about how others lived long ago, how to embody the church's beliefs in our own place and time.

Where exaltation of the contemporary forces us to rely on our own meager resources, constantly reinventing everything in our own image, and traditionalism attempts to freeze the church in time, traditioning is about the future. Tradition and traditioning, are not (impossible) replications of some moment in history but the full reception of a gift that continues to have generative and transformative power for our life together as a Christian people. This, in part, is what the apostle Paul offered the Corinthians when he said to them "what I received from the Lord, I handed on to you. . . ." Rather than establishing a liturgical text, Paul is using the church's liturgical tradition to critique the present life of the Corinthian community and to reshape their future relationships. The convergence in worship patterns that has accompanied the ecumenical liturgical movement of the Twentieth century, imperfect as these patterns may be, and which are taught in many of our classrooms and enacted in many of our chapels, provide liturgical examples of and the means by which to respect the church's tradition *and* to help that tradition speak in our own day. They intend the same future orientation.

Jeremy Begbie, in one of his explorations of the intersection of music and theology, describes the traditioning process this way:

> I become an apprentice to a tradition provided by others, a whole set of tried and tested skills, an accumulated knowledge with a very long history. I learn standards of excellence; I submit my choices, preferences and tastes to standards already held and tested by others. I learn what is considered 'musical' and 'unmusical,' what counts as good phrasing and poor phrasing, what makes a composer 'great' rather than mediocre. In time, I may question this stream of convention and wisdom, modify it, enlarge, dispute, and even reject some of it. But I cannot ignore it.[21]

20. Pelikan, *Vindication of Tradition*, 29.
21. Begbie, *Resounding Truth*, 43.

Through the traditioning of corporate worship, we receive what the Church has handed on and attempt to live faithfully out of this gift, to practice and play the "music" of the liturgy in such a way that we join our music with that of the saints and angels. Such faithful practice and play enables us some days to hear echoes of an earlier time, connecting us to our histories, and some days to hear melodies and harmonies that are more modern than we care to hear, challenging the comfort of our present. In each case, we are confronted by a melody in our own time and place and offered an invitation to participate in its music. Worship thus provides a context in which we absorb—and perhaps model—a tradition "so that the language of the tradition becomes one's own, so that one can speak it, and not only in traditional terms."[22]

Traditioning in the seminary chapel does not occur by talking about worship, as we might in the classroom, but in worshiping. As French theologian Louis-Marie Chauvet argues, "one does not *tell* the liturgy; one liturgically tells the story that one memorializes. The 'liturgification' [as he calls it] of the telling of stories about the early times is the best way to manifest their continuing foundational role in the identity of Israel [and the church]."[23] Means of grace, whether we call them sacraments or ordinances, he writes, "allow us to *see* what is said in the letter of the scriptures [echoing Luther's sense of sacrament as "visible word"], to *live* what is said because they leave on the social body of the church, and on the body of each person, a mark that becomes a command to make what is said real in everyday life."[24] Not only does it leave a mark, but it takes shape in our very bones, as James Fowler suggests as he describes the shape of faith development: "with liturgy we deal with the kinesthetics of faith. Through the teaching power of sacramental worship faith gets into our bodies and bone marrow."[25]

When we separate the traditioning process of the classroom from that of the chapel, and when we emphasize the expressive over formative role of worship, not only do we suggest that worship is the place of expression and emotion and the classroom the place of information and intellect, but we also overlook the necessary incarnational character of Christian formation, the active engagement of body, mind, and heart

22. McFague, "Between Athens and Jerusalem," 90.

23. Chauvet, *Symbol and Sacrament*, 194.

24. Ibid., 226

25. Fowler, *Weaving the New Creation*, 181.

through which our lives are "patterned" to see the world and to take our place in it as Christian people. Formation by our participation in worship, as John Westerhoff argues, is a form of apprenticeship that binds us (*religare*) to a tradition.[26] We do learn doctrine in the classroom, but we begin that long doctrinal formation "by participating in a liturgical community that symbolically shares and celebrates its sacred narrative."[27]

The process of traditioning offered through the seminary chapel thus leads us away from "what I want" to what the church knows and needs from us. We are led from knowledge *about* worship to a way of worshipful being in the midst of others. We begin to "liturgify" a way of being in the world, in community, and in the church and begin to inhabit a worldview and a particular set of relationships—both incarnate and transcendent.

Inhabiting

If corporate worship is a process of traditioning that enables a set of patterns, practices, and beliefs to take root in our bones, we might say that it is also a process of inhabiting—both in the sense of "coming to dwell in" and "making a habit of"—those patterns, practices, and beliefs. At the same time, modern rationalism has convinced us that we can learn to worship or to act faithfully, morally, virtuously, by talking about it in explanation and commentary. This is the dominant mode of theological education. But as already noted earlier, we can learn such things in this way no more readily than we learn to love by reading about it. In loving and being loved we learn to be loving persons, in acting morally we learn to be moral persons; in worshiping we learn to be a worshiping people. We learn these things by putting on the habit of loving, acting morally, and worshiping. In explanation and commentary—things necessary for our growth—we become primarily theoreticians rather than practitioners of the Christian life, we can know *about* worship and liturgical leadership but not be able to inhabit it.

Similarly, our Protestant suspicion and supposed rejection of habit ("supposed" because our church lives are filled with good and bad habits,

26. Westerhoff, "Formative Nature," 147.

27. Westerhoff, "Formative Nature," 150. George Rupp argues similarly "shared commitment through common tasks does not depend on particular ethnic or geographical qualifications" ("Communities of Collaboration," 202).

liturgical and otherwise), joined to our inclination to talk about every-thing, often blinds us to the ways in which the practice of the Christian faith in our bodies, minds, and hearts truly and really requires the devel-opment of habit and ritual. As Martin Connell recently observed, "there is a general antipathy toward the influence of religious rituals on personal formation and decision-making...even though US citizens go to church in much higher proportions than do citizens of any other nation in the Western world, the influence of the ritual behavior of church-going on those who attend seems to be negligible, at least by their confessions."[28]

Chauvet's concern for "liturgification" of the telling of stories pro-vides a link between traditioning and inhabiting, a process and link de-scribed well by Minnesota essayist Paul Gruchow. In a 1995 collection entitled *Grass Roots: The Universe of Home*, Gruchow reflected on the importance of place and home, recounting how, after his mother's death, his family asked of each other "Do you remember the day . . . ? Do you remember the time when . . . ? Do you remember how mother . . . ?" Gruchow wrote,

> To tell what we remember, and to keep on telling it, is to keep the past alive in the present. Should we not do so, we could not know, in the deepest sense, how to inhabit a place. To inhabit a place means literally to have made it a habit, to have made it the custom and ordinary practice of our lives, to have learned how to wear a place like a familiar garment, like the garments of sanctity that nuns wore. The word habit, in its now dim original form meant to own. We own places not because we possess the deeds to them, but because they have entered the continuum of our lives. What is strange to us—unfamiliar [and uninhabited]—can never be home.[29]

Where traditioning is "keeping the past alive in the present", inhabiting is making that past live in ourselves. We inhabit not only places, but also identities and relationships. As we do so, we begin to find a sense of com-fort in our selves, in the roles we are called to play, and in the presence of those we love and who love us. Traditioning, if it is to be more than an intellectual exercise, must have the character of inhabiting, of learning to wear the tradition like a familiar garment. Inhabiting comes only in re-peated practice over time, as we live into and dwell in, practices and roles.

28. Connell, "Aversion to Ritual," 386.
29. Gruchow, *Grass Roots*, 6.

Inhabiting is the process of accepting something not only intellectually but also existentially. It is the way we pour ourselves into something and assimilate it as part of our existence.[30] It is the way in which we giving ourselves over to something and take that same thing into ourselves. As Michael Polanyi argues, religious ritual "is potentially the highest degree of indwelling that is conceivable. For ritual comprises a sequence of things to be said and gestures to be made which involve the whole body and alert our whole existence. Anyone sincerely saying and doing these things in a place of worship could not fail to be completely absorbed in them [and] would be partaking devoutly in religious life."[31]

Sometimes we are not aware of the extent to which we have inhabited a particular tradition. We only discover the habits of our bodies when confronted with practices that are new to us, or which seem to belong to others. Seminarians experience this in schools of their own denominations as well as in ecumenical settings. They discover that not everyone shapes and enacts worship the way their local churches do. When we say "I don't bow or kneel" or "I don't clap or dance" we are giving voice to rules that are written not only in our minds, but also in our bodies, in our muscles and our bones. We also discover that though "I" may bow or kneel, but this community does not, I will soon no longer bow or kneel. When there is an argument between mind and body, bodies more often win (which is why ritual practices are both so powerful and potentially dangerous). Lack of attention to our bodies is, in part, why celebrations of the "joyful feast" of the Lord's Supper so often seems like a funeral service.

When Chauvet argues that "Christian faith cannot survive without religion, and therefore without rites"[32] he is claiming that faith is not about something primarily in our heads, in our intellects—although it does need careful thought, but about practices, patterns of intentional action repeated over time, rituals that we undertake in order to cultivate and nurture the habits of holy living. As Gerard Lukken notes, "Even where people wish to free themselves of ritual, there quickly arise other latent but established patterns of action."[33] As Christian people, we need

30. Polanyi, *Personal Knowledge*, 59.

31. Ibid., 198.

32. Chauvet, *Symbol and Sacrament*, 337.

33. Lukken, *Rituals in Abundance*, 45.

the habits and rituals that are so central to Christian worship in prayer-book and non-prayerbook traditions alike. Chauvet rather graphically challenges our protestant resistance to ritual when he argues that the "demon of ritualism one pretends to expel returns at a gallop bringing seven others worse than himself, disguised as a dogmatism or moralism more dangerous and no less naïve than the religious 'magic' one wants to get rid of" (see Luke 11:26).[34] Our inhabited lives abhor a vacuum. If the seminary or church does not, or will not, engage us in practices of worship that shape explicitly Christian lives, that is, in practices that habituate us, enclothe us, indwell us in the Jesus tradition, then other cultural forces will gladly step in to fill the empty space. Humanity is a ritualizing organism; where rituals, traditions, and habits are missing, we will create them or seek them out in communities of practice and tradition that may be incompatible with or antithetical to the Christian faith.

On the other side of suspicion of habit and ritual we discover a kind of subconscious "mindfulness" that is present in our bodies, a way of being in our bodies that has been trained through repetition to the point that what we do now feels "natural"—that is, we now wear the habit, the practice, rather than resisting it. Such patterning in our bodies is less about ideas than about the patterning of our lives, less about learning a text than about becoming a "text", less about intellectual knowing than about knowing experientially, phenomenologically, in our bodies. But, what we learn through ritual is neither mindless nor anti-intellectual ("rote" many Protestants might say). To the contrary, Thomas Driver argues, "Its form of intelligence is more similar to that of the arts than to conceptual theology, just as…poetry is of a different order from that of philosophy or literary criticism."[35]

Knowing at this experiential level comes not by shedding habit or ritual but from deep patterning in a practice or identity, by "in-habiting" a tradition. It comes by so fully putting on the habit that it now feels so natural that we are one with it. This kind of knowledge is not what normally occupies liturgical scholars or "professional" worship leaders when the critical apparatus is in full operation or when the mechanics or choreography of a particular service or liturgical action has our attention. That is the kind of knowledge we share in the classroom. Instead, it is

34. Chavuet, *Symbol and Sacrament*, 337.
35. Driver, *Magic of Ritual*, 84.

the kind of knowledge that comes with the singular attention required when we give ourselves over, when we hand ourselves over, to prayer, song, and even play. It is the kind of knowledge that comes from a life that practices the faith one professes, from a faith written, inhabited, in our bodies as much as it is in our minds. Ellen Charry writes, "the Church has stressed participation in Christian community and practice as a way not only of reinforcing the knowledge of God but also of shaping the mind so that knowledge of the love of God fits into a life prepared to interpret it properly."[36] When worship is an extracurricular part of pastoral formation in seminary, when communal sacramental practice and prayer are optional activities on the schedule rather than part of our "natural habitat", "we lose any sense of being formed in community, participating in a tradition that allows us to act unconsciously, with ease and delight, out of a deep sense of what is natural to us and to our milieu. We are, in short, a people without 'habit', without common custom, place or dress to lend us shared meaning."[37]

Imagining

Thomas Driver, as quoted earlier, compares the kind of knowledge found and developed in worship to that of poetry. It is an apt comparison because it helps us think somewhat less about the past and present and more about how we might imagine our future. And, by combining imagining with traditioning and inhabiting, we begin to see the possibilities for the *critical* appropriation of the church's practices (in contrast to an uncritical traditionalism).[38] Critical appropriation of the church's practices means that we are attentive to what can be and what should yet be. It means we are able to see through and beyond our present practice ("the way we've always done it") to imagine what the church intended from the beginning and to see the way forward in relationship to that intent. For example, think of the strange tension between some churches' practices of "fencing" the Lord's table and the accusation against Jesus that "he ate with tax collectors and sinners" (Mt. 9:11). Or think of Paul's description of the baptized community in which there is "no longer slave or free, male and

36. Charry, *By the Renewing*, 28.
37. Lane, *Solace of Fierce Landscapes*, 10.
38. Cahalan, "Three Approaches," 85.

female" (Gal. 3:28) and the church's historical support for slavery and segregation or of its continuing pastoral and liturgical disenfranchisement of women. Standing before or around the Lord's table singing, in unison, "One bread, one body" enables us to see, hear, and know that what is happening in this liturgical moment is very different from the way of the world and that the way of the world need not be so. Being told in the classroom that we are one body does not *mean* in the same way as singing in unison as we share from a single cup and loaf of bread.

Our imagining is not only critical appropriation; it is also a form of creating and recreating. But, our creative imagining is never *ex nihilo*, creation from nothing. Our imagining is formed by experiences, relationships, practices, and traditions. As a formative place of imagining, the seminary chapel offers a place in which to foster a Christian imagination formed by the liturgical and sacramental practices, the musical repertoires, and the artistic contributions of a larger (ecumenical/catholic) community. The imagining that happens here is less about reshaping worship and more about how we understand our selves, our world, and God. This is in contrast to much of what is said about creating "contemporary worship"—in part because it has identified itself as an "anti-tradition" without awareness of the traditions that are its predecessors. The imagining we undertake in the context of worship is less about our own creativity and more about the Spirit working to recreate us. The habits and dispositions in which we are traditioned and that we come to inhabit through worship are imaginative works of the Spirit within us. And when fully inhabited they "become structures of expertise and the resources for improvisation in meeting new and unexpected challenges,"[39] this, too, is a work of the Spirit.

Good improvisation— in prayer as in art and music—is always the result of deeply inhabited patterns and practices, the result of being so deeply formed in the traditions that we are able to respond naturally, even instinctively, to new situations as they arise. It is not only a sign of our imagination but of our success in inhabiting the tradition we are attempting to "perform." The inability to improvise, to respond appropriately from within the tradition to new situations, reveals more than anything else the shallowness of formation and the lack of experience and sustained engagement with the very practices for which pastoral leaders are given responsibility.

39. Foster, Dahill, Goleman, and Tolentino, *Educating Clergy*, 27.

Craig Dykstra has especially encouraged seminaries and churches to think about how we cultivate a "pastoral imagination" that can so respond to the needs of the church and the world. He suggests that "pastoral ministry involves a distinctive imagination and subtle and complex intelligence" that cannot "be achieved or attained" but that can come only "as a gift."[40] At the same time, he also identifies the importance of study, reflection and practical knowledge "tested and developed through broad experience, struggle and sustained engagement" as well as "the clarity of mind and spirit about what it means to worship God in spirit and in truth."[41] In worship, in ordinance, sacrament, prayer and song we are provided a means by which, even through which, we can look not toward ourselves and our own needs but toward God in Christ, grasping at the mind of Christ that we might be of one mind with him, and seeking the image into which we are called to live. Charles Wesley captures this in a stanza from one of his hymns for the Lord's Supper:

> 'Tis here we look up and grasp at thy mind,
> 'tis here that we hope thine image to find;
> the means of bestowing thy gifts we embrace;
> but all things are owing to Jesus' grace.[42]

Wesley reminds us that, in the end, our traditioning is into the Tradition that is Jesus Christ, that which we are coming to inhabit—because we never perfectly inhabit—is the likeness of Christ, and that which we imagine is, finally, the image of Christ present in and for the world. For us and for our communities this is, Gordon Lathrop writes, "an utterly new way to understand the world, and so an utterly new way to conceive and thus to live our lives."[43]

Conclusion

Formation through worship is, then, an apprenticeship in the Christian life. We practice living as Christians in prayer, song, bath, and meal; we practice a new language as we hear and tell a new family story; we prac-

---

40. Dykstra, "A Way of Seeing," 28.
41. Dykstra, "A Way of Seeing," 27.
42. Wesley, "Because thou hast said."
43. Lathrop, 32.

tice a way of keeping time that has its own new year, its own days for celebration and lamentation; we practice being a people called to holy living. Formation through worship acknowledges that liturgical experience is personal and communal *experience* that we know but cannot name. While its meaning can be interpreted (mystagogy) and anticipated (instruction), that meaning cannot be communicated other than through the ritual event itself. This is why what we say, sing, and do in worship is so important.

Therefore, when we approach questions about the role of the seminary chapel in pastoral formation through questions of tradition, habit, ritual, and imagination, we also begin to rediscover the intrinsic formational and educational possibilities of worship for the church as a whole. We discover that the liturgical sacramental life of the church is perhaps even *the* primary formative and transformative practice of the church, through which we offer ourselves to God with all that we are, in which we encounter the tangible, tastable love of God for the world, and by means of which we are compelled to loving service in the world.

Liturgical theologian Aidan Kavanagh described Christian worship as the place in which and the means by which we "do the redeemed world": "In worship alone is the church gathered in the closest obvious proximity to its fundamental values, values which are always assuming stimulative form in time, space, image, word, and repeated act. The richer this stimulation is, under the criteria of the Gospel . . . the more conscious, aware, self-possessed, and vigorously operational the given church will be."[44] Worship forms and teaches, he argued, neither by analyzing, propounding propositions, or polemicizing, nor by didacticism. "It supports, forms, and nurtures by enaging people in communal acts within which the whole of rite . . . comes into motion. The liturgy cracks open radical values, invites without coercing people into them, and celebrates this living presence deep within these same values. . . . [It] does not talk *about* God, but manifests the assembly's graced union with Father, through Son, in Spirit."[45]

To enter a seminary and to enter a seminary chapel, as new seminary students and their teachers discover, is to enter a community of particular theological, social, and political practices and conversations. Because

44. Kavanagh, *On Liturgical Theology*, 62.
45. Ibid., 115–16.

worship in the seminary, as in the local church, is the most public of a community's activities, it will reflect the ways in which these practices and conversations are being worked out. If seminary-sponsored worship is part of the formational theological curriculum, as I have argued it must be, the shape and practice of what happens in the chapel will be as central to the theological curriculum as any foundational course in theology or scripture. What, after all, is more foundational to the Christian life than the praise of God?

Works Cited

Anderson, E. Byron. "Worship and Theological Education." *Theological Education* 39.1 (2003) 117–30.

Begbie, Jeremy. *Resounding Truth: Christian Wisdom in the World of Music.* Grand Rapids: Baker, 2007.

Cahalan, Kathleen. "Three Approaches to Practical Theology, Theological Education, and the Church's Ministry." *International Journal of Practical Theology* 9.1 (2005) 63–94.

Charry, Ellen, *By the Renewing of Your Minds: The Pastoral Function of Christian Doctrine* New York: Oxford, 1997.

Chauvet, Louis-Marie. *Symbol and Sacrament: A Sacramental Reinterpretation of Christian Existence.* Translated by Patrick Madigan and Madeleine Beaumont. Collegeville, MN: Liturgical, 1995.

Chopp, Rebecca. *Saving Work: Feminist Practices of Theological Education.* Philadelphia: Westminster John Knox, 1995.

Connell, Martin. "Aversion to Ritual." *Worship* 78.5 (2004) 386–404.

Driver, Tom Faw. *The Magic of Ritual: Our Need for Liberating Rites That Transform Our Lives and Our Communities.* San Francisco: HarperSanFrancisco, 1991.

Duke, Robert. "Seminary Worship." *Theological Education* 2.1 (1965) 42–46.

Dykstra, Craig. "A Way of Seeing: Imagination and the Pastoral Life." *Christian Century* 127.7 (April 8, 2008) 26–31.

Foster, Charles R., Lisa E. Dahill, Lawrence A. Goleman, and Barbara Wang Tolentino. *Educating Clergy: Teaching Practices and Pastoral Imagination.* The Carnegie Foundation for the Achievement of Teachers: Preparation for Professions. San Francisco: Jossey-Bass, 2006.

Fowler, James. *Weaving the New Creation: Stages of Faith and the Public Church.* 1991. Reprint, Eugene, OR: Wipf and Stock, 2001.

Gruchow, Paul. *Grass Roots: The Universe of Home.* Minneapolis: Milkweed, 1995.

Jones, L. Gregory. "Beliefs, Desires, Practices, and the Ends of Theological Education." In *Practicing Theology: Beliefs and Practices in Christian Life,* edited by Miroslav Volf and Dorothy Bass, 185–205. Grand Rapids: Eerdmans, 2002.

Lane, Belden C. *The Solace of Fierce Landscapes: Exploring Desert and Mountain Spirituality.* New York: Oxford University Press, 1998.

Lathrop, Gordon. *Holy Things: A Liturgical Theology.* Minneapolis: Fortress, 1993.

Lukken, Gerard. *Rituals in Abundance: Critical Reflections On The Place, Form, And Identity Of Christian Ritual In Our Culture.* Liturgia Contenda 17. Leuven: Peeters, 2005.

Kavanagh, Aidan. *On Liturgical Theology: Hale Memorial Lectures of Seabury-Western Theological Seminary, 1981.* New York: Pueblo, 1984.

McFague, Sallie. "Between Athens and Jerusalem: The Seminary in Tension." *Christian Century* 93.4 (February 4–11, 1976) 89–93.

Mitchell, Nathan. "Teaching Worship in Seminaries: A Response." *Worship* 55.4 (1981), 319–24.

Nelson, J. Robert. "Seminary: Academy and Chapel." *Theological Education* 1.1 (1964), 53–62.

Pelikan, Jaroslav. *The Vindication of Tradition: The 1983 Jefferson Lecture in the Humanities.* New Haven, CT: Yale University Press, 1984.

Pero, Albert. "Worship and Theology in the Black Context." In *Theology and the Black Experience: The Lutheran Heritage Interpreted by African and African-American Theologians,* edited by Albert Pero and Ambrose Mayo, 227–48. Minneapolis: Fortress, 1988.

Polanyi, Michael. *Personal Knowledge: Towards a Post-Critical Philosophy.* Chicago: University of Chicago Press, 1958.

Proctor Smith, Marjorie. "Daily Worship: An Instituted Means of Grace." *Christian Century* 102.5 (February 6-13, 1985), 124–25.

Rupp, George. "Communities of Collaboration: Shared Commitments/Common Tasks." In *On Community,* edited by Leroy S. Rouner, 192–208. Boston University Studies in Philosophy and Religion. Notre Dame: University of Notre Dame Press, 1991.

Shils, Edward. *Tradition.* Chicago: University of Chicago Press, 1981.

Troeger, Thomas, and Carol Doran. *Trouble at the Table: Gathering the Tribes for Worship* Nashville: Abingdon, 1992.

Waddell, Paul. "Teaching as a Ministry of Hope." In *The Scope of Our Art: The Vocation of the Theological Teacher,* edited by L. Gregory Jones and Stephanie Paulsell, 120–34. Grand Rapids: Eerdmans, 2002.

Wesley, Charles. "Because thou hast said." In *The United Methodist Hymnal,* 635. Nashville: United Methodist Publishing House, 1989.

Westerhoff, John, "The Liturgical Imperative in Religious Education." In *The Religious Education We Need: Toward the Renewal of Christian Education,* James Michael Lee, 79–94. Mishawaka, IN: Religious Education Press, 1977.

Westerhoff, John, "The Formative Nature of the Liturgy: Cultic Life and the Initiation of Children." In *Issues in the Christian Initiation of Children: Catechesis and Liturg,* edited by Kathy Brown and Frank C. Sokol, 145–62. Font and Table Series. Chicago: Liturgy Training, 1989.

White, James. "The Teaching of Worship in Seminaries in Canada and the United States." *Worship* 55.4 (1981) 304–18.

Wood, Susan. "Participatory Knowledge of God in the Liturgy." *Studia Liturgica* 29.1 (1999) 29–52.

10

Crediting Chapel:
Worship and the Theological Curriculum

SIOBHÁN GARRIGAN

One of the joys of directing the daily ecumenical worship program at Yale Divinity School is receiving emails each year from graduates relating how chapel has prepared them for their work in the communities they now serve. One of the frustrations of the job is receiving almost as many emails each year from graduates who say: "I now see why chapel is relevant and I wish I had participated in it when I was there." This phenomenon is not new, nor is it unique to Yale: theological students who shun chapel during their education often wake up to its value, with regret, once they are in the world of work.[1] My question, then, is how can we persuade students that the learning offered in chapel is something from which they will benefit when they leave (and how do we make sure that the worship programs of our theological schools are worthy of the persuasion[2])? Students come to seminary taking for granted that they will take courses in Biblical Studies and Theology, and that these will be relevant to their future career; how do we communicate the same about the learning to be had from chapel?

---

1. Jim White's survey of worship in theological education led him to comment that, "Seminary worship formation is a crucial part of the seminary experience. Unfortunately, this is rarely recognized by many students until long after they graduate and never perceived by some faculty" ("Teaching of Worship," 311).

2. Because as White also insisted, "It is hard to teach the necessity of careful planning, preparation and conduct of worship when students may be exposed daily to the opposite" (Ibid., 313).

Compounding the problem is the fact that chapel faculty often spend a great deal of energy persuading colleagues and administrators, never mind students, that their project is *part of* the curriculum of theological education. The view that chapel is "para-curricular" or "extra-curricular" (with its implicit "not really *proper* teaching-and-learning") is common despite large numbers of alumni/ae reporting its privileged place as a pedagogical site. Like many other chapel deans around the country, however, I see my work as *teaching*. It is teaching the students who attend chapel and/or the conversations we create around it, as well as the particular students who work/study in the program. These latter students work closely with the music students who minister in organ, choral conducting and congregational song leadership, under the supervision of my faculty colleague who directs chapel music, and there are at least two hours each week with everyone together in the same room, planning and evaluating together. Thus, we teach a new generation of musicians and liturgists how to work together while ministering within a diverse educational community. Good training, I think, for our congregations.

Twenty-five years ago, Leonard Sweet remarked that, "The most prominent feature of theological education today is the rediscovery of the congregation." In a world in which seminaries and congregations had been, he felt, too long separated, he argued that: "The academy and the chapel are part of the same whole—the body of Christ. They need each other, for the church is incomplete when either is missing."[3] A generation later, much progress has been made in reconceiving the vital relationship between congregation and seminary, the fruits of which are evidenced not only in the MDiv curriculum but also in burgeoning continuing-education offerings by seminaries and the increasing numbers of visiting practitioners whose expertise is employed in seminary classrooms.[4] A significant part of this progress in many venues has also included the rediscovery of the congregation *within* the seminary, a congregation formed primarily, like all congregations, through common worship.

---

3. Sweet, "Seminary and Congregation," 426.

4. For instance, see the recent Carnegie report: "The research team witnessed the powerful and transformative effects on students participating in educational programs that were underscored by a commitment to authentic and earnest engagement with the issues and struggles of congregations and the pressing needs of our times" (Foster, Dahill, Golemon, and Tolentino, *Educating Clergy*, 9).

Of course, those who identify the congregation-like nature of the worshipping seminary community are correct to also point out its congregation-unlike aspects as well: few older people, few children, few of the usual roles or responsibilities, frequently atypical relations between worship and pastoral care, and in ecumenical communities disagreement about ordinarily agreed-upon things like creeds, ecclesiology, doctrine, Eucharist and mission.[5] It is very easy to make the argument that the group that worships in the seminary is *not* a church (although no sooner has one done so that its congregation-like characteristics reassert themselves). Frank Senn helpfully distinguished between the sorts of congregations formed by seminary and church *via* the relationship between contemplative and expressive modes of community life: " . . . the difference between seminary worship and parish worship can be defined in terms of the difference between monastic and cathedral worship."[6] He then uses this analogy to bolster his argument for the pedagogical purpose of chapel by suggesting that: "Planning worship for the seminary community with its particular needs can be a model of planning for those who, as parish pastors, will have to relate the tradition to the unique needs of a local congregation."[7]

By championing the congregational-like and -unlike aspects of the enterprise of theological education, the likes of Senn and Sweet greatly enhanced the emergent discussion of "what is seminary worship for?" In the generation since their work, however, the contexts in which theological education takes place have shifted. As the curriculum has developed, chapel has entrenched as a place for *training* (congregation-mimicking) while the rest of the curriculum has evolved in its emphasis on *teaching* (research-based learning).[8]

Seminaries today generally acknowledge that chapel is of enormous value in the life of the school, but tend to value it in the way that social

---

5. Nathan Mitchell describes the seminary congregation as "a 'tribal village' atmosphere where competition and scrutiny are intensified." Moreover, "The tribal village quickly becomes guerilla theater, with everybody participating as both actor and critic. 'Performances' are regularly rated by both faculty and peers and bad performances are met with rebuke, cynicism or ostracizing" ("Teaching Worship," 321).

6. Senn, "Teaching Worship," 329.

7. Ibid., 330.

8. While this has been more keenly felt in university-based seminaries, free-standing theological schools have not been exempt from the same pressures.

or spiritual services are valued, and not in the way that classrooms are valued. For example, the accreditation guidelines of the Association of Theological Schools (ATS) are typical in referring to it alongside "community activities."[9] While many acknowledge that chapel is the place where worship traditions/leadership techniques are demonstrated *and* the place where all the other aspects of the theological curriculum potentially come together, few credit chapel as itself a site of academic learning. Even fewer are willing to admit what Frank Senn recognized a generation ago: that chapel is a place where certain things are taught that are just not covered anywhere else in the curriculum:

> Perhaps the time has come for NAAL to lobby with the Association of Theological Schools for the upgrading of liturgical instruction in the seminaries—not only for the benefit of our disciplines, but also in the interest of the pursuit of truth. After all, certain insights into the nature of God, the role of Christ, the work of the Spirit, the character of the Church, the means of grace, and the hope of the Kingdom come as a result of cultic studies that do not come in other ways.[10]

These "insights" not only contain content but also take forms that theological education has been very slow to learn how to assess and, therefore, value.

There is, however, a chance to do so in the current climate. I would like to suggest that the most prominent feature of theological education today (and the key to assessing, and therefore valuing, and thereby being able to persuade students of the merits of chapel) is the rediscovery of the university. By this I mean *the idea of* the university and not simply those places called "University."[11] Once a location for the *transmission* of knowledge, the notion of a university is now predicated upon the understanding that knowledge is also *manufactured* there. Intellectual prowess is measured by the production of *new* knowledge rather than merely the passing-on of established knowledge. Of course, the latter still happens

---

9. *General Institutional Standards,* 3.2.4.2. (p. 140).

10. Senn, "Teaching Worship," 328–29.

11. Throughout the remainder of the essay I shall use the lower case "university" to refer to the concept of the university—that cultural phenomenon of a college of accountable learning—and to distinguish it from the upper case "University," meaning actual historical institutions that carry names like Yale, Harvard, Chicago, etc.

(indeed, the generation of the former is dependent on the circulation of the latter) but it is not the ultimate goal of the university enterprise.

Thus, as the tenure and promotion standards of North Atlantic centers of academic activity testify, professors are expected to invent and not merely to profess; "an original contribution to the field" being the essential criteria for career advancement and/or funding. As a result, such-and-such a place is seen as a good place to go to learn such-and-such a subject precisely because such-and-such a subject is being *learned-about* and not just instructed there. In this re-conceptualization, even the conventionally conservation-oriented functions of the University (such as its museums or rare book collections) are now awarded funding not merely to conserve but according to the degree they are set in the service of "research." Such a shift is reflected in everything from curatorial decisions (what aspects of a collection gets displayed), purchasing permissions (what gets bought, which collections are invested in), and who gets to work in these collections—in addition to conservationists and librarians, professional researchers are now paid, often handsomely, to incorporate collections into their original new work, and archivists are rewarded for making discoveries about (and not merely archiving) collections.

This shift, I will argue below, actually helps the task of making chapel's value as a learning site more apparent to students (and faculty/administrators), because the mission of theological education has changed in recent years in tandem with university education in general. Seminaries that are and are not part of research Universities are increasingly held to the ethos of the university in multiple aspects of their administrative and intellectual life. As the assessment criteria of the ATS demonstrate, the expectation of scholarship as the driving engine of an institution, of excellence in teaching, and of research-based learning on the part of the student is not confined to University seminaries. Furthermore, the expectation of research and publication is not confined to University faculty. *All* theological schools, and not merely those in Universities, are now held to standards of practice and measures of success that previously were the hallmark of University-based operations.[12]

---

12. "A theological school is a community of faith and learning that cultivates habits of theological reflection, nurtures wise and skilled ministerial practice, and contributes to the formation of spiritual awareness and moral sensitivity. Within this context, the task of theological scholarship is central. It includes the interrelated activities of learning, teaching, and research." *General Institutional Standards,* 136.

In his seminal article on worship and theological education, Ron Anderson identifies three (un-resolvable) tensions that anyone who has worked or worshipped in a seminary chapel can confirm: "the tensions between self-expression and formation, unity and diversity [and] the seminary and the local church."[13] To these I would like to add a fourth arising from the rediscovery of the university in theological education: the tension between creating and conveying knowledge. The rediscovery of the university may have established a focus on the creation of knowledge, and theological education may be embracing the intellectual and ecclesial opportunities this introduces, but seminary chapels often remain hostage to non-university expectations, putting them in tension with the wider world of theological education as well as the local curriculum.

For example, when my New Testament colleague includes one of his recent articles in his syllabus, it creates a nice buzz because it is seen as another sign that this is a cutting-edge, academically-exciting place to study; however, when I include a revised liturgical form in chapel, I risk being seen as a maverick, hostile to authority and irresponsible to my students. It might be back-handedly complimented as "creative," but it will not be seen as "demonstrating our excellence as a centre of research-informed theological scholarship"—the hallmark of the university enterprise today. As Senn remarked, in an early articulation of the research-based nature of the chapel dean's work, and a concomitant intuition of this same tension, "we must be granted the freedom to draw conclusions from our own studies or the studies of others without laying our jobs on the line."[14]

Chapels are credible university sites because they create knowledge in an environment that can test it in a transparent way. In addition to knowing how to perform the existing rites of many churches in a great variety of cultural milieus (transmission of knowledge), what sort of knowledge is created in chapel? To name but a few, you can come to our chapel and learn new liturgical forms and new leadership techniques that will enable you to:

- Revitalize the worship of your congregation
- Start and/or sustain collaborative ministry

13. Anderson, "Worship and Theological Education," 126.

14. Senn, "Teaching Worship," 326. He adds, "Of course, there may not be much more agreement among us than there is among non-specialists concerning what constitutes a liturgical 'norm.'"

- Get pastoral and musical staff to work together
- Navigate the worship-wars in your congregation
- Make worship more participative in your congregation
- Lead multi-cultural worship
- Lead a circle dance or start a dance choir
- Facilitate disability accessibility in embodied worship
- Enhance the performance of authorized texts without changing the text
- Create an inter-faith service
- Respond to contemporary issues (ecology, globalization, violence, poverty, etc.)
- Host a conversation about ecumenism
- Gain all sorts of theological knowledge—including deepening knowledge *of* God as well as *about* God—that is found nowhere else in the School.

Additionally, if you are interested in teaching liturgical studies, you will be interested in the new ways of connecting chapel and classroom we have made through our programming. And if you are interested in ecumenics you will be interested in the new model of ecumenical worship we have been developing.

However, the notion that something "new" is being created in chapel through rigorous, research-based and professionally-accountable teaching and learning with students, can be met with a high degree of suspicion. The persistent idea that the purpose of the chapel is to be only a demonstration chamber (while advances in scholarship happen in classrooms), derives from the lingering presumption that chapels should merely convey and not create knowledge, that is: a resistance to the revitalization of the university when it comes to this one aspect of theological education. Such a view is often communicated in the argument that when it comes to song-singing, or any other liturgical art, seminary worship is about training in "best practices," as illustrated in this conversation with former faculty colleagues:

— *Colleague X*: "May I ask, if your goal, as you state, is to have represented as full a range of liturgical styles as possible across a year's schedule, then will you be inviting people into the rich tradition of Anglican choral song on a regular basis?"

— *Me*: "I expect we will do Anglican choral song, but not on a regular basis."

— "And you mean to do it properly, without any interference."

— "Such as?"

— "Imposing new words on ancient texts, making people sit in a circle, and so on."

— "I expect to work with whichever Anglicans wish to host it and discuss with them how the service would be performed in this time and in this place, and I expect that not calling all human beings 'men' will be an important change to consider."

— "In that case it is not Anglican choral song. [*Turning to the Chair:*] I don't see why we cannot enforce a space where students experience the best that the tradition has to offer."

— *Me*: "Whose tradition?"

— "The Christian tradition."

— *Chair*: "Here at Yale we are blessed with such fabulous resources; we get the *best* organists, the *best* choral conductors and we have great instruments; we really must use them."

— *Me*: "We do use them, every day. But you are only talking about people trained in the western canon, and because we are a multicultural school, we also have a large range of other traditions represented in chapel which do not require an organist or a choral conductor to lead them. So on most days they will lead, but on other days, musicians from other traditions will lead, too."

— *Chair*: "But how can you ensure quality?

— "What do you mean?"

— "We are Yale, it needs to be the very best."

— "I'm not going for 'best'; I'm going for worshipping authentically and through that discovering together what ecumenical worship might look like in a variety of different contexts."

— *Colleague X*: "So people just standing there clapping and going all free-form; that's what you want?"

— "I want Anglican choral song one day, Pentecostal praise another day, Methodist Eucharist another, and I want each led in ways that invite others to participate in these traditions, ways that can be reflected-upon critically."

— *Colleague Y*: "But surely you must agree that just as there are some forms in music or in poetry that are patently better than others, so there are liturgical forms that are the best we've got, and we should highlight them?"

Some might read this exchange as an example of the so-called worship wars; however, I encountered it as being about pedagogy. What was at stake for me was not so much the western canon of sacred music but the western canon of theological education (which can be more concerned with the University than the university). The epistemology of my way of running chapel led my colleagues—each esteemed in their own research and teaching[15]—to feel the loss of control implicit in information no longer being handed down as secure and reliable in any and all circumstances, with the expectation that others will in turn take up the practice of it, regardless of race, gender, class, theology, denomination, circumstance, location or any other contextual or cultural factor. It replaced it with the tension described above, wherein one holds both the transmission *and* the generation of knowledge in care.

In a sense, this fourth tension has a great deal in common with Jim White's framing of the debate about the role of worship in seminary chapels with the question, "How much is teaching worship simply the traditioning of what is common practice in our churches?"[16] In 1981 he presented the results of his survey of nearly all North American theological schools and tried to assess "how much people teach worship in a purely descriptive way, that is, 'this is what Methodists do' and how much they teach worship in a normative way, that is, 'this is what Methodists

15. And none of them Liturgical Studies faculty, it should be noted.
16. White, "Teaching of Worship," 315.

should do."[17] The play between descriptive and normative has been an influential way of describing and assessing common worship in theological education ever since, with most everyone agreeing that both are needed. However, in the current climate, while both are still needed, more is also usually demanded and this is why this fourth tension also goes beyond White's original question: chapel is clearly expected to be so much more than mere traditioning, yet it is also criticized when it goes even a short way beyond it.

Beyond the possible (and probably unconscious) desire to train ministers for a church that no longer exists, what seems to actually be at stake is not so much the knowledge itself (new knowledge is not only allowed to be, but often also supposed to be, controversial in university contexts), but its epistemology—and it is here that the deep conflicts that characterize this fourth tension lie. For example, if a Spiritual is learned by singing it *something different is learned* than by simply visually studying it or verbally discussing it. The learning is happening at the level of the body. It becomes body-knowledge, and generates new theological questions and ideas.[18]

Before exploring how such an epistemology might be appropriately valued in theological education, it is necessary to explicate my claim that chapel is nowadays part of the rediscovery of the university in theological education. The ATS definition of "Learning" clearly incorporates university values: "Learning should cultivate scholarly discourse and result in the ability to think critically and constructively, conduct research, use library resources, and engage in the practice of ministry."[19] To demonstrate how chapel fulfills such learning, I shall compare it to a seminary activity the status of which in the theological curriculum is not contested: the New Testament classroom. By doing so I hope to excavate the nature of the tension between transmission and creation that the university values of modern seminaries demand.

17. Ibid.

18. One cannot help but wonder the degree to which it is a feminist epistemology, pointing to a misogynist culture. There is a basic body-fear at the heart of the resistance to the epistemologies in play in chapel, and body fear is, in our culture, associated with fear of the feminine. See: Tatman, *Knowledge that Matters*, 2001.

19. *General Institutional Standards*, 3.1.1.2 (p. 137).

1. This tension is not an "either-or" conundrum. Just like the New Testament department will require the learning of Greek and the study of the canonical texts that compose the Bible (transmission), so the worship program will require the repeated performance of a large matrix of basic practices. But just as NT departments today teach hermeneutics as they go, and just as they are training the student to think critically, to interpret, to query, to test at every stage and not merely to receive and repeat information passed on to them, so worship programs in educational venues are not the harbingers of either "this is just the way it's done" (descriptive) or "this is just the way it ought to be done" (normative) performances. Increasingly, they are also saying, "this is another way it could be done" and "how would *you* do this, given your particularity, and given the worldwide church, and why?" And "what does it mean when you do *this*, or *this*?"

2. New academic knowledge is of an incremental nature. My NT colleague writes an article for a peer-reviewed journal. Its main point is that new research changes our understanding of a particular word in one of Paul's letters. It's a tiny point. It will require a whole article to say it because, like a mathematician showing the working-out of an equation, she will need to refer to all manner of established exegetical norms and proven hermeneutical methods. Similarly, while some congregations may have encountered a sung response to intercessions, no Presbyterian church had previously experienced the whole of Form E being set to instrumentation by jazz saxophone and mean-tone organ with extensive congregational sung response. Such was the result of our chapel musicians, steeped in ministry and study, now taking one step further by combining, deconstructing and pushing the knowledges they already held in their hands. It was new, but like most of the work of the university, it was new in an incremental vein, moving one small pebble on the existing shore.

3. Knowledge is subject to many stages of testing. Like the sorts of academic materials that are used as resources in the NT syllabus, chapel worship has to be tested before it is publicly suggested. Just as the NT section leader reads many drafts of a student's exegesis paper before letting them present it, so services have to be thoroughly researched, carefully planned, crafted through repeated revisions of drafts, and

only performed after this process has been approved as complete (or as complete as possible).

4. Knowledge is peer reviewed/refereed. Revised liturgical forms risk missing important things that only other experts can identify and hold you to account about: so just as an NT article might be sent back to the author for revision by the peers who reviewed it prior to publication, so liturgical ideas will warrant significant critique and should not be performed without the requisite revisions.

5. Just like the field of NT struggled at one time with a latent "the Bible is the Bible is the Bible"—dictated by God, to be lived but not studied, so chapel worship still faces the notion that "the liturgy is the liturgy is the liturgy"—designed by God, beyond human criticism. No theological school assumes you will read the NT the same way when you leave as when you arrived. Just because you've read the Bible doesn't mean you know exegesis, and theological schools are founded on the premise that you attend them to learn it. Analogously, just because you have participated in Christian worship does not make you skilled in designing or leading it. Theological schools need to assume that just as you are re-learning to read the Bible there, so also are you re-learning to worship. How can we demand that people re-learn to read the Bible, but let them leave with only the same ways with which they came for worshipping the God made known in that Bible?

6. Just like new pieces of NT scholarship, the emergent forms of knowledge that are produced in chapel can be contentious and controversial. For example, having an African American woman provocatively dance in the Gospel prior to its verbal proclamation in an Episcopal rite was thoroughly interrogated for its "episcopo-suitability." But the most controversial example of all: we ask people who arrive in good time not to plop down in the nearest seat when they come in the door, but, rather, if they are physically able, to move farther into the space and to the middles of the rows of seats, so that those who need them can have those precious end-row, center-aisle, near-door seats. Those who need them are those who come later, or have children, or who are too large to move down the rows, or too troubled to sit deep in a crowd, or who might need to pop out to the restroom a lot. In preaching, bulletins, the newsletter, and small announcements before services, we regularly contextualize this practice within Paul's injunction to "welcome one

another." We extrapolate a theology of hospitality as the prerequisite for worship. We describe the technique's intended effects, creating a vision of a welcomed and welcoming people. Yet people resist it to the hilt, either moving begrudgingly or sitting in those seats defiantly—or not coming at all because they objected so strongly to the suggestion that they sit in such a way that welcomes others: "I should be able to sit where I want in church, damnit!" It is the technique about which I hear most complaints from people in school and most positive praise from people when they have left, because then they know that actual tried and tested techniques—with accompanying, accessible theological reasoning—are needed to cultivate hospitality in our congregations in the world today. They also see that while they are controversial in their testing-ground, they make a great deal of sense in real life.

7. When my NT colleague introduces a new piece of research, no one freaks out that she has abandoned "the tradition." She is understood to be adding one more small but significant pebble to the strand of her students' education. It is taken for granted (and rightly so), that the tradition is in tact and taught with respect in her classroom. Indeed, it is understood that it is out of respect for that very tradition (preserving it as a living tradition) that she has introduced the newly relevant materials. The same is in fact exactly true of chapel, even as it is frequently criticized as abandoning the tradition when it introduces even the smallest creative nuance.

8. NT classes are pedagogically multi-faceted. The process by which knowledge is transmitted and produced comprises multiple components. You can't just read at home and then take the final exam: you have to show up at lectures, engage in sections, write exegesis papers, pass a mid-term, receive and act on feedback from your professor, and so forth. So with chapel: it can't be measured *via* a comparison to any single classroom technique. It is a place where you need to: receive information (like a lecture and the required reading); develop critical methods and theories (lecture, reading and section); plan very carefully, researching liturgical forms in the library in video and text, and then creating multiple drafts with other people in a process of honing and rehearsing ideas (research, section, study groups, meetings with teachers); try things out without needing them to be perfect first time round (drafts of papers, presentations); finally put something out there

which is publicly accountable (final papers); receive feedback, evaluate, and reflect whether and how you would do things differently next time (read marks).

However, there are differences, perhaps the most significant one of which is that the NT classroom is seen as part of the curriculum while chapel is seen as a "community activity." What makes the NT classroom credible is its assessment procedures. A student who attends the lectures, participates in sections, and completes exegesis and other papers effectively will receive academic credit. Students going to chapel receive no credit. Why not award credit for chapel?

Some insist that the pastoral function of the chapel is compromised if it is a creditable activity. For example, after the tragic suicide of one of our students, I was planning a memorial with some key people. An administrator requested that for this service I suspend my notion of chapel as a teaching-learning space in order to do something "entirely pastoral," to respond to the "pastoral need." This implies that the teaching component of what we do in chapel can be separated from the pastoral, and this reminds me of the advertising hoardings around New York City at the moment: in them a young girl simply stares out at you, expressionlessly. The words underneath say: "Every time you scream at a driver, you are teaching her something." It's not just when we turn on our "parenting" that our children are learning from us: we are in a permanent state of parenting and they are learning how to treat themselves and others from us, every single moment. In chapel, we never switch into an additional mode of "now we're going to teach you this" or "now we're just going to play around with this for a little while to see what we might learn"; seeing as how it is always a genuine time of prayer and praise, then what is there to be "suspended" re: teaching when we are hosting a memorial service for the school?

It seems to me that the solution is to see chapel as part of the curriculum. Then, both NT classroom and chapel would be seen as *both* teaching-learning sites *and* pastoral-spiritual hosts. Chapel is already valued for doing the latter, what needs to be created are mechanisms for also valuing its teaching and research capacities. However, is it really any less inappropriate when a student has committed suicide for a class to proceed without addressing the pastoral need as it is for chapel to do so? If our theorizing in theological education is a Christian praxis, if our teaching is a ministry, if our exegesis is in the service of the church and world, then at least part of the debate, it seems to me, needs to be less about the "problematic" status of chapel as both pastoral and pedagogical site, and more about claiming/redefining the notion of classroom or the status of the classroom as such. Certainly the work I see of most of my colleagues would be worthy of such an articulation.

Returning to the question of crediting chapel, some say we cannot give credit for chapel because it would be coercive to mandate attendance in a seminary like ours. This is true. And others say that chapel is not credit-worthy because if a student's performance as a liturgical leader in chapel is subject to assessment by their faculty, that ruins the space of worship, making it like the preaching classroom; neither faculty nor students would be able to come and "just worship" were this the case. This is also true. However, who said that the creditability of chapel had to derive from these mechanisms alone? Rather than perceiving that chapel can't be assessed like we normally assess things, and therefore we can't assess it, I suggest chapel presents a challenge to "how we normally assess things" and, carefully undertaken, the alternative modes of assessment and accreditation that it enables could have a profoundly enriching and educationally improving effect on the supposedly standard modes of assessment that "count" in theological education.

Moreover, it may not be quite as alternative as it at first appears. Like many schools, it is already the case in ours that the writing of papers with footnotes is not the only mechanism for earning credit. For a start, field education is based upon an immersion in practice model, so it is not true that only "classroom" teaching is valued as credit-worthy. Furthermore, it is not the case that all modes of creditable assessment are based primarily on demonstrated advances in individual performance: we award credit for a host of activities such as the Gospel Choir, the classical choir, and the weekly Colloquium on worship, music and the arts. Furthermore, credit is awarded for a wide range of activities in the school because the classroom methodologies of my colleagues are so wonderfully diverse: a preaching colleague assesses students for all sorts of experimentation in body-practices; an ethics colleague requires students to journal extensively, another requires the viewing of films and TV clips as an essential component of a Bible class; another required the creation of an artistic product, not an essay, as the final "paper" for his class on Job. (Note how none of them requires the mere regurgitation of accepted wisdom. All are fully participating in the work of the university, and students gain credit for successfully fulfilling these creative, critical, interpretative tasks alongside those that root them in the transmission of knowledge.)

I think that the main reason that chapel is not seen as a credible site within the university enterprise, not seen as *part of* the curriculum of theological education, is that students do not get credit for the learning they gain there. Only when an activity is creditable is it credible in our context. However, as noted, to gain credit a program needs to be appropriately assessed, and so I would like to suggest two possible conversation starters by which worship might become creditable in theological education.[20]

Credit for Participating in the Worship Program.

In this model, the assessment would be focused on the program. If the program conducts services from across the spectrum of the tradition/s; if these are carefully planned, beautifully executed, properly assessed and substantially reflected upon; if the other aspects of the theological curriculum are indeed coming together there; and if there can be seen to be multiple original contributions to the field; then it should be safe to assume that by simply participating in common worship, students are learning something worthy of credit. One learns by bodily participation and, therefore, in this model, one would get credit for just going.

Of course, for this to work, there would need to be certain checks and balances. The person/people leading it should be expert in liturgical studies, knowing the liturgies of many traditions *and* the politics and theologies of ecumenism if they are in a multi-denominational setting (which can only come through extensive study). They should also be expert in the pastoral and pedagogical arts of liturgical leadership (which can only come through extensive experience as a liturgical leader). It is not fair to a Bible or Theology professor, or a local pastor, to stick them in charge of a creditable worship program. The attitude: "you've led worship, so you can direct chapel" is not much different from saying: "you've proclaimed the gospel, so you can teach New Testament," and that is not acceptable in today's seminaries.

20. I am imagining chapel being credit worthy on a credit/no-credit basis, rather than grades or distinctions.

In addition to relevant scholarly expertise, the people leading chapel must be expert practitioners, able to model good worship leadership. But most of all they must be good teachers, able to empower others to ritual agency as students of the worship program and as trainee leaders of liturgies. The chapel program must show breadth as well as depth of scholarship, and thus perform a range of rites and in a variety of ways. There must be opportunities for student as well as faculty leadership. There must be venues for shared planning. (Planning is consistently reported to be one of the most educative aspects of the chapel experience). There must be venues for discussion and assessment afterwards. And if all this happens, then, because we learn by osmosis, students could get credit simply for participating in such a rich learning-experience.

Assessment in this mode would not be about any individual's performance. It would be about the transmission and generation of intersubjective knowledge, about body knowledge—and not just knowledge, but expertise. In chapel you learn primarily *experientially*; you learn with many more parts of your body than the part (left side of brain) that you are mostly engaging as you sit in an archetypal classroom. You open yourself to meeting not only the Mystery but also the mysterious aspect of yourself who learns by doing, thinking, feeling and imagining—and all at once.[21]

Those emails from graduates are nearly all about this model of experiential formation, and the knowledge gained through it that proved vital in the local church: knowing how to adapt; knowing how theological realization and change feels in the bones; knowing how to host a conversation about worship; knowing that many alternatives might work equally well. "When a child died whose parents had been alienated from church, I knew how to handle it." "When a farmers' market started next door, I started a contemporary worship service on Saturday evening as a point of mission as well as support." "When a visiting youth group didn't want to robe, like we do, we could have a really good conversation about it, and enjoy the resulting differences." Underneath these manifold sorts of knowledge, however, is a *confidence*, a knowing that there are liturgical traditions that exist and that are relevant and accessible in any situation. You are not on your own. You don't have to make it up *ex nihilo*. You can trust your body to do what it and the congregation you serve needs it to

21. For an extended account of how these four ways of learning impact one's ministry with a congregation, see Troeger and Everding, *So That All Might Know*.

do—because your encounters in chapel taught your body what those are. Furthermore, you know stuff about God from those encounters that you learned nowhere else in your theological education, and this is the greatest source of confidence of all.

If students received credit for all this, perhaps one per year for three years, fewer might regret not having gained these knowledges from chapel once they leave. However, while the actual model of experiential learning through immersion in a good program may have proven effective, the assessment procedures are problematic. ATS assessment requires evidence of "outcomes" and emails to the chapel dean three years after the event won't cut the mustard. For worship to be creditable, we need to demonstrate progress in learning. Additionally, participation in a program needs to be proven, and this would be very difficult in the above model without imposing a system for monitoring attendance—something that is not easy to manage while preserving the principle of voluntary attendance; therefore, we might consider the following, which, while keeping the experiential quality of this mode of learning, seeks explicit ways of measuring its outcomes.

Students Taking Responsibility for their Learning in Chapel

Most models of accreditation in theological education are based on a professor assessing the performance of the student. This first struck me as odd when I was working in Galway. Theology and Fine Art shared a building there, with the vast majority of the students being painters, sculptors, photographers and film-makers. It became apparent from staff-room conversations that the Art professors had a very different pedagogy than the Theology faculty. Their main goal for their students was that they should be able to accurately assess themselves. "There is no point," one remarked, "in my just giving them a grade, because for the rest of their lives they'll only have themselves to ask if they have made the grade." And he saw his work as being to teach them how to do that, so he discussed grades with them constantly as part of the wider discussion of their work and, at the end of four years, he required them to give their own final grade, alone. There were, as in the college as a whole, an average of 15% with distinction and one or two failures, which suggests students came to an accurate and sanguine state of self-assessment.

Bearing in mind the above protections, perhaps people could get credit for chapel using similar methods to the new MDiv assessments. Students would create a chapel "portfolio" and manage it themselves, discussing it every semester with a supervisor. They would opt into a system in which they committed to attend chapel regularly, to read *The Reader* (our weekly newsletter with educational information about the week's services), and to participate in our regular lunchtime roundtable discussions. They would occasionally help to plan chapel with others and they would reflect on their learning with faculty and peers. They would monitor their own attendance, reflections and insight-development. They would keep a personal folder of annotated bulletins, and through journaling and conversation with liturgy professors they would evaluate what worked and what didn't work in the worship they attended, and they would discuss how these things might work in their own congregations. They might have two or three assigned readings each semester to further develop their reflection. They would be guided in self-assessment each year by both the chapel faculty and their own academic adviser. If they deemed themselves worthy at the end of the year, they would get three credits.

Now, in schools like ours, with no formal honor code, a high-grade culture and a lot of sheer naked ambition, this might not work. Every two years, I teach a course on Liturgical Theology which incorporates self-assessment by the students. As well as talking about self-assessment in class and in written correspondence (the students set their own paper questions), I meet with each student three times per semester to guide them in a process of self-assessment. It is quite staggering how few students can do it, even after a semester's intensive training and encouragement. They find it hard to describe their performance even when they have set the task, and the criteria for assessing it, themselves. This helps me understand the problems some ministers encounter in the parish. By training people to meet an external standard only, by failing to train people in methods for accurately assessing how they're doing, we send into ministry people who think they are either never good enough (future burn-out victims), or really quite brilliant (worse).

Given that self-assessment would be a huge culture shift in theological education (at least in this University), this model might work to keep chapel in its *para*-curricular status rather than achieving its desired integration into the curriculum. However, it is at least a viable discussion-starter for considering how credit might be awarded for the learning students are gaining in chapel.

Acknowledging the pedagogical value of chapel will take some work, but it is already being done in chapels throughout North America. Acknowledging the community-forming, pastoral, spiritual, prayerful, praising and worshipful aspects of the classroom, it seems to me, might involve more reflection on the nature of the *university* that is being revitalized in theological education these days. Sallie McFague claims that the seminary is "a *strange* institution and should remain such."[22] She identifies common worship as the place where the seminary's essential strangeness lies, arguing that the worshipping life of a community signals to the University that something *else* is going on here than just University business as usual. "We need to worship together as a signal to the university of a presence in its midst committed to the fear and love of God and as a witness to the church that we are a community dedicated to the task of helping it to reflect on its faith."[23]

Inevitably, much has changed since 1975 when McFague spoke these words during her installation as dean of the Vanderbilt University Divinity School. The pressures of assessment and the professionalization of many aspects of cultural life, including both ministry and academia, were just beginning. Her vision may seem, therefore, to be at odds with everything I just proposed. However, I think her words are as true today as they were then. It is not that worship programs—or any other aspect of the seminary curriculum—became a willing handmaid of university culture, subsumed by assessment and goal-driven thinking in the intervening years. It is rather than the most constructive aspects of university striving seeped into the seminary enterprise, and opened up a space for what was already going on in many of its chapels to become recognizable as being of curricular value. The university is not an absolute bastion of secular materialism any more than the seminary is full of do-gooding saints. Rather, the seminary's worship enriches the life of the institution of which it is a part the more it makes original contributions to the field of strangeness. Far from making it less strange, universitification of worship as part of theological education made it moreso, demanding ever more

22. McFague, "Between Athens and Jerusalem," 93.
23. Ibid.

evolution into the strangeness that is in the inevitable affect of being a sign of God's *koinonia* on earth.

Works Cited:

Anderson, E. Byron. "Worship and Theological Education." *Theological Education* 39 (2003) 117–30.

Foster, Charles, Lisa Dahill, Larry Golemon, and Barbara Wang Tolentino. *Educating Clergy: Teaching Practices and Pastoral Imagination: Media Pack.* San Francisco: Jossey Bass, 2005.

Mitchell, Nathan. "Teaching Worship in Seminaries: A Response." *Worship* 55 (1981) 319–24.

McFague Teselle, Sallie. "Between Athens and Jerusalem: The Seminary in Tension." *The Christian Century* (February 4–11, 1976) 93–95.

Senn, Frank C. "Teaching Worship in Seminaries: A Response." *Worship* 55 (1981) 325–32.

Sweet, Leonard I. "Seminary and Congregation: Uneasy Alliance." *Theology Today* 40 (1984) 426–30.

Tatman, Lucy. *Knowledge that Matters: A Feminist Theological Paradigm and Epistemology.* New York: Continuum, 2001.

Troeger, Thomas H. and H. Edward Everding. *So That All Might Know: Preaching that Engages the Whole Congregation.* Nashville: Abingdon, 2008.

White, James F. "The Teaching of Worship in Seminaries in Canada and the United States." *Worship* 54 (1981) 304–18.